AUTHENTIC
and Free

Wishing you blessings & love as you continue shining as the authentic you!

♡,
Courtney

AUTHENTIC
and Free

A Journey From Shame to Self-Acceptance

Courtney Long

Be & Love YOU Publishing
Phoenix, AZ

Published and distributed in the United States of America by: Be and Love YOU Publishing.

Be and Love YOU Publishing
3844 N. 32nd St, Suite 9
Phoenix, AZ 85018
www.beandloveyoupublishing.com

Each individual's journey is unique. The author does not prescribe the use of any technique as a form of treatment for physical, emotional, mental, spiritual, or medical problems without the advice of a physician. Ideas shared in this book should not take the place of medical treatment or mental health care. If you choose to utilize techniques shared in this book, the author and publisher assume no responsibility for your actions.

As a work of creative nonfiction, this book is based on the author's life and includes some fictional elements for creative effect. Conversations were recreated based on the author's perception of actual events. Characters' names and identities have been changed, with exception of those who gave permission to author. Some of the characters represent composite characters.

Cover Design by Heather Brown, www.culturalsponge.com
Cover Photo by Ila Alagia-Wist, www.butterflybeautiesphotography.com
Editing by JoSelle Vanderhooft, www.joselle-vanderhooft.com
First paperback edition: July 2012

ISBN-13: 978-1456309305
ISBN-10: 1456309307
Library of Congress Control Number (LCCN): 2012908159

Acknowledgements

Did you know that it takes a community to write a book?! I didn't before I began writing, and now that I'm finished, I no longer feel alone! As I reflect on all the beautiful souls who contributed to the creation of this book, my deepest, most heartfelt gratitude goes to:

Amy Pershing, LMSW, ACSW, Executive Director and Co-Founder of Pershing Turner Centers; Clinical Director, The Center for Eating Disorders, my therapist, for being the bridge to connect my lost soul to nourishment, self-acceptance, and self-care.

Elmas Vincent, the Lightpreneurs™ Guru, my business coach, for being a guiding light. **Julie Tufte**, my best friend, for endless emotional support and comic relief. My beautiful **Mom** for all her love and having the courage to be authentic; my caring **Dad** and sisters **Kelly** and **Tracy** for their love, compassion, and support.

JoSelle Vanderhooft, my editor, for her insightful editing and attention to detail; **Heather Brown** of Cultural Sponge for her awesome cover design work; **Ila Agalia-Wist** of Butterfly Beauties Photography for a colorfully creative Authentic and Free photo shoot.

Dr. Kimberly Landino, ND, **Laurie Geraghty**, LCSW, DTR, **Dr. Pamela Traum**, DC, and **Gabrielle Marie Loomis**, for facilitating my healing; **Richard Seaman**, **Linda Bennett**, and **KC Miller** for teaching me to shine my light and stand in my power; the **Southwest Institute of Healing Arts** for empowering me to awaken my inner gifts.

Michael Suszczynski for being a supportive, loving mirror; **Lora Pirie** for her feedback and support every step of the way; **my inner child** and **inner teenager** for their courage to heal.

My friends, family and God/Spirit/Universe for honoring the authentic me; **my clients and colleagues** for sharing their courageous journeys of authenticity; my previous romantic partners including

Kasey, Nathan, James, Brent and Leah for walking alongside me for valuable soul lessons.

And finally, all who contributed feedback, editing assistance, and LOVE: Brenna Dugan, Janet Grosse, Christine Pierce, Christian Ghattas, Mike Hegeman, Lisa Bufton, Pamela Rose Anders, Luisa Valdez, Taylor Grace, Holly Hakes Peterson, Lisa Hecke, Tamira Mehler-Burns, Rowan Mehler, Lynea Adams and Chrystal Kubis.

Thank you, thank you, thank you!

Dedicated to my beautiful cousin,
Jamie Lynn Slaybaugh
and
LGBTQ youth worldwide

May you have the courage
to spread your wings and soar
in AUTHENTICITY and LOVE!

CONTENTS

Introduction   1

I: Hungry Caterpillar

1.   If You Weren't You, Who Would You Be?   9
2.   Bunnies & Brides   13
3.   Troublemaker   23
4.   Where Do I Fit?   29
5.   Can Dreams Come True After All?   35
6.   Hungry for Love   45
7.   Something "Different"   51
8.   Dance Like No One's Watching   59
9.   A Way to Feel   67
10.   Knight to the Rescue   73
11.   Milkshakes Make Everything Better   81
12.   Praying for Forgiveness   89
13.   Silver Platter   95
14.   Don't You Remember?   101
15.   Craving the Crown   107
16.   Can't We Just Be Happy?   113

II: Cocoon of Self-Discovery

17.   Sweet Freedom   119
18.   Dreams Shattered   127
19.   Looking for Me in All the Wrong Places   133
20.   Who Am I?   147
21.   Anyone Up for Adventure?   155
22.   Just One More Workout, Then I'll Be Acceptable   163
23.   Being of Light   171
24.   Fasten Your Seatbelt   177
25.   Don't I Know You from Somewhere?   183
26.   Confessions   191
27.   A Magical Hike   199

CONTENTS

28. Seismic Activity   205
29. The Strength of Surrender   213
30. The Uniting of Souls   221
31. Mom, There's Something I Need to Tell You   225

III: Love Cocoon

32. One Step at a Time   233
33. The Gift of Love   239
34. You're Going to Eat *That*?   247
35. The Ultimate Judge   253
36. Journey into the Subconscious   259
37. Mystery Solved   265
38. What Are You Afraid Of?   271

IV: Butterfly Wings

39. Will I Ever Feel Good Enough?   287
40. Mirror Reflections   297
41. No More Hiding   303
42. Bisexual Beauty   309
43. Out and Proud   319
44. Self-Love   325
45. Celebration of Wings   331
46. I Am Beautiful!   343

Introduction

Tragedies were plastered all over the news during autumn 2010. Holding my breath, I read the headlines as they appeared over and over:

- *Bullied Gay Teen Commits Suicide*
- *Teen Takes His Own Life After Years of Anti-Gay Bullying*
- *Fifth Gay Teen Suicide Leads to Serious Concern*

Sick to my stomach with devastation, my heart sank. These youth had a whole lifetime ahead of them, with the potential for love, acceptance, support, and connection. Instead, tragically, their lives ended in hopelessness and fear. They had not yet discovered their own strengths and inner light. They had not yet learned the beauty and blessings of being lesbian, gay, bisexual, transgender, queer or questioning (LGBTQ).

My mind drifted with concern to all the people in this world, regardless of sexual orientation, gender, age or race, who struggle with self-doubts. I too, used to be very depressed, with low self-esteem and heavy doses of guilt and shame. Just like many others, I was hungry for love, connection, and the freedom to be my true self. However, in an effort to "fit in," I denied my deepest hungers.

As I talked with local community members about the suicides, I learned that these recent headlines didn't describe a one-time occurrence: LGBTQ youth commit suicide on a regular basis at a rate much higher than their straight, non-transgender counterparts. It's not difficult to see why. Many youth are kicked out of their homes by their own parents because they are LGBTQ or expressing themselves in an authentic way. Churches and other institutions that could inspire and help LGBTQ youth and adults often hurt and reject them by saying that being gay, lesbian, bisexual, transgender, queer or questioning is sinful and sick. Our media is also filled with anti-LGBTQ social messages that subtly and overtly tell this vulnerable population that there's something wrong with them, or that they deserve to be hated and discriminated against.

As I watched more and more suicides of LGBTQ youth appear on the news every week, I wondered, *since when is being one's true self a reason for hatred and discrimination?* How could these LGBTQ youth and adults know how beautiful and precious they are? How could they transform shame into self-acceptance?

And what could I do to help? At first, I had no idea. How could I make a difference as just one person? I still had insecurities about my own bisexuality, which I still chose to hide at certain times. I was still on my own journey of self-acceptance and unsure if I had reached any destination.

One day during that same autumn, my business coach Elmas Vincent and I met at a local coffee shop. Due to Elmas's playful sense of humor, our meetings were usually light and jovial. Today, however, Elmas was anything but playful as we discussed the recent youth suicides. As he looked me directly in the eyes, I felt my breath catch. I knew that he was about to share something profound.

With intensity in every word, Elmas said, "Courtney, you have to tell your story. It's time to write your book."

The silence that followed seemed to last forever as I considered what he had just said. I then laughed with utter nervousness. Anxious energy raced through my body. *He's kidding, right?* I wondered. *Tell my story? Is he CRAZY? I haven't told my story to anyone beside my therapist. Does he know how fucking scary that would be and what that would mean?*

Wanting to tremble—or better yet, grab my tea and go—I remained very still instead. The truth of what he had just said washed over me like a wave of calm stillness pushing up from the bottom of the sea. The Universe had planted Elmas in my life for many reasons, I realized, and clearly this was one of them—to plant this seed and give me the kick in the butt I needed. I *had* said I wanted to help, after all. However, I was terrified! I hardly opened up to anyone, especially not strangers en masse.

"You're right," I said, gazing back at him. "I just don't know if I have the courage."

"You do," he said with a smile. "I'll talk to you in a few weeks once you've started your book."

As soon as I arrived home, I walked to the closet, grabbed a chair to stand on, and pulled a heavy box down from the top shelf. I set the box down on the carpeted floor. I was relieved my partner was not yet home from work. I didn't want her to see what I was doing.

Do I dare open this box? I wondered. *It's like opening a hidden vault of secrets.* With a deep breath, I removed the packing tape and peered inside.

There they were, just as I had left them years ago… my journals. Colorful spiral notebook after colorful spiral notebook. On every cover I had printed in big, bold letters: "Private… Do NOT read… or else." The covers were bent and torn, reminding me of the many times I had opened each notebook and poured my heart out on the pages. When I was a teenager, my journal had been my place of escape, the one I could confide in… my best friend. At times, my only true friend.

If I opened these spiral notebooks, I would be delving into darkness… and deep secrets I had kept hidden from everyone… at times even from myself.

Elmas was wrong, I thought. *I can't do this. Relive all that pain? Share the things I did in the privacy of my own closet? Share the things my mom said to me? It would devastate her… and probably destroy our relationship.*

Standing up to put the box of journals back in the closet, I paused. A force much greater than my own fear pulled me back down to the floor. *Oh, what the heck?* I thought. *Maybe I'll just read a few entries. It might be kind of interesting. But I won't be sharing these with anyone else, that's for sure.*

I had no idea what I'd be getting myself into. For the next two hours, I poured over journal entry after journal entry, tears streaming down my face. I recalled falling in love, experiencing the heartache of breakups, and many memories I would have liked to have forgotten.

If Elmas saw this stuff, he would understand why I can't share it, I reasoned. As if my younger self had anticipated this moment, two journal entries backed up my feelings:

"I've decided that no one can ever read my journals. It's all I have. No one can ever know my thoughts while I'm still alive."
—Journal, age 16, Thursday, 4/11/96, 11:40 p.m.

"I have been wondering—what am I going to do with all my crazy journals? They are me, like right down to the core of my soul. My innermost, deepest, craziest thoughts. Many of which I don't share with anyone. Not even my best friends. I would be mortified if anyone ever read them... well, maybe they can... long after I die."
—Journal, age 19, Monday, 4/19/99, 12:13 p.m.

Throughout my life, I thought that if people knew my true thoughts, they would lock me away in a psych ward, never to be loved by anyone ever again. Embarrassed and sometimes terrified of the repulsive, disgusting person I felt I was, shame clouded my existence. All I wanted was to be loved, but I had no clue how to love myself.

Glancing at the mirror across the room, my reflection stared back at me. *Am I willing to face my fears?* I asked myself. *Can I risk sharing my deep, dark secrets? Am I willing to handle the potential criticism and judgment? What if people read my story and do not like me anymore? What if my family becomes angry with me for breaking our unspoken code of silence? Is it "safe" to speak my truth? What if I end up all alone?* These worries swirled around my mind for the next several weeks.

Over the next month, I recalled what I had learned in my life coaching classes: that I came to earth to be my true self and to help others. I came to be a vessel of light and love, and my purpose is to empower others to love themselves and celebrate who they are. *How can I inspire them if I don't first accept and celebrate myself?* The longer I thought about it, the more sense this made. *Despite the fear, I must do this. I must have the courage to be myself and speak my truth.* If my story prevents one person from harming themselves and instead inspires them to see their inner light, then my endless hours writing, crying, feeling, and healing will have been well-spent.

The result of that decision is the book you now hold in your hands (or have open on your computer or e-reader). Two years after making that choice, I am now stepping fully into my fear and take the risk to open my heart to you, my dear reader. As you open the pages of this book, you peer into what I consider sacred. The deepest parts of me I could possibly share, including actual excerpts from my previously forbidden journals. The parts of me I did not want anyone to ever see.

This book is for anyone who has struggled with self-doubts or has been told that they are less than beautiful. The deeper truth is that no matter who you are, what you've done or didn't do, no matter what anyone has said or done to you, and no matter your sexual orientation, gender identity, race, age or belief system, *you* are good enough, lovable, and beautiful inside and out—right now. You don't have to change or "fix" yourself—nor beat yourself up. Just be you. I accept and love you for who you are. May this book inspire you to accept and love yourself too!

To feel whole and complete, we must shine light on all parts of ourselves, our light *and* our darkness. I bare my soul to you now with love, gratitude, and the intention of inspiring you to remember who you are… your essence, power, and light. I hold up a clear, bright mirror so that you too may see the beauty of the authentic YOU!

With love,

Courtney

An Affirmation

Nowadays when my inner light shines, I remember that…

I am a human, spirit, daughter, sister, proud aunt, godmother, Guide to the Authentic and empowerment coach; I am creative, beautiful, unique, intelligent; I feel good about who I am.

And in other moments...

I am not smart enough, too skinny, too fat, too serious (*Why can't I lighten up?*), too silly, too nice, too bitchy; I am not doing enough to help others; my stomach is too fat; my body is misshapen. No one likes me… How could they? I don't even like myself.

But who am I really?
Who *IS* the authentic me?

PART I:

Hungry Caterpillar

Chapter 1

If You Weren't You, Who Would You Be?

"You are always a valuable, worthwhile human being… not because anybody says so… but because you decide to believe it and for no other reason." —Wayne Dyer[i]

January 23, 2012

The woman stared distantly through the coffee shop window. Although she hardly noticed the sheets of rain pouring down from the sky, she felt the heaviness of the raindrops as though they were pounding against her heart. Her mind focused on something else entirely.

"Don't I know you from somewhere?" a tall blonde interrupted the woman's deep thought as she approached. "You look so familiar."

"No, I don't believe so," the woman replied, her tone sullen. "My name is Sarah. I'm just waiting for my friend."

"Oh, okay. Hmm… well, have a good day."

The woman walked away, glancing back and quizzically shaking her head. Sarah watched her go and returned to her quiet contemplation. Her long, auburn hair fell down around her face as she anxiously massaged her coffee cup.

Suddenly, the door to the coffee shop flew open, and a woman who felt like sunshine itself hurried in out of the rain. Dressed in a turquoise dress with a matching butterfly necklace, she flashed her contagious smile at passers-by as she shook out her umbrella, then ran her fingers through her short, light brown hair. Approaching Sarah, she reached her arms out for a big, loving hug.

"It's raining buckets out there, Sarah!" she said before settling into the chair directly across the table.

"Yeah, strange weather for Phoenix, isn't it? I got you a tea."

The woman smiled, tilting her head with compassion. "Aw, thank you!" Quickly switching gears, she looked Sarah deep in the eyes with concern. "Sarah, how are you?"

Sarah sighed, looking down solemnly at the table. "I could be better. Things have been a mess with my kids. And being single gets old after a while. Just stuff like that."

"Anything I can do to help?"

Sarah looked into her friend's smiling face and felt her own scrunch with curiosity. "How do you do it? You always seem so…. at peace inside. I mean, you absolutely glow."

The woman beamed with delight, sitting up taller. "Wow, really? That's good to hear. I do feel at peace. For the first time in my life, I feel like I can truly be myself. It's liberating!"

"I wish I could relate." Sarah's shoulders suddenly hunched.

The woman's expression lost some of its shine as she took a deep breath. "You know, Sarah, it wasn't always this way."

"Huh? What do you mean? It seems like you have everything together, like you couldn't be happier. You've been that way ever since we met!"

The woman chuckled. "That's funny, because some days I feel like punching and screaming. You know, stress, anger, that kind of stuff."

"Trust me, I get it."

The woman stared off into space for a moment, her expression thoughtful. "I actually like anger."

"Huh?" Sarah leaned back.

"Well, when I was younger, I thought nice people didn't get angry. I thought I had to be sweet and follow all the rules. Most of my life I was angry, but I stuffed it down. Now it feels good to let that anger out, you know, in healthy ways."

Sarah giggled as her friend playfully pounded her fist on the table. She then shook her head in confusion. "But why were you so angry?"

The woman thought for a moment. "Because I had to fit into boxes that I didn't belong in," she said at last. "And I hated my mom's rules and the way she hurt my feelings sometimes."

"But you didn't express your feelings?"

"Well, actually I did, but not on the outside. I took the anger out on myself, criticizing myself for every little thing I did. I obsessed over being thin, so I exercised like a maniac."

Sarah tilted her head. "I'm confused. Isn't exercise healthy?"

"Not when you use it to punish yourself. For me it was an addiction, a way to cover up how stupid, ugly and fat I felt. I never felt good enough. I don't like talking about it, but I hurt myself. The woman shifted uncomfortably in her seat, looking down.

"Sarah, I was even suicidal a few times."

Sarah's eyes widened with surprise.

"Wow, really? I can't imagine that!"

"Yeah, well... I still don't feel confident every second. But when I look back at pictures of myself as a teenager with my shoulders all slouched, it's hard to believe that was me."

"You looked miserable?"

"No, actually I smiled a lot, and everyone thought I was so happy. But there was sadness just beneath my smile. I see it when I look at old photos now. I hated myself, and I hated life. There could have been a beautiful rainbow right in front of me, but if so, I wouldn't have noticed."

Sarah placed her elbows on the table. "Wow."

"Yeah. There were happy moments too, but overall, I just felt like something was deeply wrong with me, and I couldn't place my finger on what it was. I was so busy trying to make everyone else happy and trying to be who I thought they wanted me to be that I didn't know how to just be ME."

Sarah's eyes widened in bewilderment. "Courtney?"

"Yes?"

"If you weren't you, who would you be? I mean, you help so many people just by being yourself. Don't you kind of think you're exactly who you're supposed to be?"

An ear-to-ear grin came over Courtney's face.

"Exactly! It took me a looooong time to realize this. But sometimes..." She hunched down closer to the table and invited Sarah to lean in close.

"Sometimes I even LIKE being me," she whispered.

11

The two women laughed.

"That's some heavy-duty stuff," Sarah said. "But I just don't understand. Why didn't you like yourself before?"

Sarah's emerging smile made Courtney smile, too. "Well, it starts with a castle. And a knight in shining armor. And…" She looked at the clock. "How much time do you have?"

Sarah winked. "Courtney, if this can help me accept myself, I'm all ears."

Chapter 2

Bunnies and Brides

"Wherever you go, no matter what the weather, always bring your own sunshine." —Anthony J. D'Angelo[ii]

Summer's end, 1986

Leah and I were playing in the cold, grey, musty basement. Despite the room's dreariness, the fantasy world through which we were flitting was all color, delight, and pure excitement. My parents and two older sisters were upstairs, far away in a distant land. Thank goodness, because I was tired of rules and "have-tos." Down here, Leah and I were free to play and be ourselves.

As cousins and best friends with only one year's difference in ages (she was five, and I was six), Leah and I were like two magnets. We felt intensely drawn to one another and most content when connected. We spent every day of the summer together and even had matching pink Mickey and Minnie Mouse bathing suits. She was my most beloved and treasured playmate.

Like many other good little girls, we had plenty of make-believe children and adoring husbands, roles dutifully played by our many baby dolls and stuffed animals. They were the only people allowed into our special world, after all.

"This one's my daughter, Isabelle," I bossily informed Leah as I grabbed a doll wearing a purple dress. The doll reminded me of Leah with her super thick, straight dark brown hair. She even had intense brown eyes and thick eyelashes like Leah. Both were beautiful.

"Well, this one's my son, Chad," Leah said, grabbing a boy doll and grinning through her cute freckles.

We showered our children with love and tenderness as we brushed their hair and sang softly to them. I moved a strand of my wavy, light blond hair away from my face as I placed my sweet little Isabelle into her crib.

Just then, Leah informed me, "Our husbands are home from work! Time to serve dinner."

I turned to see Leah holding two large stuffed bunnies on either side of her. The Easter bunny had brought them to me last spring. With brown fur and white bellies, at four feet each, they were taller than her!

"Welcome home, husbands!" I declared.

Leah handed me mine, and I welcomed him home with a passionate kiss. After enjoying our dinner of plastic play food, all the kids had to go to sleep. Thank goodness, because then Leah and I could enjoy romantic slow dancing with our adoring husbands.

Partway through the song "Endless Love," Leah suddenly stopped dancing. She dropped her bunny and put her hands on her hips.

"I'm tired of this bunny. I have a better idea. Why don't you be my husband?"

After smiling at Leah's cute spunkiness, my face then contorted in a look of confusion. I looked around to see who she was talking to. Could it be? She was indeed looking at me.

"Huh? You want *me* to be your husband?"

"Yeah, it will be more fun to slow dance."

"Sure, but we're two girls. How would we kiss?"

"Just like this, silly."

Leah stood up and placed the back of her hand against her mouth. She motioned to me to do the same. I then felt her hand on my waist, pulling me close against her. My feet wobbled for a moment as my balance readjusted. I felt uncertain and unsure of what was happening. Then the palm of Leah's hand joined with mine, and our bodies pressed closer together. Leah's lips made the squishing sound of a kiss against the back of her hand. I stood back and looked at her.

"I guess it works."

We then leaned in and pretended to kiss romantically and passionately. *This feels a little weird,* I thought. *But I think Leah is onto something. This* does *feel better than the bunny husbands!*

"Okay Leah, I guess I can be your husband now. What's my name going to be?"

"Duh. Lionel Richie!"

I shook my head and rolled my eyes.

"Leah, I already told you. When you're old enough to get married, Lionel Richie will be *too old* for you."

"I don't care. He's handsome."

I giggled at her as we sat down on the velvety blue couch to rest, continuing to create the life of our dreams. Beyond all the romance, sweet children, and bright, beautiful future, what more could we ask for?

Suddenly, Leah pulled a bag of red licorice out from behind the couch's pillow.

"Where'd you get that?" I asked. She certainly did not get it from *my* house.

"I brought it from home, since your mom hardly ever has candy around here. Do you think our kids want some?"

I gasped in horror that she would even *think* of feeding our little children red licorice. *It's not healthy! Why does Leah eat so much candy, anyway? It's supposed to be a treat, once in a while, not something to eat every day.*

I scowled at her, but Leah didn't seem to notice as she handed me a few pieces. "Here you go."

"No thanks," I sighed.

"What do you mean? You don't want any?"

I shook my head. The truth was that it did look deliciously tempting. But it was close to dinnertime and already past my afternoon snack time, which always took place between 3:00 and 4:00 p.m.

"Court, you're not worried that your mom will find out, are you? Just have some, anyway. She won't know."

My eyes widened with dismay. "No way! What if she comes down here? I would be in *huge* trouble." My body tensed with nervousness

15

as I envisioned mom's furious wrath attacking me. There was no telling what my punishment would entail… being spanked, shamed, and screamed at (meaning complete humiliation in front of Leah), or grounded for a few weeks like my sisters often were. The actual punishment would pale in comparison to the shame of realizing what a rotten person I was for disappointing the person I ached to please the most—my mom.

"Suit yourself!" Leah sniffed, nose in the air, as she reached for more licorice.

I crossed my arms angrily. *Leah's going to spoil her dinner. Why is she breaking the rules? And if she gets to, why can't I?* Sometimes I wished my mom would lighten up a little. *Oh well, it could be worse, I guess. At least I get to have candy sometimes.*

Leah then informed me that little Isabelle was crying. I went to her crib and took the sweet little one in my arms. Kissing her head, I reassured her that everything was okay. We sat in the rocking chair, and I soothed her back to sleep. The rocking motion must have soothed me too, because I soon forgot about the candy. Instead, my mind was drifting far away.

I saw an image of myself wearing a long white wedding gown and marrying the man of my dreams. Like me, he had blond hair and gray-blue eyes. And just as the fairy tales promised, once I married my handsome knight in shining armor, all my troubles faded away and I lived happily ever after.

My daydreaming ended abruptly as my aunt called from upstairs, "Leah, c'mon, it's time to go home!"

Although I adored my Aunt Suzie, in that moment, her voice sent chills down my spine. *Why do adults always have to boss us around?* I wondered.

The thought of Leah leaving broke off my daydream of a perfect future and left me frowning. Sure, we would reunite soon, but departing from our fantasy world was as pleasant as ripping a Band-Aid off tender skin. We sighed, hugged, and reluctantly said our goodbyes.

As Leah climbed the stairs, I tidied up our bunnies and dolls and cringed when I heard the front door slam. My heart felt a little emptier now that my best friend had left. I turned the light off on our special play area and slowly, reluctantly climbed the basement steps myself.

Back to the real world, I thought, feeling a twinge of dread. I opened the door on the savory scent of beef roasting in the Crock-Pot. Tiptoeing into the dining room, I prayed Mom would be in a decent mood. When her crabbiness showed up, it showed up in a huge way, like a thick cloud of smoke filling the entire room, making it difficult for me to breathe.

"Courtney, you need to help your sister," Mom barked from the kitchen. As a tall, powerful woman, Mom towered over and intimidated me. She reminded me of a Roman emperor pounding down her staff with swift command. Fear forced me to obey her orders without question, like any humble servant would. In our house, after all, it was Mom's way or the highway.

I glanced at my older sister Kelly, who winked at me as we quietly set the table. She was so pretty with her dark brown hair, rich brown eyes, smooth skin, and cute dimples.

So far, so good, I thought. *Mom seems to be in a good mood, though with her mood swings, that could change any second.* I never knew when she would have an explosive emotional outburst; therefore, I remained on guard at all times, prepared to defend myself against attack. *At least it's Saturday. That means Dad's home, and he's always nice to us.* His smiling face lit up the dining room as he entered.

"Hi, Smiley," Dad said as he patted me on the back.

"Hi, Dad." I grinned at him as he pulled out a chair from underneath the table and sat down.

As I was placing the remaining napkins on the table, suddenly, my heart jolted at the sound of Mom's agitation. "Tracy, dinner's ready! Come downstairs right *now!*"

Argh, why does Mom have to yell so loud? Can't she be nicer? Tracy was just upstairs, not committing a crime. Sometimes Mom told me I was overly sensitive and dramatic, but even so, my insides trembled each time she yelled. I knew she often felt achy from her fibromyalgia, but still, did she have to take her pain out on us? I never knew what might set her off; but I could count on an explosion anytime we forgot

17

to use a coaster on the living room coffee tables, forgot to rinse the dishes before placing them in the dishwasher, opened more than one cereal box at a time, or stated an opinion that differed from hers. Mom believed there was a "right" way and "wrong" way to do things and see the world, and if we didn't agree with her, we were wrong. I was frightened to form my own opinions and intimidated into believing hers.

Thankfully, she did not yell at me as much as she did at my sisters and Dad. I was her baby. Still, it didn't matter who her anger was directed toward; it elicited a traumatic, painful response in my body. I took a deep breath and felt relieved one minute later when Tracy showed up. Thankfully, Mom quickly calmed down.

I grinned at my big sister, who also had brown hair, beautiful chocolate brown eyes, and cute dimples. She just radiated warmth and filled the room with joy. The rest of us joined my dad around the table.

As we passed around Mom's delicious home-cooked food, I was smiling, sure, but deep down I was anxious. The hot, humid Michigan summer was fading, and first grade would start in just three days. My stomach had been hurting for days from the anxiety! As though that wasn't bad enough, now, my mom was pushing the bowl of lima beans my way.

"Here you go, Court." After handing me the bowl, Mom brushed her curly light brown hair away from her face.

"But Mom, I don't like lima beans," I pleaded.

"You have to try at least one bite. Maybe your taste buds have changed."

I raised an eyebrow doubtfully, since I had just tried them two weeks ago.

"Courtney, if you're hungry, you'll eat them," she stated matter-of-factly.

Oh well, I thought, *at least I can plug my nose to hide the taste.* As I reluctantly placed the smallest spoonful that I could get away with on my plate and passed the bowl to Kelly, my mind wandered. *What will school be like?* I wondered. *I will have to be away from my mom for the whole day… every day?* As crabby as she could be sometimes, I felt quite attached to her and could often be found glued to her hip. Sure, I'd gone to preschool and kindergarten, but I'd never been away from her for a whole day. *Who will take care of me? I'm not ready yet for this big girl stuff.*

I interrupted my parents' conversation. "Mom, I have to ride the bus all by myself, right?"

"Yes… and you'll be fine," she replied nonchalantly, oblivious to my fears.

My expression soured. "How will I know where to go when we get to school? What if no one wants to sit with me on the bus?"

"The teachers will be waiting to show you where to go." She paused thoughtfully. "Hopefully school will help you stop being backward."

"'Backward'? Mom, what does that mean?" Kelly asked defensively on my behalf.

"It means shy."

"Don't worry, Court, you'll make friends," Kelly interjected, as though she would take all my fear away if she could.

My two older sisters loved to nurture me. From a very young age, they dressed me up like one of their baby dolls. Once we even put on a Barbie and the Rockers concert for our parents, complete with 80s regalia of lace gloves, bangle bracelets, big teased hair and all. Both my sisters were smart, outgoing, and so pretty with their long eyelashes and stylish taste in clothes. Neither of them wore ugly glasses like me. *Will I have tons of friends like Kelly and Tracy do? What if the kids see my pink glasses and call me "four-eyes"?*

Despite my family's attempts, this conversation did not soothe my fears. *Why do I have to go to school, anyway?* I wondered. *Why can't I just stay home and play with Leah in the basement all day long? Or make crafts?* I adored making holiday ornaments, beaded bracelets, and bookmarks. In fact, sometimes I sold them to my family members for fifty cents per beaded bracelet. *Can't I just make crafts for a living?*

"Don't worry," Dad said, interrupting my downward spiral of anxious thoughts. "Your smiley face will charm everyone."

Raising an eyebrow and cocking my head to the side, my reaction spoke a loud and clear "Yeah, right." Sometimes Dad was far too cheerful and optimistic.

My parents often told me what a happy baby I had been, smiling all the time—except, of course, for when I came out of the womb with the umbilical cord wrapped around my neck three times. Maybe I just wanted to be different from my sisters, who had both arrived smoothly with beautiful, thick, curly black hair. Instead, I had purple skin and white hair, which made my poor mom cried in shock. But apart from my unique entrance into the world, I *did* smile a lot. My dad and I had that in common.

Dad was someone I looked up to, figuratively and literally. He stood six feet tall with wavy black hair and had warm, grayish-blue eyes like mine. His skin was always very tan from installing cable towers outside for his business and maintaining our three-acre yard on evenings and weekends. He was friendly and outgoing to everyone he met, which must have helped him greatly as an entrepreneur. But while he worked really hard, he was always home by 5:30 on the dot for dinner. If not, he got in big trouble with Mom. Sometimes, even then, I wondered if he was just as scared of her as my sisters and I were.

Mom seemed tense a lot of the time and she showed it by yelling. When she yelled at me, I could not figure out why or what I had done wrong. I often wondered if she did not care for me being so smiley and happy. Or… did it bother her when my sisters and I laughed and had a good time? Although I tiptoed across our home's eggshell-covered floors, trying desperately to cheer her up, sometimes I lost my cool and asked her to stop yelling. She'd then get even angrier and insist that she was just being passionate. *Huh?* My sensitive body just could not understand this communication style.

But it wasn't as though Mom was *always* yelling. Sometimes she smiled or laughed, too. I could tell that she *really* loved us. Often, I cuddled up next to her while she read me endless books. We also had fun together grocery shopping (she always let me choose my favorite Kool-Aid flavors), going to the mall, and doing craft projects—hence my wish that I could just do crafts for the rest of my life. Mom cross-stitched the most beautiful pictures, which she loved to give as gifts. She said it helped her stay calm. I also appreciated her weekly homemade cookies—snicker doodles, peanut butter, and Mom's special twist on chocolate chip.

While Dad worked, Mom had stayed at home to raise my sisters and me—until that week. When I started school in just three days, she would start working at my parents' company installing cable.

What if she isn't home by the time I arrive off the school bus? Will I be okay? I sighed as my intestines twisted and turned with worry and anticipation.

Chapter 3

Troublemaker

"What if the question is not why I am so infrequently the person I really want to be, but why do I so infrequently want to be the person I really am?"
—Oriah Mountain Dreamer[iii]

Autumn's beginning, 1986

Sitting outside on the lush, green grass of the castle lawn, my beautiful satin pink dress fell gently around my legs. I was brushing out the wrinkles with my white lace gloves when suddenly a large, proud lion approached me.

"Why, hello!" I declared.

"Hello there, young princess. What can I do for you today?" he asked.

"Walk with me around the castle grounds, will you? It's such a beautiful day."

He held out his paw, upon which I balanced myself as I stood up to greet the sunshine. Together, we elegantly strolled around the castle grounds in peace and calm. Occasionally we looked up and admired the shapes and textures of the heavenly clouds.

"Look at that one," I exclaimed. "It looks like a butterfly!"

The lion smiled. Like me, he much preferred to be outside. It was far better than being inside the confines of the box-like castle walls where we had to live by the queen's rigid rules. But suddenly, our stroll came to a crashing halt as a blinding light flooded the world and immediately transported me to a different land.

"Good morning," my mother said. In a voice filled with excitement and love, she continued, "It's time to wake up for your first day of school!"

I opened my eyes and saw Mom standing in my bedroom doorway. Immediately my stomach filled with butterflies as I remembered what today was.

"Oh man, it's that time already?"

Wiping the cobwebs out of my eyes, I silently thanked my lion friend for keeping me company during my dream. My heart raced as I thought about the impending day... my first (gulp!) day of school.

After getting ready, I hugged my sisters, who wished me good luck then rushed off to junior high and high school. Mom neatly tied my hair into a ponytail then braided it—my absolute favorite hairstyle. With lunchbox in hand and schoolbag over the other shoulder, I was ready—at least on the outside. On the inside, I felt a pit of fear in the bottom of my stomach. Mom walked me down our long, winding driveway, taking pictures of me all along the way. *She sure is excited for me*, I thought. I felt a little excited too, but mostly scared to get on the bus without her.

After one last hug, Mom stayed in our driveway, and I crossed the street to join the other neighborhood kids. I avoided small talk as we waited for the bus. Once it arrived and we climbed the stairs, I was astonished. The seats were so big that I could not see over the one in front of mine!

After a zigzag tour of our small suburban city to pick up other kids, we finally arrived at my new elementary school. Just as Mom had said, the teachers were waiting for us. Soon enough I found my teacher, Ms. Stout. She was a plump older woman with short, curly brown hair and warm green eyes. She really liked teddy bears, as I discovered as soon as my new classmates and I entered our colorful, teddy bear-themed classroom. I found my seat and breathed a huge sigh of relief. *So far so good.*

The day went by like a whirlwind. We learned all sorts of new things, like handwriting, addition, and where to go for lunch and recess. New friends were hard to come by, but I did smile at a few girls. One had short red hair and freckles. The other had long, straight blond hair and seemed just as shy as I was. The boys I avoided completely.

Recess I spent playing on the swings alone, wishing someone would talk to me. However, I refused to look up out of fear that someone might actually try. After more learning in the afternoon, it was time to go home. I breathed a huge sigh of relief once I made it to the bus. Yippee, I survived!

As I stared out the window, my mind drifted to Leah, who I would see again this weekend. I wished she could come to school with me, but she was a year younger and lived in a different city.

Even though the day had gone well, my stomach arrived home in twisted knots. Thankfully, Mom was home already from her first day of work. After she greeted me at the end of the driveway, we spent the afternoon chatting about how our days had gone.

As the weeks went by, school grew on me. I enjoyed learning, and I focused on getting good grades like my sisters. I felt intense pressure to be smart, responsible, charming, sweet, and nice at all times. If I smiled enough, I thought that maybe no one would notice how unsure of myself I felt. Once in a while, Mom volunteered at school. Once she even made cinnamon-flavored cookies in the shape of teddy bears for Ms. Stout's birthday.

I eventually befriended the blond-haired girl named Abby and redheaded girl named Jennifer. Like I had suspected, Abby was quiet, shy, smart, and responsible. Jennifer, on the other hand, was confident, playful, and as the youngest of seven children, a bit of a troublemaker.

About two months into the school year, I noticed a yellow note taped to my locker when I got to school one morning that said "Kick me" in large letters and unfamiliar handwriting. In smaller letters at the bottom, it said, "Just kidding, from Jennifer." I thought it was both funny and weird. Jennifer was always playing jokes, though. Thinking quickly, I decided to be funny back.

Just before our first lesson of the day started, I quickly and sneakily taped a note to her locker. It said, "I hate you… just kidding, from Courtney." I thought my sarcasm would make her laugh. I obviously did not hate her.

Thankfully, our lesson was engaging. Otherwise, my focus would have been on the note waiting outside the classroom on Jennifer's locker. Ms. Stout showed us a giant-sized picture of a green caterpillar and then asked if anyone knew what a caterpillar did.

A young boy named Brent raised his hand. "It makes a cocoon and then when it bursts out, it's a butterfly!" he exclaimed with a big grin.

"That's right." Ms. Stout flashed a smile, too. She then showed us giant-sized pictures of a cocoon and a beautiful orange-and-black monarch butterfly.

"Wow, cool!" many of my classmates cried in unison.

Ms. Stout explained, "When in the cocoon, it looks like nothing's happening. But underneath the surface, all kinds of changes are taking place. The caterpillar goes through what is called a 'transformation' to become the beautiful butterfly. What many people do not realize, though, is that the caterpillar goes through many changes while it's still a caterpillar."

She must have noticed the quizzical looks on our faces, because she continued, "The caterpillar eats and eats until its skin becomes too tight! It has to shed or 'molt' its old skin. It forms a new one. Each stage in between molts is called an 'instar.' This happens about five times before the caterpillar forms a cocoon and is ready to become the butterfly."

My sponge-like brain was really soaking up this information. Wow! No wonder I liked butterflies so much! They were so pretty and reminded me to be hopeful and positive, kind of like my dad. Besides, they did some really cool things!

After completing colorful caterpillar and butterfly handouts, the bell rang for recess. However, before I could go outside to enjoy myself, I discovered that I was way out of my league as a jokester. Just before Jennifer got to her locker, my note was intercepted, but not by her.

Oh no, not the teacher! I agonized.

As the rest of our classmates hurried eagerly to the playground, Ms. Stout announced that Jennifer and I had to stay back and talk to her. I felt incredibly embarrassed… and terrified. *Something must be wrong*, I thought. I never got in trouble at school. I was a good girl. But the feeling of shame in my stomach was telling me otherwise.

With note in hand, Ms. Stout looked at me with a piercing stare. If I had a tail, it would certainly have been between my legs.

"'I hate you,' the note says. Courtney, is that how you talk to a classmate or friend?"

"No," I said, looking down at my feet as shame squirmed painfully through my insides.

"Please explain." Ms. Stout's look turned more inquisitive now.

"Well, um… well, she said 'kick me.' I was trying to be funny."

"Is this funny?" Ms. Stout asked, her voice going to a higher pitch.

The answer was so obvious, I wondered if she really needed me to answer. "No," I dutifully responded.

Ms. Stout turned to Jennifer. "Jennifer, did you laugh?"

"No. It hurt my feelings," she replied, also looking down at the floor.

"Courtney, what do you say?" Ms. Stout demanded.

"I'm sorry, Jennifer. I didn't mean to hurt your feelings. I'm sorry." Somehow, I held back the waterfall of tears swelling in my eyes.

"Jennifer, do you accept her apology?"

"Yes."

"Okay. Go ahead to recess. But I had better not see notes like these ever again!"

"Yes, ma'am," we said simultaneously and scurried along.

Jennifer hurried far ahead of me, and I felt lonesome as I headed to the playground alone. Walking to the swing set, I hoped Jennifer would meet me there like on most other days. Instead, Jennifer ran off to play kickball with some other kids. I played alone all recess, my head hung low in sadness, fear, and shame.

The guilt created a fog in my mind the rest of the day. During the bus ride home, my mind raced like a hamster wheel. *What was I thinking? I really messed up. I do not hate Jennifer. I did not mean to hurt her feelings. Ahh… what is wrong with me? Will she ever forgive me? Getting in trouble is the worst thing ever, especially with Ms. Stout. I really disappointed her. Does this mean I won't be a straight-A student anymore?*

Apparently, I could not trust myself not to say something stupid. In fact, I felt extremely stupid inside. From this moment on, I made an unconscious vow never to upset anyone ever again.

At least a light appeared that evening. We had my favorite dinner: Mom's homemade lasagna with white sauce, salads, and buttery garlic bread. Doubtful that I actually deserved this delicious meal, I joined my family at the dinner table and ate, anyway. Another bonus was that my Granny and Boppa Long and Granny Bova had come over for dinner, too.

"Want to know what I learned in school today?" I asked excitedly. I then began sharing all about the caterpillar, cocoon, and butterfly. My grandparents seemed fascinated, especially my grandfather. As an avid reader, he was knowledgeable in all sorts of things. My secret plot was to avoid the topic of me hurting Jennifer's feelings and getting in trouble with my teacher. I felt terrible enough already without any more shame or guilt trips.

Granny Bova had pretty, snow-white hair and fidgety hands, and she knew just as well as my mom how to make me feel bad about something I did. If I had told her, she would have made a long drawn-out "Aww…" sound, as if to say, "You're a bad kid, and you're going to get in so much trouble!" I guess it was her way of keeping us kids in line. Granny and Boppa were accustomed to guilt too, as they were practicing Catholics. Dad's family lineage had taught him not to rock the boat and to avoid conflict and confrontation at all costs.

I followed Granny Long's and Dad's lead in being sweet, compliant and putting everyone else's needs ahead of mine—preferably with a big smile on my face. This night was a perfect example. I did not dare let anyone know that I had hurt my friend's feelings today at school. Apparently, I was not as sweet as I pretended to be, but I could not risk anyone ever finding out.

Chapter 4

Where Do I Fit?

"It's never been true, not anywhere at anytime, that the value of a soul, of a human spirit is dependent on a number on a scale." —Geneen Roth[iv]

Autumn 1990

Over the next four years of elementary school, I spent as much time as possible outside by myself. My refuge was in riding my bike up and down our long, winding driveway or journaling on a blanket in the yard. Thankfully, our house rested upon three acres, so I had plenty of outdoor play space. I found comfort among the hills, trees, green grass, dandelions and many little hills on our property. The large, swaying weeping willows became my fortress. Their long, loose, limp branches formed walls under which I found solace and protection from the harshness of everyday life.

Inside our house and at school, I instantly detected others' bad moods. I was uncertain how to shield or protect my caring heart, so the discomfort from absorbing others' feelings was unbearable. Things were especially bad when it came to Mom; whenever she yelled or seemed unhappy, all the muscles in my body tensed and tightened. I wanted to take her bad moods away not only because I cared about her, but because I wanted to feel peaceful in my own body.

Needless to say, with all of this tension, sometimes I just needed some breathing space. Whenever I connected with nature's deep wisdom by playing or journaling outside, my body relaxed and my mind quieted. I often stared up at the blue sky, admiring its vastness and knowing deep within that there was something bigger than me out there. *I guess that's what they call God*, I thought. I did not understand who or what God was, but we seemed to have a good relationship. I prayed to him often.

The start of fifth grade brought new friends and more pressure than ever to look cute. I realized I'd need to focus on my looks if I ever wanted to impress friends or, more importantly, attract a boyfriend. With Mom's shopping assistance, I followed the latest trends by wearing stylish hats, vests, and skirts over leggings, accessorized by slap bracelets and troll dolls. After mall shopping one evening, Mom took Kelly and me for an even better treat.

"Ready for some ice cream?" Mom asked with a smile.

"Sure!" I exclaimed. Ice cream happened to be my favorite dessert.

As Mom drove us to the ice cream parlor, from the back seat of the car, I stared out the window, admiring the red, yellow, and orange autumn leaves. I then thought of my sister Tracy. She had recently moved away to college, and I missed her so much. I felt happy for her, though. At least she no longer had to spend weekends and summers grounded for breaking the rules. *I bet she gets to make up her own rules now. How cool!*

As we continued driving along, Mom made an announcement: "Your dad and I have decided to switch churches."

My brow furrowed. From the passenger seat, Kelly quickly glanced at my mom. "Really? How come?" she asked.

"Well, we don't like the new priest. And besides your Catechism classes, we've only been going on Christmas and Easter."

From the back seat, I secretly gritted my teeth. I had felt quite guilty about that, especially since Catechism had taught me the importance of going to church every week to show my dedication to God. *On the other hand*, I thought, *that doesn't make sense. I feel closer to God outside in nature than I do in that cold building sitting on hard wooden pews, reciting words I do not understand.*

Outside, when I feel God whispering to me or comforting me with a nice breeze, he seems peaceful and loving, like he wants me to be happy. So why does that church say we should be afraid of him? Why do they say that it's holy to suffer? Can't I just be happy? Do I really have to suffer my whole life to get into heaven? And why would God be so willing to punish us for our sins if he's the one who created us? Didn't he create 'sin' too? Suddenly, I felt overwhelmed and confused.

"Mom, where will we go now?" I asked.

"To the Lutheran church I attended as a little girl. It's not as strict. I think you'll like it!" She seemed excited.

I hoped that I would. I already felt a little nervous about the idea of attending a completely new church, but it *had* to be better than the Catholic church: kneel, sit, kneel again, hold my hands in just the proper position and say just the right phrase to receive communion. I always worried I'd get something wrong. Our Catechism teacher could be so mean and demanding, too; she scolded kids for staring out the window, staring off into space or forgetting their Bible verses. I stared into space all the time, since the lessons were so boring. Good thing I knew how to pretend-listen by nodding and smiling. *Yippee! No more Catechism!*

Before I knew it, Mom, Kelly and I were walking into the ice cream parlor.

"Do you have a crush on anyone?" Kelly suddenly asked me as we sat down in the restaurant with ice cream menus in hand. She asked as though she had every right to know. I, on the other hand, was more private about these things than my boy-crazed sister.

"Kind of," I reluctantly and obediently answered. I was not in the mood to be teased.

"Oooh, tell me about him."

Just then the waitress came to take our orders. *Good timing,* I thought. *Maybe after she leaves, I can change the subject.* Mom and Kelly ordered. As the waitress turned to me, I ordered my usual toffee and chocolate sundae.

"Oh, I'm sorry sweetie," she said with sympathy. "That doesn't come in the kids' size."

"I usually get the adult size."

"You can eat that whole thing? Wow!"

As she took our orders to the kitchen, I felt confused and a bit uncomfortable. *Sometimes figuring out this life thing isn't easy,* I thought. Thankfully, I had Mom to tell me right from wrong.

"Mom, what's wrong with me getting the adult size?" I asked.

"Nothing!" she responded in her usual matter-of-fact tone.

"But you said the other day that I still have baby fat."

"Yes, you do," she said firmly. "I only told you that because you asked about your weight, and I want you to know it's nothing to worry about. You will have another growth spurt and outgrow it soon."

I sat in puzzlement, looking down at my poofy stomach. My gaze next drifted to the extra chub on my arms. I remembered hearing dozens of times what a chubby baby I had been. I suddenly felt disgusting, like I just wanted to burst out of this shell of baby fat. *I'm almost eleven years old*, I reflected angrily. *I'm not a baby.*

While Mom and Kelly talked about Kelly's latest boyfriend, I tuned out the conversation and reviewed the menu again. It said the kids' sizes were for ages twelve and under. If so, then why had I been eating the adult size for months? This alarmed me, since I wasn't as thin as some of the other girls at school. *Oh no*, I thought. *I got something wrong again.* A familiar feeling of shame welled up in the pit of my stomach.

Within the blink of an eye, our sundaes arrived. Mom and Kelly dug right in while they continued their conversation. I slowly dipped my long spoon into the toffee-and-chocolate-covered vanilla ice cream and lowered the bite into my mouth. It didn't taste very good. *That's weird*, I thought. *I usually love this sundae. Maybe they left out some of the toffee crunches.* About midway through, I lost my appetite. *That's enough. I should not be eating this big sundae, anyway. If I'm ever going to get a boyfriend, I had better start thinning out.* I decided that my body could not be trusted. It had certainly betrayed me, with all this baby fat.

"Aren't you going to finish your sundae?" Kelly asked.

"No, I'm done."

"Are you okay, Court?"

"Yeah. Can we go home now?"

I remained silent the whole way home, stuck in a place of shame and self-loathing.

Not surprisingly, that night I had a nightmare. It started out like my reoccurring dreams in first grade. I was the princess again, only this time, I was stuck in the castle without any doors to let me outside where I could be free and happy. I panicked, stuck inside the castle with no help and no way out!

I then noticed a ball of red light in the hallway. As I stared in confusion, it grew larger and larger until the light started to fade and a curious creature materialized underneath. She stepped forward into the dim lighting.

"You're so stupid. What do you think you were doing earlier, ordering that *huge* sundae?"

Her cruel and demeaning voice sent painful shivers down my spine. As she stepped forward, I instinctively stepped back. *How does she know what I did earlier? Who is she?*

My legs began to tremble as her shriveled up, wrinkled face twisted into a look of wrath. Her pointy eyes looked like daggers ready to pierce my heart. What frightened me the most was that she resembled me, except far taller and stronger. As she pointed her crooked finger my way, my insides froze in fear. In a snarling, accusatory tone, she continued: "Why don't you answer me, fool? You must be even more stupid than I thought. Why did you order that big sundae, little Courtney? Do you want to get even fatter than you already are?"

My blood bubbled with anger and my heart pumped faster and faster until it became one continual buzz. I wanted to stand up for myself. I wanted to say, "Don't you dare talk to me like that." But instead, the old familiar feeling of shame came over me. Just like Dad, I needed to avoid rocking the boat. Who was I to know what was best for me, after all? I was just a kid. Shoulders slouched, I made a confession.

"I know, I messed up again."

"Yes you *did*!"

I wanted to ask why she had to be so mean. Instead, out of the instinct to survive, I chose to agree. "I'll do better next time." My head hung low as I stared at the floor.

"Yes you *will*. Start listening to me, kid. I'll show you the ropes. You are way too sensitive. Time to toughen up."

I prayed I would live to see the end of this interaction. As she stared me down, questions raced through my mind. *Why is she calling me "kid"? Is she older than me? Why does she look like me?*

The creature started to fade back into the red light.

"Wait! Hey, what's your name?"

"C.I.B."

"C.I.B.? What does it stand for?"

"I'll tell you later. Be patient, stupid."

She faded fast, and I felt relieved to still be alive. *Great,* I thought. *I have to see her again? That was so scary. C.I.B., monster... whoever she is, I'll be happier if she never comes around again.*

Thankfully, my next dream was much more pleasant—a preview of Monday's algebra test.

Chapter 5

Can Dreams Come True After All?

"You don't need the acceptance of others. You express your own divinity by being alive and by loving yourself and others." —Don Miguel Ruiz[v]

Spring 1993

Even though three years had passed, I never forgot C.I.B. or her foreboding promise to return to my dreams. I had been on the lookout ever since, bracing for her snarling reappearance. Since my imagination led to daydreaming during classes, I feared she could show up any time I closed my eyes, day or night. Much to my relief, this had not happened. I began to shrug her off as just a bad dream and absorbed myself in a far more important subject—my new prince charming.

A tall, dreamy blond with sparkling blue eyes, he had soft, smooth skin and a great sense of humor. This dream come true often cracked jokes and made me laugh, a perfect balance to my way too serious side. My beloved cuddled up next to me on the couch and we began to—

"Hellooo? Where are you?"

I saw Abby's hand waving in front of my face. She laughed as she sat down in the desk next to me.

"Oh, oops. I must have gone into a daze." I sat up straighter, realizing I had completely lost track of time.

"We're in homeroom, remember?"

"Oh yeah. I have to finish my science homework!"

"Who were you thinking about... *Brent*? Brent and Courtney sitting in a tree... K-I-S-S-I-N-G."

My cheeks instantly turned hot. "Aren't we a little old for that song?" I looked both ways to make sure no other classmates were listening. When none of them glanced over, I continued in a hushed voice: "Okay, you caught me. We've been spending a lot of time together at his house. His mom lets us go to his room alone."

"Awesome! Does your mom know?"

"No way. She'd kill me!"

"And?"

"Students, time to wrap up your conversations and focus on your homework," our homeroom teacher announced.

"And what?" My voice turned into a whisper.

Abby tilted her head down and raised her eyebrows as if to say, "Oh come on."

"Okay, fine. We've been kissing… a *lot*. And making out. It's been awesome. He really likes me." Beaming, I felt sparkling lights dancing all around me.

Abby's smile turned into a quick frown. "So if he likes you so much, why has he been flirting with Brittney?"

"Huh?" A black curtain came down, covering my beams of light and crushing my spirit. *She'd noticed it too?* I thought maybe I'd been imagining things. "I know he's a big flirt. But I trust him."

"Courtney, don't be so naïve. Look at them." Abby pointed across the classroom.

My gaze followed the direction of her finger. Sure enough, there was Brent, sitting awfully close to curly, chocolate-brown-haired Brittney as the two of them laughed. *Why does he keep touching her hand*, I wondered. *Why is he sitting so close to her? Doesn't he realize I'm in the same exact room? Doesn't he care? Why isn't he sitting by me?*

My eyebrows raised and sparks of jealousy filled my entire body like a firecracker ready to explode. This was the last straw. Despite all the lovey-dovey stuff, I would not put up with this.

"How dare he!" My rage scared me. I did not want to lose control, especially not at school.

"Yeah, what an asshole, huh? I saw them flirting yesterday, too. I was waiting for a good moment to tell you."

"But I thought he really liked me. We talk to each other all the time. What about all the cuddling, the time alone, the—"

"Students, quiet, please. Get to your homework," our teacher now demanded.

But my science homework would have to wait. My mind was reeling. *What did I do wrong? Why aren't I good enough for him?* Things were bad enough already this month. I had just gotten over mononucleosis, which had exhausted me for weeks. At the same time, depression had set in. I even wrote a poem for English class explaining the deep, dark hole I was in. Brent was the one light in my life. *And now he's not there for me?* I needed to sit with this before I decided what to do. At least later tonight, I could express this firecracker energy in my journal.

Thankfully, my family did not notice my angry mood that evening. As usual, they seemed caught up in their own stuff. Mom focused on dinner and Dad remained in his whirlwind of thoughts about work. Kelly noticed that I was quieter than usual, but I just told her I was tired. After unloading the dishwasher and doing my homework, I raced up to my room, where I delved into my journal.

> *"One of the things I hate the most is facing the world every morning. I'm not sure why. Probably because I'm so confused right now—about my friends, school, my family, the way I look, the way I've changed, and mostly about Brent. No matter how hard I try, I can't get rid of this low feeling. I just want to hide from everything. I've tried so hard to be strong and to help myself. But it hurts. Everything hurts. Life hurts."*
> —Journal, age 13, Monday, 3/8/93, 6:52 p.m.

At this point, Brent had called for our nightly phone call. I didn't know what to do or what to say to him, so there was a great deal of silence on my end.

> *"Brent and I are on the phone. He has no idea that I'm crying. He has no idea that I feel this way. He is*

supposed to be here for me... at least that's what I thought. It seems like we're over.

My head hurts and my stomach hurts, but Brent doesn't care. I need to lose weight. Every time I look at myself, I seem to get fatter and fatter. I can't help it. My legs are so big that I can't stand to look at them. And I hate seeing all those little skinny stick-people everywhere... at school, on TV and the magazine covers. I want to feel good about myself. I want to be able to happily show off my face and my body.

What is wrong with me?"

—Journal, age 13, Monday, 3/8/93, 7:18 p.m.

Who does he want me to be? I wondered. *Obviously, I'm not good enough for him. If I were, he wouldn't flirt with other girls.* That night, after we hung up, I cried myself into a deep sleep.

Before long, I heard a familiar, creepy voice in the dark.

"Courtney.... Coooouuuurtneeeeey..."

I gasped as chills ran down my spine.

"Remember me?"

I hesitated to answer, hoping that if I remained motionless, perhaps the voice would go away. Unfortunately, it did not. Instead, its energy intensified.

"Hey, stupid! I know you remember me. I'm that voice in your head. You know, the one who beats you up all the time. You feel that deep, dark feeling in the pit in your stomach right now, don't you? That's from me."

I took a breath of despair. C.I.B. had reappeared at last.

"So *you're* the one always telling me I'm not good enough?"

"Yep, that would be me!"

Although the room remained dark and I could not see her, I imagined her beaming with her chest puffed out, feeling very proud of herself. Proud was the opposite of how I felt toward her.

"You need to leave, right now!" I was surprised at how forcefully the words escaped my mouth. I hoped she would not sense the timid fear behind them.

"I can't. Sorry kid, you're stuck with me."

I was growing quite tired of her snotty, demeaning tone.

"What do you mean?"

"You need my help."

"Huh?"

"Well, you want to be liked by other kids, right?"

"Of course."

"You want a boyfriend who won't flirt with other girls, right?"

"Well, yeah."

"How will you know how to act if you don't have me? I'll keep you in line. You don't want to be a nerd, do you? You want to be loved, right?"

Still, I was not convinced, and apparently, C.I.B. noticed.

"Aren't you tired of rules… school, church, especially your mom's? Where do you have any say?"

My mind drifted to our strict eating times at home. Earlier in the week, I wanted a snack after the 4:00 cutoff time, and Mom bit my head off. But I wasn't hungry at the 3:00 snack time!

Yeah, C.I.B. has a point. When do I get to decide when to eat? Why can't I follow my own appetite? I'm tired of Mom's rules and how mean she can be. She says I don't have to be perfect, but that's not how she acts. The other night, Tracy called from college while Mom was at the grocery store. I forgot to tell Mom until the next morning, and she grounded me for the rest of the day. She even took the phone out of my bedroom! I couldn't even call my friends. It was a mistake, okay? Why do I have to be punished for making a mistake? I didn't mean to forget. Then the other day, she told my dad I was being a "little asshole" because I argued with her about practicing my flute. I had a stomachache! Her meanness is annoying, just like C.I.B.'s.

"And now your own boyfriend is walking all over you, too? Isn't it time *you* were the one in control?"

I visualized how being in control of my own life would feel. *Would it feel as great as riding my bike after school?* It was thrilling to know that I was the one controlling my bike, speed, and destination. I was the one feeling the wind in my hair. Even though Mom did not allow me to ride beyond our street, I snuck away with Abby after school all the time. We rode all around town, often stopping at the local dairy parlor for ice cream. I felt so tired of school, rules, and pretty much everything.

"C'mon, we have some work to do. I'll help you."

C.I.B.'s proposal sounded too good to be true. *What kind of help can she give me?* I wondered. Just as I opened my mouth to ask, I heard an even more familiar noise.

Ring, ring, ring! Ring, ring, ring!

I woke abruptly to the sound of my alarm clock ringing. *Oh man, I still didn't get a chance to ask what her initials stand for. What a weird dream. Good thing that's the only place C.I.B. has appeared. I would NOT want to meet her in real life.* Reluctantly, I tossed back the covers and got out of bed, dreading the day ahead. *C.I.B. was right,* I thought. *I do have some work to do.*

On the bus ride to school, I scribbled vigorously in one of my notebooks. Later that morning, I spotted Brent in the hallway. As I walked up to him, I refused to look at him out of sadness and disgust. He had broken my heart.

"Brent, I have something for you."

His smirk quickly faded as I handed him a note and the necklace he had given me.

"Courtney, what's going on?"

Without uttering a word, I quickly turned away and walked to my locker. The note would explain it all. My body shook as I wondered when he would read it. I wondered what he would think when he read that I would no longer tolerate his flirting with other girls. I wondered when he would realize that I was claiming my power back and that I was breaking up with him.

I felt empowered and strong. At the same time, however, obsessive, worried thoughts spun through my mind. *How can I hurt him like this? Will I regret this later?* Never before had someone held and loved me the way he had. I thought we had such a special bond. I thought I could trust him. *I guess I was wrong. Apparently, there's not much in life that I can trust.*

"What's wrong?" Abby asked as she met me at my locker.

"I'm so upset, Abby. I'm breaking up with Brent."

I was not sure which emotion to show: sadness, fear, hurt, or anger. For the sake of appearing strong, I decided to hide them all.

"I think you did the right thing. Don't worry, he was a jerk, anyway."

I sighed as I swapped my geometry book for my lunch bag.

We made our way to the cafeteria and found our usual seats with our friend Janelle and a few other kids. Janelle was a sweet, funny girl and smart, too. She didn't seem to know it, though, or at least didn't want to flaunt it. She slouched her shoulders and seemed more interested in listening than talking. She hid behind long auburn hair that loosely framed her face. I really admired her and tried slouching my shoulders and hiding behind my long hair too.

"Oh no, not again. Janelle, you're not eating lunch again?" Abby asked, pointing with concern to Janelle's unopened, untouched lunch bag.

"No, I told you, I need to lose weight."

Abby raised an eyebrow. "You don't need to lose weight! You look great like you are. When will you understand that?"

"Thanks, but I'm not hungry, anyway."

Abby rolled her eyes.

My appreciation for Janelle also included mimicking her eating habits. Suddenly I had lost my appetite, too. I looked down at my half-eaten applesauce. *That's enough*, I thought. *Janelle is far from fat... she's tall and thin. If she thinks she's fat, then what does that say about my body? I'm the one still carrying baby fat. Thank God I've lost some of it, but still not nearly enough.* I ate half of my ham and cheese sandwich, just enough to get me through the rest of the afternoon. As Janelle threw her lunch away, I threw away the remainder of mine, including the cookies my mom had packed. I reminded myself to tell her later that I no longer wanted mayo on the sandwiches. That should help cut down on some unwanted calories.

We were engrossed in conversation about the upcoming weekend when one of the cheerleaders came up to Janelle and whispered in her ear. As Janelle's expression changed to one of shock and disgust, the cheerleader left as quickly as she had arrived. Taking a deep breath, Janelle then turned to me and reluctantly reported the news. Brent was officially 'going out' with Brittney. He even gave her my necklace. I was crushed—and enraged.

"Oh my god, Court, I'm so sorry," Janelle and Abby said simultaneously.

"What? How could he? I thought he loved me." I sat there in disbelief, unable to think of anything else to say.

The rest of the school day and bus ride home were a blur. Upon arriving home, I fumbled to get my house key into the lock. Somehow in my fury, I managed to open the door and walk inside. Upon calling out to confirm that no one was home, I threw my backpack down on the entryway floor and then I joined it, sinking to my knees, crying in agony. I felt sick to my stomach as thoughts of Brent and Brittney raced through my mind.

"It's like I meant nothing to him!" I screamed. "He just tossed me away and forgot. He forgot about the memories. Well I want to forget, too!"

I certainly did not feel like watching my usual soap opera or eating my usual snack of cheese and crackers or pretzels dipped in melted chocolate chips. Instead, I went directly to the series of thin, long rectangular mirrors in the living room. *Why do I always look and feel so disgusting?* I scanned my body in the mirror. *There, I spotted it. That must be it!* My eyes narrowed in on my thighs.

"You're so fat, Courtney," I said. "You're disgusting, like the scum of the earth. Look how fucking fat your thighs are. They're so gross! Maybe that's why Brent didn't love you anymore."

Why didn't I notice this before? I wondered, feeling even more alarmed. *There must be something I can do. I have to lose weight—and quickly.* I needed to fit in, which meant covering up any and all flaws. I thought back to the hundreds of magazine covers I had seen over the years while helping Mom unload the cart at the grocery store. The headlines had said things like "30 day weight loss plan," "Get your body beach-ready for the summer!", or "Lose weight through exercise." That was it! I hurried to the cabinet under the TV, where I pushed aside VHS tapes and dug out Mom's exercise videos. *This will work for now. But I will need more soon... very soon.*

In my panic and rage, I hardly noticed the sound of the garage door as Kelly and Mom arrived home. But when I heard it, I frantically grabbed my backpack and scurried to the kitchen table to pretend that I had been doing homework.

After eating minimal portions at dinner, cleaning up, and finishing my homework, I changed into a T-shirt, shorts, and tennis shoes and slipped one of my mom's exercise videos into the living room VCR.

I'll show them, I thought. *I'm gonna be thin, and maybe then Brent will miss me and want me back. Of course, I wouldn't take him back... but still. Maybe he'll want me back.*

As I began working out, Mom peeked her head in momentarily, looking surprised. Thinking quickly while attempting to hide my tears of anger, I announced that our gym teacher wanted us to get in better shape. The answer satisfied Mom long enough to leave me in peace.

Feeling awkward and uncoordinated, I followed the leotard-wearing exercisers through grapevines and knee lifts and spun around in circles. I had never done anything like this before! By the time I was finished, I felt I had gotten a good workout. I had worked up a sweat, after all.

As I turned off the TV and unlaced my tennis shoes, Brent popped into my mind. I pushed the thought away and instead reassured myself I would do the same exercise video the next day. Smiling with satisfaction at my accomplishment, I knew that somewhere, C.I.B. was smiling too.

◎

Over the next few weeks, my stomach turned and twisted in painful knots at school. I pretended not to care when I saw Brent walking past with Brittney or sitting next to her in class. I was tired of feeling angry, hurt, and depressed. Therefore, I remained laser-focused on my goal, determined to lose just the weight I needed to. After my evening workouts, I wrote about my progress in my journal.

"I need help so bad. I don't know why, but I haven't written in here about my little food problem. It's no big deal, I guess. But I hate myself more and more every day. My legs are so fat. I look completely out of balance. They keep getting bigger too, even though I don't eat near as much as I used to. Sometimes I skip lunch, but mostly I have applesauce and a juice box. My snacks have been cut down, but at breakfast and dinner I just don't get second helpings. I'm okay. I'm not weak; simply exhausted from school and loss of sleep due to exercising. I personally don't give a shit if I get sick or become anorexic. I just want to be skinny. I want to look good for myself. I want to be able to say that I'm better than those little fucking stick people. Maybe they look disgusting, but that's better than being humongous. I want a way out of this body."

—Journal, age 13, Thursday, 3/25/93, 6:49 p.m.

"I started eating again. But I'm eating healthy foods, and only a teeny little bit of fatty foods (I need the fat anyway because of my body changes). I've started to exercise continuously, and my body feels great. My legs are in such pain right now, but I'm very happy about it. I already lost a few pounds. I feel a lot better about myself, which has taken me out of the depression."

—Journal, age 13, Thursday, 4/1/93, 6:52 p.m.

"Every time I look at myself, I seem to get fatter and fatter. What is wrong with me?"

—Journal, age 13, Thursday, 4/15/93, 8:53 p.m.

Chapter 6

Hungry for Love

"There is nothing wrong with you. You are not broken and you don't need fixing. You are brilliant and represent limitless potential."
–Panache Desai[vi]

January 23, 2012

As the rain continued pouring outside the coffee shop window, Sarah sat up straighter in her chair, nodded her head and leaned in closer.

"I love that you broke up with Brent. You stood up for yourself!" Sarah high fived Courtney across the table. "I bet he had low self-esteem too, or he wouldn't have needed other girls' attention."

"Ooh, that's true; I hadn't thought of that!" Courtney half-smiled.

"But still, it's so sad that you thought it was your fault. You blamed your body. Were you even overweight?"

"Nope. I'd lost my baby fat by then. I was thin, but that's definitely not how I saw myself." She pulled out a teenage picture to show Sarah. "My thighs weren't that big, right?"

Sarah raised her eyebrows. "Seriously, Courtney? Uh no, not at all."

"When I looked in the mirror, my thighs looked as wide as two elephants put together. Sometimes they grew to three or four elephants." Courtney shook her head as she laughed.

"Well, you were hardly the size of elephants. How did your body image get so distorted?"

Courtney paused to reflect, her expression somber. "I don't know, but all those mean self-doubts in my head probably distorted a lot of things. Like, I thought I was responsible for everyone's happiness. No matter who it was, if someone in a room wasn't happy, I assumed I did something wrong, and I tried to fix it right away."

"So you were super nice to everyone else, yet super mean to yourself. Right?"

"Exactly," Courtney nodded.

"That's exactly how I am. Why do we have to be our own worst critics? Is there a cure for that?" Sarah chuckled.

Courtney shrugged her shoulders then stared through the window as if the answer might be lurking outside in the rain.

"I think most of us are so used to criticizing ourselves that we have no idea what awesome, beautiful, powerful beings we are," Courtney said at last.

Sarah gave a wary look as Courtney continued: "Every human being has tons of strengths… and talents… and light inside."

"You really think so? Everyone?"

Courtney nodded.

"That means me too?"

"Yes, Sarah, you too!" Courtney smiled affectionately. "From the day we were born, all of us have been lovable, good enough, whole, and complete. No matter what anyone says or does to us, nothing can change that."

Sarah frowned. "Courtney, I like your theory, but if it's true, then why don't more people know this?"

"Good question. Maybe because it's a whole new way of thinking."

"Hmm… my parents encouraged me, thankfully. But I guess my self-doubts overrode the positive stuff, you know?"

Courtney nodded in agreement. "Trust me, I get it! Even though my mom had her bad moods, she was really empowering too. Always so proud of me for doing well in school and attended all my band concerts. Mom told me I could do or be anything I wanted, and she encouraged me to be confident. I always appreciated that."

"But even so, you were raised in a religion that taught you were born into ugliness and sin."

"Yeah, exactly. I bet religion factors in for a lot of people. Thankfully, now some religions are talking about strengths and inner light. But that's not how mine was growing up!"

"Mine either." Sarah looked down at the table in deep thought. "I was raised Catholic too, and now that I think about it, before communion we always recited, 'Lord I am not worthy to receive you…'" She glanced up from the table. "Oh my gosh, Courtney I was taught that I was unworthy!" Sarah's jaw dropped to the table.

"Yeah, and 'unworthy' is another way to say 'not good enough.'"

Sarah's eyes widened. "Wild! I never thought about this!"

"I totally relate, Sarah. I thought that the only reason I had a chance of going to heaven was because Jesus died for my sins… not because I actually deserved to go there."

The two women sat in silence, breathing in the significance of their conversation. Then, Courtney continued: "I wonder how those religious teachings affect people's self-esteem. I mean, it's one thing to be humble and learn from our mistakes. Yet that doesn't mean we need to feel unworthy or shameful."

Sarah nodded, "I wonder if that's why so many people sabotage themselves, you know, by drinking a ton or neglecting their self-care. Because they feel unworthy from deep within?"

"That's what I suspect! You know what else I wonder? What if kids learned from a very young age that they are good enough just as they are? That it's okay to be themselves, even if that means being unique or different?"

Sarah's eyes lit up. "How cool! What if they knew it's okay to have flaws and be 'imperfect'?"

Courtney's eyes drifted off. "Sarah, I wonder if that would help with bullying."

"What do you mean?" Sarah's head tilted to the side.

"Well, hurt people tend to hurt others. Bullies put someone else down to make themselves feel superior. What if they didn't feel inferior to begin with? Would they really need to bully anyone?"

"Ooh," Sarah said. "Do you mean that bullies have low self-esteem?"

"Yes! Their air of superiority is just an act."

Courtney nodded, "That's my theory anyway."

Sarah's face soured. "Well, the kids who bullied me were ruthless. I felt powerless around them, you know? Like I was a complete idiot."

"I'm sorry, Sarah. That doesn't sound like fun at all!"

"No, it wasn't, that's for sure! Were you bullied?"

Courtney paused.

"Hey, are you avoiding the question?" Sarah asked with a sideways glance.

"No. It's just uncomfortable to talk about. I was bullied a little, but mostly I blended in, you know, trying to be cool just like my friends."

"I tried that, but it never seemed to work for me," Sarah giggled. "My quirkiness was too obvious."

Courtney joined in the giggling. "I did all kinds of things to fit in, like not raising my hand in class every time I knew the answer, because I didn't want to be teased for 'sucking up' to the teacher."

"It's wild when you think about it. What's wrong with intelligence?" Sarah shook her head.

"The bullying comment that crushed me the most was at an evening band concert. My parents were there, and one of my good friends sarcastically said, 'Oh look at the happy family,' like there was something so wrong with us. I felt so offended. She had no idea how tense and crazy it could be at home. And we actually *were* happy a lot of the time. My parents took really good care of us, and we went on all kinds of fun family vacations. We did other fun stuff too, you know, like singing to old records at home, bowling, golfing, stuff like that. I was very blessed. And what was wrong with that? Oooh, I was furious."

"Uh Courtney, I think you're still furious," Sarah pointed out, observing Courtney's flushed cheeks. "She was probably jealous, don't you think?"

"Yeah, probably. But I had no idea back then! Another friend tried to beat me up at the bus stop because I 'stole' her boyfriend. Oh, and other friends called me a 'slut' sometimes because of my luck with the boys. It's funny how I'll never forget these comments."

"Did you ever stand up for yourself?"

"No way! I was too scared, so I just swallowed my feelings. I thought maybe my friends were right, that I really was a 'slut' and 'too happy.' Just like I believed the things my mom said to me, like that I was 'overdramatic, over-reactive, and overly sensitive.'"

Sarah's forehead furrowed in concern. "Courtney, just because you believed those thoughts about yourself does not mean they were true. You were just like everyone else, wanting to love and be loved."

"Thank you for understanding, Sarah," Courtney said as tears welled in her eyes and fell down her cheeks. After staring out the window for a few moments, she continued: "I wanted to be loved and accepted so much that I pretended to be someone else. I thought I needed others to latch onto—friends, a boyfriend, *someone* to show me who to be. If I pretended to be like them—to like the same clothes, movies, and music as them—maybe they would look beyond the ugly truth about me. Or better yet, maybe they wouldn't notice how truly nerdy, stupid, fat, ugly, and gross I really was—or thought I was."

"Courtney, you were really confused. You're not stupid, fat, ugly, or gross. Maybe a little nerdy, though." Sarah's expression remained as deadpan as her voice.

"Hey, thanks a lot!" Courtney said sarcastically.

Sarah flashed her a smile.

Courtney sighed through a faint but promising smile. "The love I got from others wasn't consistent. But I still hunted for it, because I was hungry beyond belief. I was hungry for love, acceptance, and peace. I wasn't sure even they existed."

"Do you know they exist now?"

Through her tears, the corners of Courtney's mouth turned upward into a smile. "Be patient. We haven't gotten to that part yet."

The two women laughed.

"Well, it sounds like you weren't living the life of a princess like in your dream."

"No, and I didn't realize that something interesting was about to happen. I would have a choice... to be Courtney or to continue hiding."

"Oooh, tell me more."

Chapter 7

Something "Different"

"Be yourself; everyone else is already taken." —Oscar Wilde

Winter 1994

A year and a half later, my classmates and I entered high school. This meant a whole new ballgame, including new school subjects, loads of homework, and boys that were cuter and more charming than ever.

With all the pressure I put on myself to do well in school, I just needed a break sometimes. Thank goodness I could escape into my journal. Thankfully, I also had another place of safety and comfort… Leah. She never made fun of me or judged me. All I sensed from her was unconditional love and admiration.

Sometimes I wondered why she loved me so much. Even so, I loved escaping to see her on weekends. Seeing her sweet, freckled face made my heart smile.

"You're coming over later, right?" I asked, as we spoke on the phone. "Kelly's going out, and my parents have their Friday night bowling league, so we'll have the whole house to ourselves."

"Yeah, for sure. I can't wait. Do you want to dance?"

"Of course!" I giggled giddily.

Since it was the weekend, I decided to put off homework until Sunday. Thankfully, this meant I had time for a workout before dinner! Now, I was guaranteed a good night. The deep sense of accomplishment after each workout inflated my ego and sense of dominion over my own world. Recently, I had ordered a new step aerobics video and was using it as much as possible. With each ache and pain, I felt a deep sense of accomplishment and satisfaction. With each squat or lunge, I felt more like the master of my world.

Today, I decided that the instructor on the video was not working me hard enough, so I took matters into my own hands. I paused the video to perform extra knee lifts and jumping jacks. Once I had used every ounce of energy I could muster, my job was done.

After stretching and showering, I skipped down the stairs to join my parents for dinner. Kelly had already gone to her boyfriend's house for the evening. As I sat down, I reflected, *I'll have to be very careful about what I eat, since I don't want to negate the workout I just did. Every calorie counts, after all.* Thankfully, my parents were too busy talking about work to notice what small portions I took.

After an uneventful dinner, I escaped to my bedroom to wait for Leah. I had just enough time to review a few journal entries from the past year. As I did, I felt proud of my progress.

> "For my New Year resolutions...I need to be nicer and more pleasant to be around. I realized tonight just how bad and obnoxious I look when I'm a bitch around here. And I have to stop whining and interrupting. I have to. The biggest promise is for me to work as hard as I can to like my body and feel good inside. I'm going to do step aerobics every day. The videos can help me, I know. And no matter what anyone says, I need the help."
> —Journal, age 13, Friday, 12/31/93, 11:11 p.m.

> "I'm pretty sure I've become obsessed with exercising. I do this little thing in my head where I make myself feel fat every time I skip a night of exercising. And the thing is, I never skip more than two nights a week. The only time I don't do it is when I absolutely can't. Why do I have to be so hard on myself? But the good part is, I've lost my stomach, my love handles, my cheeks, a lot of my legs, and a part of my butt. I feel a whole lot better too. It's so great."
> —Journal, age 14, Tuesday, 4/19/94, 10:30 p.m.

"Court! Leah's here!" Mom called from downstairs. I closed my journal, tucked it safely beneath my bed, and ran downstairs to greet Leah and Aunt Suzie.

Thankfully, Mom had loosened up enough to let Leah and me stay home alone. I was fourteen years old, after all, and I no longer needed a babysitter. After hugs and kisses, Aunt Suzie, Mom, and Dad left. We quietly ran to the front window and watched Aunt Suzie's green car and my dad's gray Blazer pull down our long, winding driveway and turn out of the neighborhood.

"All right, time for some fun!" I informed Leah with a huge grin. "I'll turn on the music."

We ate ice cream and lounged back with our feet on the table. We had a blast dancing in almost every room, like we were the queens of the world. Good thing Mom couldn't see us. I was sure she would not be happy about us putting our glasses on the table without coasters or playing the music so loudly.

"Remember when we used to play with baby dolls and stuffed bunnies?" I asked Leah with a sly smile on my face.

"Mmm-hmm." She nodded, turning her head to look at me with curiosity.

"Well, we still have our own special world… you know, only you and me know about it. No one else would ever understand, anyway. I'm glad it's just you and me. But anyway, this time our play feels, umm… a little different."

We looked at each other with completely straight, serious faces for a moment. Leah knew exactly what I meant. After a few moments of serious staring, simultaneously we both cracked up, laughing from deep within our bellies.

We walked into my parents' bedroom with its antique oak furniture, oversized four-post bed, quilted green bedspread, and Mom's favorite teddy bears keeping watch. It was a good thing the teddy bears could not tell on us, I thought as we opened the drawer of my dad's dresser.

There in its usual spot was Dad's stack of adult magazines. We pulled out the latest one and giggled as we climbed up onto the bed.

With excitement, we flipped it opened and gawked at the naked women page by page. It felt naughty but curiously good.

Some were blonde and White. Others were Black or Latina. Although each woman looked different, they had something in common: beautiful, voluptuous, curvy bodies. I did not want to tell Leah, but as we flipped through the magazine, my own body felt a little funny—especially 'down there.'

As we flipped through a few more magazines, my mind spun into a tizzy. *Why does my body feel so weird? Why are we being so sinful? We are both girls. We know this is wrong. So why does it feel so good?*

I bit my lip. *I want to look at these pictures, but I shouldn't. Can't I just look with one eye open and the other turned away?* The women's bodies intrigued me. They were so curvy, sexy, and sensual.

Why don't I get this excited about men's bodies? I loved flirting and getting attention from boys at school. I had boyfriends on and off since age ten. What was going on? *Aren't I supposed to like boys... and boys only?*

"Leah, let's put these away. I'm bored." I hoped Leah would not notice my sudden shift in mood, or the fact that I was lying. She glanced at me mysteriously.

"Okay, no problem, Court."

We closed the magazines and neatly stacked them back in the dresser in just the order we found them. If my parents ever found out, we would be in *huge* trouble, and I would be beyond mortified. Suddenly, I felt anger toward Dad for having these magazines anyway. *Does Mom know? Does it upset her? Why does he look at these? Why do I?* I felt disgustingly dirty inside.

"Hey Court, wanna watch *National Lampoon's Christmas Vacation*?"

"Again?"

"Of course!" Then in her best Aunt Bethany voice, Leah asked, "Clark, is the tree on fire?"

We giggled until our cheeks turned pink. We wandered into the living room and placed the movie in the VCR. It happened to be December, but to us it would not have mattered. We adored this movie and watched it year round. Every so often, images of the naked women popped into my mind, distracting me from the movie. They seemed to haunt me the rest of the night.

About three-fourths of the way through the film, my parents came home. I was relieved, as I was tired and ready for bed. Leah and I turned the movie off and headed upstairs. As usual, we reserved my bed for the stuffed animals and both slept in cuddly sleeping bags on the floor.

Comfortably tucked in with the lights out, my mind was reeling. *What if I go to hell for looking at those magazines? Why do I like the women's bodies? What is wrong with me? Well, hopefully God will forgive me,* I consoled myself and drifted into a deep sleep.

◎

The following Monday morning, I woke up with a strange feeling and an impression that something had happened. *Was that real? Or did I just dream that?* I pulled the cobwebs from my eyes and changed into my shorts, workout bra, and tennis shoes for my early morning step aerobic workout. The bus came at 7:00, which meant I needed to wake up at 4:45 each day if I was going to get in a good vigorous workout, breakfast, and shower. I entered my sister Tracy's old bedroom. Now that she was away at college, I had converted it into my workout room, fully equipped with TV, VCR, hand weights, and an aerobics step. As the video instructed, I stepped side to side while doing chest presses to warm up. As I started to wake up, I realized it had just been a dream. I dreamed that Leah and I had kissed. *That's so weird,* I thought. I pushed the thought away as we transitioned into squats and knee lifts.

That day at school, my teachers lectured about algebra, correct sentence structure, and Civil War history. I half listened, and half focused on my dream. It was a good thing my mind could hold so many thoughts at once.

Leah and I kissed? Why? What does this mean? Do I want to kiss her—a girl? Is that why I dreamed it? How embarrassing. I had never seen a girl kissing another girl. It was totally against the rules—and maybe that was why it felt so exciting!

I attempted to tuck that dream away and pretend it never happened. However, the further down I pushed it, the more it popped into the forefront of my mind.

After weeks of being totally distracted at school, I courageously decided to tell Leah about my dream. Maybe if I told her, my mind could stop reviewing it, like a never-ending bad movie, I reasoned. Just in case she freaked out, my back-up plan would be to laugh it off.

That afternoon after school, we hung out at her house in the basement. I was a nervous wreck.

"Leah?"

"Yeah?"

"Um… there's something I want to tell you. Promise not to tell anyone, okay? Actually, you have to *swear* not to tell anyone… ever."

I put out my pinky requesting a pinky swear. With a look of hesitant curiosity, she did the same. Pinkies intertwined, we shook.

"Okay, so, um… I kind of had this dream. It was really weird. You know how dreams can be so weird sometimes."

"What was it about? Get to the point, Court." Leah shrugged one shoulder and shook her head as though my dream could not possibly be any big deal.

"Okay, fine." I took a deep breath, still not really wanting to tell her, but ready to take the plunge. "You pinky swore, remember?"

"*Yes!* Now tell me!"

I swallowed and took a deep breath. "Okay… Well, it was really weird… and I don't know why I dreamed it… who knows…"

"Court, c'mon already!"

"Well, I dreamt that we kissed. Isn't that weird?"

My body tensed up as I awaited the wrath of her judgment, like a guilty puppy waiting for my beating.

"You and I?"

"Yeah, you and I."

This was by far the longest moment of my life. *Did time just freeze or something?* My body froze as well…my stomach tensed, and even the hairs on my back raised. I heard the dramatic background music played in soap operas during moments like these. Suddenly, the sweet sound of Leah's voice pulled me back to reality.

"Really? Cool! That's awesome."

"Huh?"

Is she serious? Mouth open, I stood in shock and disbelief. Time froze again as I absorbed her statement. My fear melted away instantly. "Yeah, well Leah, I guess it was kind of cool."

Just then, a seductive look came over her face. Looking at me directly with intense brown eyes, she spoke words I'd never dreamed I'd hear.

"Court, we should try it sometime."

I sat in silence. I did not even know what to say.

Chapter 8

Dance Like No One's Watching

"Nothing in life is to be feared. It is only to be understood."
—Marie Curie

Spring 1995

Over the next few months, the possibility of kissing Leah consumed my thoughts. Although I'd previously wanted to end the 'bad' movie playing in my mind, now it seemed quite appealing. In fact, maybe I wanted to produce this movie myself.

But really? Kiss Leah? Is that allowed? Wouldn't that be going against the rules?

I was quite curious and kissing her sounded really exciting. I imagined the feel of her lips and the warmth of her body being so close to mine.

But no, I can't do that. No way. It's weird.

In my bedroom late one night, I journaled vigorously instead of brushing my teeth and going to sleep.

> *"I'm afraid of what Leah and I are feeling toward each other. I don't think I'm bisexual or anything, but I keep having these dreams that we plan on kissing. We talked about it, and we think that one time when we get totally trashed, we'll end up kissing. I do not want this to happen. To me, this would be an even bigger sin than having sex outside marriage. But does one kiss change everything, like our sexuality?"*
>
> —Journal, age 14, Wednesday, 12/28/94, 10:31 p.m.

My pen paused on the paper as my mind drifted off. *On the other hand*, I thought, *I am tired of being such a* good *girl... so sweet and working so hard in school. When do I ever get to have fun?* Heat bubbled within my chest and back—the same call to action feeling I experienced just before exercising. I wanted to feel powerful and strong, like I was the one directing my life. I also wanted the thrill of doing something "bad" for once.

Immediately, I scolded myself. *Kissing a girl is an atrocious sin! Do you really want the punishment of burning in hell?* I sighed as my whole body deflated like a balloon. With sadness and defeat, I felt called to take the responsible road yet again. *It just isn't worth it to kiss Leah... if I do, who knows what scary punishment will come? I don't want to be around to find out.*

I laid my head on the pillow and drifted into a restless sleep.

"Good morning, Court! Guess what?!" I heard Kelly's voice in the dark as she opened my bedroom door. Her body glowed in the doorway, backlit by a flood of light.

"Uh, good morning, Kel. What?" Covering my eyes with my hand, I pulled back the covers.

"I got us tickets to see your favorite band at an outdoor concert!" She bounced up and down with excitement.

"You're kidding! You mean Hole? Courtney Love? The one and only?"

I was suddenly fully awake and joining her in a dance of joy.

"Yes! It's this summer. The only trick will be convincing Mom to let you go."

"Yeah, good point." I frowned at the upcoming challenge, but felt hopeful too. I had recently turned fifteen years old, and Kelly was already twenty. She was plenty old enough to escort me. However, Mom did not like the fact that people did drugs at concerts. She wouldn't even let me watch MTV, just in case I saw sex or drugs. *Why is she so overprotective? She seems to think the world is a scary, dangerous place. Is it really that bad?*

Over time, I was becoming increasingly frustrated with her rules, especially when they interfered with what I wanted. I hopped out of bed, gave Kelly a big hug, and got ready for school. When I arrived downstairs for breakfast, Mom was in a bad mood as usual. Either I was imagining things, or she had become increasingly crabby over time. *When will this menopause stage be over?* I wondered.

"You need to clean your room when you get home from school," Mom barked in her usual authoritative, imperial tone.

"Okay," I responded, attempting to hide the attitude I couldn't help but feel.

"And make sure you wear a jacket. It's chilly out today."

"Mom, I don't need to. It's been warming up lately."

Placing her hands on her hips, she glared down at me with wrath. I cowered in my shoes as her gaze pierced my heart. *Oh no, why did you just say that, stupid Courtney?*

"Courtney, I already told you… you can have happy teenage years or teenage years like hell. It's your choice."

My whole body cringed as her voice whipped at me again. "Remember that I can make your life miserable for the next three years. Now, put on your jacket!"

Oh my god, she's such a bitch! Reluctantly, I grabbed my jacket, fighting back tears and trying to calm my trembling lip. I prayed she did not notice how much she had affected me. *Well, she wouldn't care, anyway,* I convinced myself. *She doesn't love you, Courtney. In fact, she hates you. You don't deserve to be loved.*

Jacket on, I walked through the front door and into the cool air outside, feeling such a sense of relief as I stepped away from my mom's anger and headed to the bus stop. As soon as I got on the bus, far out of my mother's sight, I took my jacket off. *Why does she boss me around, like she knows everything and I'm a complete idiot? When do I get to make decisions?* I stared out the window, hardly aware of my classmates hopping into the bus. *What does she mean she can make my life miserable? It already is.*

◎

Soon enough it was the weekend, and thankfully my parents were going out bowling and Leah was coming over to dance. Each time she visited, we had gotten gutsier, most recently sneaking into my

61

parents' supply of rum. We happily blended it with various flavors of Kool-Aid and replaced the small amounts of rum we drank with water so my parents would never notice. It didn't take much to give us a nice buzz. I felt the warmth of the rum burning down my throat and oozing down through my body, until I felt a pleasant, tingling sensation in my shoulders, arms, legs, and especially "down there."

"I'm hot," Leah declared as she began taking her shirt off. "Let's dance in our bras and underwear!"

"Okay," I said, surprised to hear myself agree with no hesitation. I must have had more rum and Kool-Aid than I thought.

We took off our outer layers of clothes and danced. It felt so freeing and fun! I was certain no one else had a special, secret world like ours. I felt like we were at a disco, dancing away to "Gonna Make You Sweat (Everybody Dance Now)" by C+C Music Factory and numerous other upbeat songs. I imagined a fog machine and multi-colored strobe lights pulsating all around us.

Leah looked sexy as she swung her head from side to side, her beautiful black hair flowing in what seemed to me like slow motion. I wanted to kiss her. I really did. *Who cares about all those fears and doubts? I want to do it.* I felt the excitement, curiosity, and nervousness building inside me. Just because I wanted to, though, I still was not sure I could be brave enough.

We started to dance a bit closer, and her hands joined with mine. We took turns twirling each other around, laughing so hard and yelling out with joy.

"Woo! This is great! Courtney, why isn't school this much fun?" Leah asked with a smile.

"Yeah, it's the best!" I said with delight.

"So do you want to do it?"

I swallowed. *Is she serious?*

"Do I want to do what, Leah?"

"Kiss, silly! You've been avoiding the subject for months. When do you want to do it?"

I stared at her, unsure what to say. I did not utter a word, and even so, Leah sensed my answer. She wrapped her arms around my waist and pulled me close. It felt so good to hold her. I felt overwhelmed by all the love I had felt for her since we were little kids. Now, the feeling was still that of love… but different. I brushed her hair from the side of her face. *Wow, her skin is soft. Wow, her eyes are pretty this close up.*

Before I knew it, we had both leaned in and our lips met. Pulses of energy electrified my body. *Whoa,* I thought. Then, for once, my thoughts ceased to exist. All I felt were my lips locked with hers and the most intoxicating, invigorating sensations in my body. Her lips were so soft, and her energy so sensual. She smelled and felt so good. My whole body felt alive. *I* felt alive!

At some point, we stood back and looked at each other. Leah giggled, as did I.

"Wow, Leah, that was… um, amazing!"

Her flirty smile showed me that she agreed.

◎

"Hey" I said, greeting Leah as our families entered the back of our church together two weeks later.

"Hi," she said with a secretive smirk.

We got in a single-file line and made our way to a pew near the front— Mom, Aunt Suzie, Leah's step-dad Uncle Tom, Dad, me, and Leah all in a row. We whispered among ourselves for a bit, waiting for the service to begin. I loved our new Lutheran church. The people seemed friendlier and less uptight than at our previous Catholic church, and I was certain that God was happier with my family and me now that we attended regularly. It seemed we were always at church, whether for Sunday services, the youth group, or the hand bell choir that Leah and I had joined.

As the organ blasted the opening hymn, my mind drifted far away, back to the kiss. Leah and I had not talked about it afterward. We had gone to sleep like usual that night, and the next morning Aunt Suzie came to pick her up, just like on any other Saturday morning. I guess Leah and I did not need to talk about it. Both of us seemed to feel a sense of peaceful satisfaction that finally, after months of escalating anticipation, we had done it. We had finally given into temptation, and our reward, the kiss, felt incredible.

However, "incredible" wasn't the only feeling the kiss had brought me. The last two weeks had given me plenty of time to tear our beautiful experience into shreds. The next morning after the alcohol had worn off, I found myself alone with loads of guilt and confusion. *I can't believe I kissed her*, I thought. Then my inner voice turned much harsher and in fact, downright mean. *What were you thinking, stupid Courtney?*

"Please recite with me The Lord's Prayer," our pastor requested. I was grateful for the reprieve, but my mind again drifted off after we all recited the prayer in unison. Interestingly, out of hundreds of sermons, I had never heard our pastor mention homosexuality. However, our church certainly did not tolerate homosexuality. Our youth group leader had a short haircut, stocky masculine appearance, and had never dated men. Aunt Suzie suspected that she was a lesbian, and I heard kids in youth group sniggering and gossiping about it too. If it were true, however, our leader did not dare tell anyone. I wondered what might happen if she did: would she be disgraced and kicked out of the church? Would God still love her? If *she* couldn't be honest even though she was respected and loved, I decided I had better never say anything, either.

I had also heard the youth group kids saying that being gay is a sin, according to the Bible. This left me feeling terrible. Just as church taught me, I had been born a sinner, and kissing Leah had proved it. I considered asking God for forgiveness during communion, but just in case God had not noticed, I did not want to incriminate myself by admitting the horrifying truth.

In fact, I did not want to admit it to myself. A few weeks later, one evening after school, I finally make the confession to my journal:

> "All right, I was too ashamed before to write about this. I felt too guilty, and it would be horrifying if anyone ever read it. But I have to tell you. I think I'm bisexual. Leah and I have kissed, and we've pretty much made out two different times..."
> —Journal, age 15, Wednesday, 3/8/95, 10:29 p.m.

After finishing my journal entry, I laid my head down to go to sleep. However, I was soon panicking. *Had I really just admitted it? I wrote down that Leah and I had kissed. What if someone finds my journal? What if someone finds out?* For the remainder of the evening I tossed and turned in turmoil with far more questions than answers. *Why did kissing Leah feel so right if it was technically wrong? If I am going to hell for this, what about asking for forgiveness for my sins? Can I just continue kissing her if I keep asking for forgiveness at church?* I was so confused. I certainly wanted to kiss her again—and I had a few more times since our first kiss. It was hard to admit to myself, but I was liking each kiss more and more.

Though it's not like I can have a relationship with Leah, I thought. *She's my cousin. Kissing is just something that we do. She's the only girl I could ever do this with... the only girl I would want to kiss.*

Obsessive thoughts raced through my mind like a funnel cloud. *What's wrong with me? I don't see any other girls kissing girls.* Though I had heard that my favorite singer Courtney Love was bisexual. That made me feel somewhat better. *But what would my friends think if they found out? And my parents? Would I be kicked out of church? No one can ever find out... ever!*

Hours into the night, I just longed to be at school, because that would mean that this sleepless, gut-wrenching night would be over.

Chapter 9

A Way to Feel

"I have a right to feel what I feel. What I am feeling is a temporary experience that cannot harm me." —Iyanla Vanzant[vii]

January 23, 2012

"Hold on," Sarah exclaimed, slapping her hand down on the table. "*You* kissed a girl when you were a teenager? I didn't know that!"

"Ha, yes and not just any girl... my cousin!"

The two women giggled.

"Why didn't you come out?" Sarah's head tilted to the side.

Courtney shrugged. "I never even considered it. Only one person in our whole high school was 'out,' a lesbian named Dana."

"Were you afraid of what your parents would think?"

Courtney glanced pensively outside the window, then back at Sarah. "Yeah, of course. I think they were a bit homophobic when I was really young. But my sister Tracy's best friends in high school, Carlos and Adam, were gay. They were absolutely wonderful, and my parents loved them."

"Awesome!" Sarah smiled. "So that changed their minds about gay people?"

"Yep. Isn't that cool? It gave me a lot of respect for my parents, that they were willing to open their minds. But besides Carlos, Adam, and Dana, I didn't know any other LGBTQ people. And definitely not anyone who was bi. I felt so weird and alone."

"Yeah, that's how I felt, too. I didn't know any other lesbians. It took me a long time to catch on and realize that a lot of women fantasize about being with other women. Same goes for a lot of men feeling attracted to other men. It happens more than people are willing to admit."

Courtney sipped her tea, her expression concerned. "Oh my god, a *ton* of people are attracted to the same sex. So many are still closeted or won't let themselves explore. It's sad… and yet, I can understand. When I realized I was probably bisexual, I thought I would be outcast from society forever. Some moments I thought it was pretty cool, and other moments I hated it."

Sarah grinned. "Oh, do tell more about the *cool* part."

Courtney looked at her with playful suspicion.

"I can't help it! I like the juicy stuff!"

With a giggle, Courtney obliged. "Well, it felt daring and thrilling to break the rules… to kiss a *girl*. Like a chance to finally live on the edge, doing what I wanted to do for once. Our secret world was something that no one else—not even my mom—could control."

"Ha, like you were the queen of the world? Yet instead of having to kiss a king, you had the power to kiss another queen." Sarah winked.

Courtney smiled. "Yeah, I guess I liked making my own 'rules.' Rule number one: Love is love, regardless of sex, gender or appearance."

"Ooh, I want to live in *your* kingdom," Sarah joked. "But seriously, who in society decided that girls couldn't kiss girls and guys couldn't kiss guys?" Her brow furrowed.

"That's what I wonder. Hey, ever hear of "two-spirits?"

Sarah shook her head. "No, what's that?"

"Traditional Native American tribes viewed gay and gender-variant people as sacred. They called them 'two-spirit,' because they embodied both male and female energy in one body. Two-spirits were given special roles in the tribe, like shamans and healers. From what I understand, when someone came out, the tribe gathered to celebrate."

Sarah's eyes widened. "Really? I had no idea! That's incredible."

"Yeah. So if homosexuality was seen as positive, then what happened? Who said something was wrong with it? As a teenager, I thought God said so. I didn't realize that God doesn't discriminate."

"Right, and whatever or whoever God is, God didn't make mistakes when we were created."

"*Yes!*"

Courtney and Sarah high fived across the table.

"I wish I would have known about the two-spirit concept as a teenager. I didn't realize how subjective my religion's and society's rules were, especially about homosexuality. I was so worried about what other people might think that I had no idea how to listen to my heart."

"So did you even tell your friends, like Abby or Janelle?"

"Oh my gosh, no way. I thought for sure they would ditch me!"

"Wait, let me make sure I understand. You had friends, but you didn't let them in, right?"

"Exactly. I mostly talked about superficial things, like school or boys. My self-hatred was so loud, like someone screaming through a megaphone in my head. If I let someone get close to me, I was afraid they would hear it. So, even though I had awesome friends, I felt really alone most of the time." Courtney's sad gaze drifted out to the falling rain.

"I can relate to that. I still feel alone a lot of the time." Sarah looked down with a half-hearted smile.

Courtney looked at her, nodding in agreement. "Well, hopefully hearing the rest of my story will help change that."

Sarah looked up with a glimmer of hope in her eyes. "Courtney, I wonder what your friends would have said if you'd taken the risk to share your true feelings with them. Maybe they would have accepted you!"

"Hmm, that's a good question. Though I didn't know then and even now I'm not sure. Oh. Speaking of feelings, I really couldn't talk about them, because I didn't know I had them—well, beside 'happy' and 'depressed.'"

Sarah frowned.

Courtney continued: "Remember, I thought I needed to be happy all the time, like my dad? I had no idea it was safe to feel different emotions, like sadness or anger. I didn't realize there are reasons we have emotions."

"I thought so." Sarah frowned. "But you know, that's a good question. What are emotions for, anyway?"

Courtney smiled. "They are supposed to provide us information and guidance. If we're willing enough to listen."

"Like what?"

"Well, if I'm angry, it might be because my feelings were hurt. Or because I'm feeling like someone has more power than me. So anger can be a call to action, a time to reconnect with our power and set a boundary."

"Ooh, that's interesting." Sarah smiled. "I'll have to start paying more attention to that."

"Emotions are not bad. The only time they create a problem is when we push them away or ignore them. Like I tried to do by over-exercising."

Sarah shook her head. "It's funny. I never thought that exercise could actually be unhealthy. I'm starting to understand now. What did your mom say about it?"

Courtney frowned. "She started criticizing it, of course... which only made me want to do it more. At meals, she started noticing my behaviors... like blotting all the fat off my bacon with tons of napkins. She tried to convince me that fat was good for me, but I didn't believe her. I'm sure she was just concerned, but to me it felt like criticism. She told me how to do everything else; she did not need to tell me how to eat."

As Sarah's eyes widened, Courtney coughed. "Wow. I guess I'm still angry. I hadn't realized. She and I had such a power struggle. Sometimes I got so mad at her that exercise wasn't even enough to calm me down."

"Courtney?" Sarah asked when her friend shifted uncomfortably in her chair. "Is everything okay?"

Courtney took a moment to respond. "Sarah," she said slowly. "Do you really want to hear this? It's not pretty."

"Go ahead. I can handle it."

After taking a deep breath, Courtney murmured, "Sometimes I used a razor to cut my arm." She looked down in embarrassment as Sarah's eyes widened with shock.

When her friend didn't look up, Sarah leaned in. "You did? I've heard of people doing that, but I don't know why they do it. Were you trying to hurt yourself?"

"No, not at all… at least not consciously. I was looking for a way to express anger… and, well, I think the best way to explain it is to read you a journal entry. Do you mind?"

"No, please, go ahead."

"I just wrote this a few months ago," Courtney said as she pulled a notebook out of her purse. "It was weird. I was really stressed, and I had the urge to cut myself, which I hadn't felt in *years*. Instead of doing it, though, thankfully I journaled instead." After fumbling for the correct page, she opened the book and read:

"Cutting. It's a way to feel. Everything else was too painful. I had to numb myself to it.

Cutting, piercing the skin was a way to feel. To be in my body. To feel something. Something that was mine and mine only. Something that no one could change or take away from me. No one else got to rule or control it. No one else got to feel it or even know about it. It was all mine. *My* body.

If I can hurt myself in this way...

If I can cut my own skin...

I can do anything.

I am powerful!

I am fucking powerful!

I wore it as a badge of honor. I'm proud to have this kind of power, strength and control. Plus, I would rather destroy myself than hurt anyone else.

Little did I know that I was piercing much more than my skin. Each stroke of the razor simultaneously pierced my heart and self-worth.

I didn't want to hurt myself. I was trying to alleviate some of my pain. The energy had to go somewhere. I didn't know how to express it outward.

71

> My arm wasn't the only part of me that bled. My
> heart bled with pain and sadness. The gut-wrenching pain
> of not knowing how to express my pain. How to reach out
> to someone. How to tell them what I was really feeling."
> —Journal, age 31, Thursday, 11/17/11, 9:09 a.m.

"That's it." Courtney looked unsure as she took a deep breath. "It was a terrible idea. I wish I'd had some healthier outlets."

Sarah's eyes were still wide with shock. "Oh my god. Courtney, that's intense. And you never reached out to anyone? Didn't anyone notice?"

"Well, my mom noticed once, but I told her I got caught in some thorn bushes in the woods behind our house. She totally freaked out with worry, but at least she bought my story."

"How did you hide the cuts?"

Courtney glanced uneasily at her arm, which now, twenty years later, appeared scar-free. "I just wore long sleeves every day," she said, shrugging her shoulders. With her opposite hand, she caressed her arm then pulled it across her chest, as though apologizing for harming it.

"Wow, Courtney, I'm glad you stopped hurting yourself like that," Sarah said compassionately.

"Me too. I remember feeling sad for myself, like no one cared. But I didn't give anyone the opportunity to care."

After taking a long, heavy breath, Sarah responded, "I'm so sorry."

Courtney rolled her shoulders back and sat back in her chair again. "Thanks, Sarah, I appreciate that. It's been a long journey of healing, that's for sure!"

Sarah nodded. "I know that was pretty heavy, but do you mind if we change the subject? I can't wait to hear what happens next with Leah!"

"Sure." Courtney paused to take a sip of her tea before she continued.

Chapter 10

Knight to the Rescue

"There is luxury in self-reproach. When we blame ourselves, we feel no one else has a right to blame us." —Oscar Wilde

Spring 1995

"Wanna go to a sleepover Friday night at my church?" Abby asked as we left biology.

Finally, seventh period is over, I thought. *Time to go home.* We had just dissected a frog, which had made me a bit queasy. I was thankful for Abby's diversion. "What's the sleepover like? I mean, what do you do there?"

"Don't worry, it won't be churchy at all. We play pool, watch movies, play games, and just hang out. It's super fun."

Since our elementary school days, Abby had broken out of her shell. With her newfound laid-back attitude, shoulder-length haircut and classic rock T-shirts, she was quickly becoming one of the cool, popular kids. I felt relieved that she still wanted to be my friend. She still did well in school but certainly wasn't an overachiever like me.

"Okay, sure, I would love to. Hopefully my mom will let me go."

We continued to our lockers, passing tons of other students along the way, all anxious to head home. As I thought about the older students heading to their cars, I fantasized about turning sixteen next year, and gaining the freedom to drive my own car.

"Did you see him?"

The urgency in Abby's voice quickly brought my focus back to my surroundings.

"Who, what?"

"James Hudson. He's so cute. He *smiled* at you!"

"Really? Are you sure?"

I doubted what Abby had seen, but a twinge of excitement fluttered through my belly. Even the *possibility* of him smiling at me felt thrilling. James had such a handsome smile. I felt sorry I had missed it.

"Yes, Courtney. He looked directly at *you* and smiled," Abby insisted.

James was two years older and extremely attractive. He had brown curly hair that fell down around his ears and the sweetest, most sparkly blue eyes I'd ever seen. He wrestled and played football and was strong and athletic, but much different than the typical jock. He was popular and got along with everybody, and there was something about him that I couldn't quite put my finger on. A softness, maybe; a gentleness. Whatever it was, I found him really down-to-earth and intriguing. But even though he'd had band with me all year, I had never worked up the courage to talk to him. Still, I would have given anything even to be his friend.

Later that evening, Mom agreed to let me go to the sleepover, as long as there was adult supervision and no drugs or alcohol. As I set the dinner table, I felt like celebrating. Then I realized I had forgotten to tell her one tiny, yet potentially deal-breaking detail.

"Mom, it's gonna be co-ed, though… you know, girls and guys, too."

"I assumed so. That's okay as long as adults are there. You *are* growing up, you know." Mom's answer was so light and upbeat that it took me by surprise. Apart from having to cut up a dead animal in Biology class, I had had one good day!

Friday night couldn't come fast enough, especially once I heard that James might be there, too. Over the next few days, my heart flip-flopped as I walked through the school hallways, eagerly scanning for James between each class period. Indeed, he must have smiled at me the other day, because he directed his handsome, twinkling eyes my way two more times during the week. During band class, we caught each other's eyes again, and this time I felt my own eyes twinkle. The thought that someone as cute as James would smile at me made me so giddy I felt like I could dance on the classroom ceiling.

That dancing feeling floated me through the rest of the week. On Friday night, Abby came over early, and we spent hours doing our makeup and choosing our outfits. I hoped James would like my jeans and multi-colored long-sleeved, striped shirt. After Dad dropped us off at the church, we excitedly hurried inside.

"Hi there," a low voice said as we walked through the doorway.

I turned and realized, much to my delight, that the voice belonged to James.

"Well hi," I answered with a huge grin on my face. I wanted to play it cool, but attempting to hide my excitement would have been impossible. I was already glowing.

"How are you?"

"I'm good, James. How about you?"

"Good, now that you're here."

For real? He is talking to me?

Indeed, he was.

"So what do we do here?" I asked, trying to think of something cool to say.

"There's a pool table... do you play?"

James' cuteness melted my whole body, including my legs, which now wobbled. I grabbed onto the wall to keep from falling over, still trying to play it cool. "My family has a pool table in our basement, and my dad and I play sometimes."

"I bet I'll win." James winked at me.

"Oh yeah? We'll see about that."

This sleepover is going to be an absolute blast! I thought, passing a bunch of other kids as I followed James to the pool table.

We flirted the entire time we played, and I let him win once or twice. In the back of my mind, I hoped Abby did not mind that I was hardly talking to her.

James and I stayed side by side the entire night. Who needed sleep? We found ourselves far too busy talking and getting to know one another to even consider it. The constant stream of fireworks exploding within my heart provided me with plenty of energy. As we all played hide-and-seek in the dark, James held my hand. Nothing had ever felt so right in my life. Even though it was well after midnight, I felt as if a bright light were shining all around us. I was barely aware of the other kids playing with us; all I felt was the playful happiness between James and me.

"Sit here," he whispered as he gently guided me onto his lap. It felt so good to be close to him. James Hudson! Liking *me*! I wasn't sure if I deserved such a handsome and sweet guy, but I wasn't about to start questioning this now. He was the knight in shining armor I had dreamed of my whole life.

Eventually, the sun rose and it was time to go home. My heart fluttered as James pulled me close for a hug. He slipped me a note with his phone number.

"Call me sometime, okay?"

"Of course!"

I was so tired and love-struck that I hardly remembered Dad picking me up. After getting home and climbing the stairs to my cozy bedroom, I slept for most of the day. As soon as I got up, I called Leah, excited to share my good news.

"Hi!" I chirped when she picked up.

"Hi. Want to come over tonight?"

"No, I'm too tired. I was at a sleepover last night."

"Oh yeah. How was it?"

Despite her attempt to sound upbeat and interested, I sensed disappointment in her voice.

"Well, I met this really cute boy, James. He's older than me. He flirted with me the whole night!"

I nervously awaited Leah's response, fully anticipating jealousy, but hoping she'd be happy for me.

"Oh. Well, I don't feel good, so you couldn't have come over anyway. See you tomorrow at church, then! Bye!"

"Uh, bye," I responded, hearing the click as Leah disconnected.

What just happened? I wondered. *I know Leah's been sick a lot lately. She's been missing a lot of school, and the doctors can't figure out what's wrong. But still, I think she just lied to me. Why would she invite me then say she didn't feel well? She's obviously upset with me.* Unfortunately, rationalizing did not soothe my hurt feelings or my guilt for upsetting Leah.

The next morning at church, Leah was downright distant. She sat beside her mom instead of me during the service and avoided my glances completely. When it was over, I attempted a "hello," but instead of reciprocating, she quickly walked away with her nose in the air.

Great, I thought. *Now that we kissed, she's going to be jealous of every relationship I have? What happened to being my best friend?*

"Why didn't Leah talk to you today?" Mom asked as I climbed into the truck with her and Dad. "That was strange."

"I'm not sure."

A rushing waterfall of tears ached to escape from my eyes, but I quickly cleared my throat and wiped away the few escapees. If only I could share the truth with my parents, just to get it off my chest. I stared out the window, tuning out their conversation as we headed home. *What does Leah expect from me... never to have a boyfriend just so I can keep kissing her? I don't understand!* The fury that rushed through me was just as bad as the sadness.

Later that afternoon, Mom dropped me off at our high school's St. Patrick's Day jazz band performance. Abby met me outside, and we gleefully chatted about Friday night's sleepover before entering the building. Thankfully, she was not mad at me for ditching her, as she, too, had found a boy to flirt with!

As we found our seats, my eyes happily zeroed in on James, who was playing the baritone sax in the second row. His curly brown hair bounced around as he swayed back and forth, soulfully expressing his joy through music. *Mmm... I could watch him all day*, I thought. And I did for several songs, lost in the music and in him.

Then, just like hat, a pin popped my balloon near the concert's end.

"What's that?" Abby frowned, pointing to my arm.

"Oh, nothing." I quickly slid my arm back into my jacket.

What were you thinking, idiot Courtney? I chastised myself. I had forgotten to wear long sleeves to cover up the self-inflicted cuts on my arm. I would die if anyone realized I was not the happy, confident "good girl" I pretended to be.

Thankfully, the conductor's announcement of the next song distracted Abby. The concert concluded after that number, and we waited around to see my knight in shining armor. After congratulating him for an awesome concert and talking for a few minutes, we parted to do our homework. I was reluctant to leave, but alas, Mom's car awaited me outside. I smiled at the thought of seeing James' handsome face the following day.

After greeting me, she dove right in: "Kelly told me about the outdoor concert. I'm sorry, Court, but you can't go."

Panic and anger welled up within me. She had no right to keep me from seeing my favorite band! "Mom, why?"

"Because there will be drugs there."

"But Kelly's going to be with me! Who cares? I don't even want to do drugs. Kelly already has the tickets! You have to let me go."

"No I don't, Courtney. I said no, and the final answer is *no*."

Once Mom pulled the car into the garage, I slammed the car door, flung open the door to the house, and ran to my room. *How dare she? This is way beyond being strict! It's so unfair!*

My blood boiled with anger. Pacing back and forth in my room, I wanted to yell at her for being so stupid. *But if I scream at her, I'll be grounded the rest of my life.* However, my anger craved expression. *Maybe I can exercise? No, Mom will flip out* again *if she hears me exercising.*

As I glancing at my bedroom window, I suddenly felt a spark of hope. I pounced onto my bed and opened my window. I snickered at the sight of the flat rooftop below.

After maneuvering the tiny knobs that held the screen in place, I disassembled and removed it completely. I looked back toward my bedroom door, making sure it was securely closed and more importantly, that no one was watching. After making sure the coast was clear, I climbed outside onto the black rooftop and breathed in the sweetness air of freedom.

If she thinks she can control me, she'd better think again. She'd freak out if she saw me up here. Staring out at the browns and greens of the woods behind our house, I dreamed of the day I could fly away and finally be myself, free of rules and restrictions. I soaked in the taste of freedom just long enough for my racing heart to calm down. I returned to my room and replaced the screen, breathing a sigh of relief that I had not been caught.

Doesn't she care that she hurt my feelings? Why doesn't she trust me?

Maybe because you suck and don't deserve to be trusted.

That thought made me feel even worse. I opened my closet door and furiously dug beneath the piles of blankets and books until I found the thing I craved. The glass bottle, with its gold and silver-embossed label felt like treasure in my hands. I crawled as far in as I could and pushed aside clothes and shoes to create a soft resting place. *Mom would be so upset if she knew what I'm doing.* I opened the bottle of rum and took a whiff. *Damn, I wish I had some Kool-Aid. Oh well, here goes.* The taste of straight rum burned my taste buds, sending jolts of shock down my throat.

Still, it felt like sweet revenge. I could not punish my mom, but I could certainly punish myself. Drinking a few swigs provided some relief from the pent-up rage inside. This revenge did not come without side effects, however. *Tomorrow I need to exercise extra to make up for these calories,* I vowed.

Chapter 11

Milkshakes Make Everything Better

"To be alive is the biggest fear humans have. Death is not the biggest fear we have; our biggest fear is taking the risk to be alive—the risk to be alive and express what we really are." —Don Miguel Ruiz[viii]

Despite the painful secrets in my closet and heart, springtime delivered fresh, new energy. The sun's reappearance after a long, dreary Michigan winter always delighted me. After the snow melted and the earth thawed out, the purple tulips' and yellow daffodils' reappearance cheered me even more. And then the spring of 1995 delivered an even more exciting treat.

"Did you know today's the first day of spring?" James asked with a playful smile.

"Awesome! Spring's my favorite season."

We walked along the path of the local park, admiring the fields of green grass speckled with endless yellow dandelions. The sun shined overhead, blessing our afterschool outing. James reached for my hand then stood still.

"Courtney, I have a question for you."

"Okay. What is it?"

He had been flirting with me for ten days now. He brought so much light and joy into my life. We had talked on the phone daily and exchanged notes in the hallways. He now occupied many of my thoughts, distracting me from my problems. My heart beat faster every time I thought of him or saw his sparkling blue eyes. I held my breath, hoping his question was the one for which I had been praying.

"Will you go out with me?"

"Do you mean like…"

"Yes… be my girlfriend. Will you?"

Sparkles of excitement danced throughout my whole body. "I would love to!"

I reached in for a loving hug. After a sweet kiss, we continued walking, this time hand in hand. *Is this real?* I wondered. *It feels too good to be true!* Although I maintained my cool, I wished I could have skipped or twirled around.

"Courtney, I know you have to go home soon."

"Yeah, before I get caught. My mom doesn't know I'm with you. She thinks I'm at a friend's house studying."

"Why didn't you just tell her?"

"Oh, well, she has kinda strict rules."

"So when will I see you again? Can I come over after school tomorrow?"

"I wish, but I can't have boys over when I'm home alone 'til I'm sixteen. I'm sorry."

My body tensed with embarrassment. James was two years older than me, and his parents did not have any weird or restrictive rules. I hated disappointing him, and I prayed that he would still want to date me.

"We'll figure something out, okay?"

James drove me home, and we said our goodbyes just in time. Two minutes after his truck pulled out of the driveway, Mom's car pulled in. I breathed a sigh of relief, started setting the table for dinner, and allowed my mind to float back into the clouds.

"Wow, you sure are happy," Mom noticed as she entered the house.

My cheeks turned pink.

"Uh-oh, looks like someone's in love!" Dad said, walking in from work as well.

"That obvious, huh?"

"What's his name?" Dad asked.

"James Hudson. He's so cute. I can't wait till you guys meet him."

"We'll be happy to," Mom said.

"Are you guys sure I can't have him over after school? I won't do anything bad, I promise!"

"Courtney, you know the rules. It wouldn't be fair to your sisters if we changed them for you."

"What if we ask Kelly and Tracy? Maybe they won't mind."

Apparently, Mom did not appreciate my idea. "You can see him on the weekends."

"He actually has wrestling matches on Saturdays. Maybe we can figure out something else?"

"Courtney!" she raised her voice in a biting tone, her anger now escalating. "What don't you understand about the word '*no*'?"

"Jeez, okay." My joy quickly deflated into frustration, defeat and despair. I suddenly wished I were invisible. *Why can't I ever make Mom happy? It seems like everything I say pisses her off. Maybe it would be better if I didn't exist at all.* I sunk down into the unfairness.

I need James in my life. I need him to keep me from slipping into a deep, dark hole. If he likes me so much, maybe I'm not such a bad person after all. Maybe I can start feeling better about myself. If Mom would not cooperate, I would just have to come up with an alternate plan.

Over the next several weeks, I ached to spend time alone with James. One day at school, I asked him to come over late that night, but not to knock on the front door. After saying goodnight to my parents, I retreated into my bedroom, turned off the light, curled into bed, and watched the clock. When the numbers on my alarm clock flashed 11:30 p.m., my heart raced with nervousness. I slowly propped open my bedroom door and glanced downstairs at my parents' bedroom to insure they had gone to sleep. I quietly reclosed my door so I wouldn't wake up Kelly in the bedroom next to mine. I then removed the screen from my window and escaped into the cool night air of the rooftop.

"Hi!" James whispered from the darkness on the ground below.

After giving my eyes a moment to adjust, I walked to the edge. "Hi handsome," I whispered back.

James instructed me how to maneuver my body to climb down from the roof. I felt relieved once my feet felt the firmness of the earth beneath them and his arms closed around me. Looking over James' shoulder, I noticed a massive amount of bright twinkling stars in the sky.

"C'mon! This way."

I grabbed his hand and led him to the backyard, just behind the pool. It seemed to be a good enough hiding spot. We lay down on the grass and cuddled up to keep warm. Although I felt a little nervous about being caught, the tension in my body quickly melted away in James' arms. I felt safe and protected, as though my knight in shining armor had just rescued me from the castle and brought me to a land of peaceful, loving bliss.

"Courtney, look at all the stars! It's amazing."

"Yeah, it is." I smiled. We both stared dreamily at the star-filled sky, mesmerized by the magical energy of the twinkling lights.

"Are you looking at any particular star?"

"Hmm… there's one I've been staring at a while."

"Me, too. I wonder if it's the same one!"

My curiosity piqued. "Do you know the Big Dipper?"

"Yes."

"On the handle of the Big Dipper, three stars in… that's where I've been focusing."

"That's the same exact star I chose!"

Our eyes opened wide with surprise as we looked at each other in silence.

Is this possible? I wondered. *Out of millions of stars in the sky, we were just staring at the same exact star. This must mean he's the one!*

"James, what do you think this means?"

"That you're the love of my life."

He leaned closer and placed his lips against mine for a soft, romantic kiss.

My heart had never felt such peace. In that moment, it was just James, me, the sky full of stars, and the magical beauty of our love.

Around 2:00 a.m., James hoisted me safely back onto the rooftop, and I climbed through the window and into my bed for a short yet deep sleep. Thankfully, our rendezvous had gone unnoticed by my family. Although I was sleepy at school the next day, my heart felt like it was dancing up there with the stars. By now, it seemed the whole school knew that we were a couple. I beamed with pride and joy as I walked next to James through the hallways.

On the bus ride home that day, I thought about Leah. Suddenly, worry smashed into me like a funnel cloud. *What will I tell her?*

> "It's too late. We've already become bisexual, and I don't know how to stop it. It'll kill her if I decide to stop now. She's already hurt enough because she's not the only one in my life. What if I leave her (in a sexual way) completely? Nothing in our friendship will ever be the same. It'll hurt her so fucking bad, but somehow I have to stop this. We can't kiss or anything else anymore, even if we're drunk. It's not right, and I don't truly want to be bi. I never truly did. And plus, this is cheating on James.... I can't cheat on James. I won't. I never could. I'm still afraid of wanting to though."
> —Journal, age 15, Thursday, 4/20/95, 9:34 p.m.

That evening during my workout, I anxiously contemplated what to do. Thankfully, each knee lift seemed to provide an outlet for the fear and frustration. I devoted every drop of energy available to the motions, hoping to create space within for a bright idea to suddenly spring to life. Leah and I would see each other in just a few days. *What will I say to her? I can't lose my best friend. But kissing my cousin is wrong. I already love James, and I know he's the one... especially after last night.*

"Courtney, turn off the VCR." My mom's voice startled me from my reverie.

Is she blind? I thought in frustration. *I'm in the middle of knee lift repetitions.*

As I grabbed a towel to wipe the sweat off my forehead, I felt certain I had misunderstood her. If I turned off the VCR, how would I know which move to do next? *Though I have done this workout so many times, I probably have it memorized.*

"Mom, I don't understand. Why?"

"Turn off the VCR. Your dad and I want to talk to you."

I slowly turned around and was appalled at the sight before me. Mom and Dad stood at the back of the room, holding a milkshake from the local fast food restaurant.

"Um, guys, if you can't see, I'm in the middle of a workout. Thanks, but I told you earlier I didn't want dessert. Can't we talk when I'm done?"

"No, right now."

"Listen to your mother, Courtney."

"I can't just stop in the middle of a workout. It's not good for my heart rate. Now I'll have to start all over from the beginning."

"Now!" Mom commanded fiercely.

Are they insane? I thought to myself, reluctantly pushing pause on the VCR. *This had better not take long. I still have 40 minutes of calorie burning ahead.*

"Courtney, all you do lately is exercise. Here, drink this," Mom demanded, pushing the milkshake my way.

My brow furrowed with frustration. "You guys, I'm trying to lose weight. I don't want this." I pushed it back toward her.

"You don't need to lose weight."

"Yes, I do."

"You're a teenager," Dad chimed in. "Don't you want to spend your time with friends or maybe doing a hobby?"

"Exercise *is* my hobby now. It's good for me. Don't you want me to be healthy?"

Turning my back to him, I rolled my eyes.

"Of course we do," Dad continued. "But you're overdoing it."

"You're terrified of eating anything fattening," Mom said. "Some fat is good for you. You can't just cut out desserts." I sighed angrily; her concern felt like criticism. She now approached me from the side. Out of the corner of my eye, I saw her again push the milkshake my way. "Here, *drink*."

What does she know about health? I wondered heatedly. "I don't want to."

"Would you rather be grounded for a week?" she threatened cunningly.

I wanted to shoot them a dirty look or better yet, punch them, especially Mom. But I knew I needed to be polite or I may be grounded for the rest of my life. I grudgingly took the cold chocolate milkshake into my hand and lifted it up to my mouth for a teeny-tiny sip, vowing that if I had my say, I would never drink a milkshake again.

"Drink the *whole* thing," Mom bossed.

Cool tears of defeat and anger slid down my flushed face. *How can they be so stupid? They pretend they're trying to help me, but instead they criticize and punish me. How dare they?*

With each disgusting sip, I felt my body getting fatter. Horrified and enraged, I plotted out the five extra workouts I would have to do to make up for the calories from this sordid dessert.

Chapter 12

Praying for Forgiveness

"When you discriminate against the black or the white, or the flower, or the lesbian, you discriminate against God, which is the basic goodness in you." —Thich Nhat Hanh[ix]

That Saturday night, Mom dropped me off at Leah's as planned. We practically had the house to ourselves after Aunt Suzie and Uncle Tom retreated upstairs to watch a movie. Although I referred to it as my second home, tonight I felt eerily uncomfortable and out of place.

As Leah and I descended the stairs to the basement, I felt a growing sense of dread. I had no idea how, but I needed to put a stop to our romantic rendezvous.

"You're quiet tonight," she commented as she settled onto the floor and reached for the remote control. I sat just behind her on the couch.

"Yeah, well, I'm tired," I said as she flipped through the TV stations.

From previous experience, I knew she did not want to hear about James, and I didn't know what else to discuss. Apart from the elephant in the room, he was the only topic on my mind.

"I made a new friend at school. She's really pretty. I kinda have a crush on her."

Why is Leah telling me this? I wondered. *Does she want me to be jealous? If so, it's working.* "That's nice," I said, attempting to hide my distaste.

"Court, you're not jealous, are you?"

Leah turned off the TV and lifted herself up to the couch. She placed her hand on my thigh and began softly caressing, as though she wanted to reassure me that I was the only one for her. I wished I could reassure her of the same. The familiar look of seduction came over her face, and she leaned in to kiss me. Unsure how to deny her and desperately desiring her lips, I kissed her back.

After a few moments of passionate kissing, Leah lifted off her shirt and began unhooking her bra.

I began to panic as my mind started up a tug-of-war with itself. *What am I supposed to do?*

Courtney, you're supposed to dedicate yourself to James, remember? James!

But I want to kiss her.

Yeah, but Courtney, it's not right. It never was.

I did the only thing I could think of: pull away.

"Leah, I'm really tired. I know it's early, but do you mind if we go to sleep?"

"You're tired already?" She gave me a suspicious look.

"Yes, it was a long week at school." I tilted my head down to show her how "tired" I was.

Leah's look of disappointment pained my already bleeding heart. "All right, I guess."

We settled into our sleeping bags. Despite feeling overwhelmed, I soon fell fast asleep.

◎

After a full night of deep rest, I woke up feeling much clearer about what I needed to do. Remaining cuddled in my sleeping bag, I waited for Leah to wake up. After what seemed like forever, she eventually rolled over and opened her eyes.

"Good morning, Court," she said, yawning.

Before losing my courage, I blurted out, "Leah, I need to talk to you. I can't do this anymore."

"What do you mean?" She leaned back hesitantly.

"You know what I mean," my voice got quieter as I heard the sounds of Aunt Suzie making coffee upstairs. "Kiss and stuff. I don't want to cheat on James."

"Court, that's not fair. We were together before you started going out with *him*."

I sighed. "I know, but I really like him, Leah. I think I will marry him someday. I'm sorry, Leah, but I just can't. I don't want to be bisexual anymore. I'm not sure I ever did."

Balancing both sadness and uncertainty, I stared off into the distance. When Leah didn't say anything, I picked up the phone, dialed my house, and asked Mom to pick me up immediately. I felt unable to witness Leah's sadness, as I had enough of my own.

"Court, you have to choose between him and me. It's that simple," she said after I hung up.

My eyes widened with surprise. "Leah, I'm not going to choose between my cousin and the boy I'm going to marry someday. That's ridiculous!"

What, now she's gone crazy, too? What is happening? I already hated conflict, and in this moment, I hated it even more. My best friend was expecting me to make an impossible decision, and it felt like no matter what path I chose, our life-long friendship was crumbling. Suddenly, I felt exhausted.

"You can't just say you're not going to be bisexual anymore. Maybe that works for you, but it doesn't work for me!" Tears of hurt and anger streamed down her face. I quickly rolled up my sleeping bag, grabbed my stuff and gave Leah one last look before heading upstairs and out the front door to wait for my mom in the fresh air.

Devastated and forlorn, I could not wait to get home to exercise. That would certainly make things better. *What am I doing? Why am I so messed up? Why am I hurting two people I love? I have to make things right. I have to confess my secret to James. Maybe then, everything will be okay.* I never thought I'd be so happy to see Mom's car pulling into the driveway. Relieved, I hopped in the passenger seat, anxious to get home, yet dreading what lie ahead.

◎

My insides were in turmoil for the rest of the weekend. The following Monday, James came over after school to watch our favorite soap opera. We sat in our usual spots on the floor, guessed which couples would say their vows, kiss passionately and live happily ever after. At this point, I simply ignored my mom's rule about not having boys over. I disliked the intense fear of being caught and grounded, but since I was afraid all the time anyway, what was the difference? As long as James left before Mom arrived home, sneaking was worth it to have the boy who was increasingly becoming my lifeline around.

Usually I felt so good when I was with him. Today, however, my heart felt like it weighed a ton from all the sadness and dread it was holding. Every muscle in my body tightened, bracing for his anger and judgment, along with the rejection that was sure to come once I confessed my secret. I felt like an actor ready to take the stage, hoping for applause but prepared to be pelted by an endless volley of tomatoes. As soon as the soap opera concluded, I entered stage right.

"James, can I talk to you for a minute?"

"Sure, what's up?"

I looked down sadly. "James, there's something I need to tell you. Keep sitting down, okay? I don't think you're going to like this."

James frowned. "Okay," he said.

"Okay, here goes. Before you came into the picture, something was happening. Well, you know my cousin Leah, right?"

"Yeah," he said hesitantly.

My body trembled with trepidation. "A few months ago, I had this dream that Leah and I kissed."

"That's weird."

I sighed. "Yeah, it was. Yet one night when we were drunk, we did. We've kissed a few times, actually."

I looked down, wishing I could take it back... wishing it were not true. I braced for the blow of his anger.

"You kissed a girl? More than once? Why?"

"I think I'm probably bisexual."

I looked him directly in the eyes now and held my breath. Immediately, tears rushed to his eyes. His face contorted in a mixture of fear, anger, and confusion. He stood up, reaching for his school bag.

"I have to go."

"No, James, please."

I grabbed his hand and forced him to sit next to me on the floor.

"I want to be with you. I don't want to be bisexual anymore. I told Leah we can't kiss anymore. We only did once since you and I have been going out. I told her it can't happen ever again. I'm sorry, James. I didn't mean to hurt you." Hot tears welled in my eyes.

"You cheated on me?" James said furiously.

I can't dare tell him it went slightly further than kissing. "Yes. I'm so sorry. It won't happen ever again. I know you'll probably need time for this to sink in. I'm really sorry, and I pray you will forgive me. I love you so much."

He left in a hurry, fighting back more tears. As soon as the front door closed, the floodgates opened. *What if he leaves me?* I thought as I sobbed. *God, why do I have to be so fucked up? Why do I have to be bisexual? Well I'm not going to anymore. I can't believe I made him cry.*

I didn't relax until he called me later that night.

"Court, I still want to be with you," he said when I picked up the phone.

My shoulders dropped away from my ears, and somehow my breathing returned to normal.

"I'm sure Leah pressured you into it. Maybe you thought you were bi so Leah would accept you. Or maybe you just didn't want to hurt her feelings."

It took a moment for it to register that James was blaming everything on Leah. Also, he was saying that I wasn't really bi. Well, I thought, that didn't matter, because I did not want to be bi anymore. If he was willing to stay with me, even though I had kissed a girl, then I would not argue. Any other guy would have dumped me for sure. I bit my lip and just felt incredibly relieved.

"James, I love you."

Those were the only words I could muster through my tears.

"I love you, too!" he assured me.

Later that night I told my journal everything.

"I confessed my secret to him. I felt ashamed... I knew he wouldn't love me any less. But I also knew that he'd look at me differently...I was so scared of what I had done,

scared of what he thought, shocked that I actually told
him that, and happy that he would still love me."
—Journal, age 15, Wednesday. 4/26/95, 8:44 p.m.

Just before turning the lights off for the night, I stared at the light
switch. *On... off,* I thought. *On... off. It seems so simple. Maybe that's just
how it can be with my attraction to Leah. Time to turn the light* off.

Chapter 13

Silver Platter

"We cannot selectively numb emotions, when we numb the painful emotions, we also numb the positive emotions."
—Brené Brown[x]

"You really like butterflies, huh?" James asked, pointing to my folder, which I'd covered in butterfly stickers. He had driven me home from school that afternoon, unbeknown to my parents. He had come inside to spend some time with me, as he was doing regularly now.

"I love them!" I said as we walked into the living room. I plopped down on the couch.

"Why do you like them so much?" he asked as he sat down beside me.

"I guess they remind me of hope and freedom. Well, and they're just so beautiful! I've liked them since I was little."

The corners of his mouth quirked into a grin. "Well, I think butterflies are awesome, especially since you remind me of one."

"What?" I blinked and blushed in surprise.

"There's something magical about you, Courtney. You said how beautiful butterflies are. Well, you're beautiful, too."

"Oh James, I love you. You're so good to me."

"I love you too!"

After a sweet kiss, we contentedly snuggled into each other's arms and I gently nuzzled his neck. After catching up on our days at school, we turned on our usual soap opera. Suddenly the phone rang. I hopped up to answer it, just in case it was my mom.

"Hello?"

"Court?" my grandmother asked.

"Yeah, it's me."

"Can I talk to your mom?"

"No, she's still at work. She won't be home for a while."

"Well that's odd. I called the office, and they said she had come home sick today."

My stomach dropped to the floor. Blood rushed through my body. "What? Oh, um, Gran, I gotta go. I'll have Mom call you later." I hung up the phone without saying a proper goodbye.

"James, you've gotta go. Right now. My mom's on her way home. She's coming home from work sick. She'll be here any minute!"

"What?" James was already grabbing up his stuff. I pushed him out of the door as quickly as possible, giving him the quickest kiss I could spare.

"I'll call you later."

I closed the door and turned to run upstairs. My stomach was already a nervous wreck, and I was anxious to hide in my bedroom. However, life had a different plan for me. The moment my foot hit the first stair, my body froze in terror.

"Cooouuurrrtneey."

The eerie voice had come from my mother's bedroom, which was just across from the stairs.

Oh no.

"I've been watching you this whole time."

I stepped back down onto the floor and turned to look into the bedroom. Swiftly, Mom propped herself up in her bed.

"Hi, Mom. You're not feeling well, huh?" I attempted in the sweetest voice I could muster up.

"No, I've been home since noon. I feel even worse now. I've been watching you and James this whole time."

The disgust in her voice sent chills of terror down my spine.

Her bedroom has a clear view into the living room, I thought. *Good thing James and I weren't making out.*

"Mom, all we did was talk. We didn't do anyth—"

"How often does James come over when I'm not home?" she snapped.

Her anger made me feel as if hundreds of daggers were piercing my skin. I feared she could see through my soul, but I lied anyway.

"Today was the first time."

"You know the rule, Courtney. No boys allowed over until you're sixteen."

"But Mom, that's not fair. I'm fifteen, and I'm mature for my age. I don't get it. When am I ever supposed to see James?"

"Stop arguing with me. You're grounded for two weeks!"

"But Mom, it's Memorial weekend. I'm supposed to hang out with James and all my friends."

"Well, you should have thought of that before you broke the rules, Courtney. Go to your room now!"

> "Immediately, I cried. I knew what had happened. I knew what it meant. It meant that my life was over. Every little bit of trust she had in me was gone, gone forever."
> —Journal, age 15, Saturday 5/27/95, 10:36 p.m.

Without the energy to argue anymore, I made the walk of shame to my bedroom. I was too shocked and numb to slam my door; instead, I shut it gently then threw myself on the floor beside my bed.

After staring blankly at the wall for what felt like hours, suddenly, a torrential downpour of thoughts flooded my mind.

How could you be so stupid, Courtney?
You deserve punishment.
You got off easy, compared to what you deserve.

Unable to tolerate such cruelty within my own mind, I fought back.

Yeah, but why does she have such stupid rules? Why is she so mean and abusive? I feel betrayed. I hate her!

Do you? She's your mom.

I thought you loved her.

                                            I do… most of the time.

If you love her, idiot, then why
do you break her rules?

                Thanks a lot. I already feel sick to my
            stomach. Do you have to make it worse?

You're no good, Courtney. You're
made of mud. You don't deserve to breathe.

              Why can't I get things right? Why can't
                I just be who Mom wants me to be?
                  Why can't I just be a good person?

Because you're not.

                              Shut up! Leave me alone!

I stood up and paced back and forth vehemently, my mind now racing with dreadful fears. *How will I survive two weeks without James? And, he can't come over after school anymore… ever again. What if he leaves me? What am I supposed to do?*

Every muscle in my body tensed with terror and fury and my pace quickened. As the energy escalated within me, it ached for an outlet. However, none of my usual tactics would suffice. I could not risk getting in any more trouble. Going on the roof was not an option. Drinking or cutting seemed pointless. None of these things hurt Mom, anyway. I couldn't possibly hurt her as badly as she'd hurt me.

After a while, I heard Mom calling from downstairs that dinner was ready. Eating was the farthest thing from my mind. Plus, I certainly did not want to see *her* again tonight. I opened my door and hollered that I had no appetite. Head hung low in defeat, I retreated back into my room.

Where can I hide? I'm a disgrace to my mom, God, and myself. Finally, I climbed as far as I could fit into my closet. As soon as I was inside, my whole body began to cry and convulse with waves of panic and hopelessness.

> "I thought about killing myself. I seriously almost ran away. I was so close, but I decided to cry instead. It was bad, so bad. I've never experienced feelings like that ever before. I seriously felt like my life was over."
> —Journal, age 15, Saturday 5/27/95, 10:36 p.m.

I can't take this anymore! Throwing one of my shoes across the room provided a split-second of relief. However, as it hit the opposite wall with a loud bang, I trembled with fear at the thought of my mom's wrath if she had heard it from downstairs.

Obviously, breaking the rules is not working. I can't stand sneaking anymore. I was jumpy every second, because I never knew when the next bomb would explode. *God, why do I have to be so afraid of my own mother? Isn't she supposed to love me and help me feel safe?* I sniffed with sarcasm. *"Safe" is the opposite of what I feel around her. It's like she's always right behind my back, holding a hammer over my head, waiting to punish me. Or, maybe that's actually God waiting to punish me for being such a no-good, low-life sinner.* I sighed loudly, tears streaming down my face. *I have to be with James. He's the only thing that keeps me going.*

I felt as though my power rested on a silver platter, and I could either keep it in front of me or hand it to my mother. *When I listen to me, I break rules and get in trouble. Mom thinks she knows my feelings and needs better than I do. It makes me so mad when she acts like that. She thinks my opinions need to be the exact same as hers. But maybe she's right?*

My head hung even lower. *Maybe I can convince myself to* like *her rules... just like I've convinced myself that I no longer like chocolate, French fries, ice cream, cookies, or potato chips.* In fact, I now felt like vomiting when I thought of eating those foods.

What I want no longer matters. Obviously, fighting back is pointless. I have to comply with Mom's rules, and not only that, but I need to want *to comply. I need to be the sweet, good person that I know I can be. That way, we'll all be happy… Mom, me, and everyone else. If I just hide my true feelings from her, and from myself, maybe I can survive.*

Just like waving a white flag of defeat, I imagined handing her the silver tray, my power's brightness now dim and dull. *Here you go, Mom, just like you wanted.* Today proved that what Mom was always saying was right—she *could* make my life miserable over the next three years. Therefore, I would do whatever I needed to survive.

Chapter 14

Don't You Remember?

"We get so much in the habit of wearing a disguise before others that we eventually appear disguised before ourselves."
— Francois de la Rochefoucauld

July 1995

If a crystal ball had predicted the many twists and turns my first year of high school would take, I would not have believed it. My life felt like a ride in a bumper car, and some moments, I questioned whether I was really in the driver's seat.

As the school year ended, the summer sun shined overhead. As its rays beat down on me, I felt just as hot inside with anger. However, I had made the decision to turn off my emotions and just do what Mom said.

On one particularly hot day, I decided to see if a swim in our pool would cool me off both inside and out. Although I felt on edge around her lately, I invited Leah over, hoping that today she would be friendly instead of being cold. Lately, I never knew what to expect from her. That day, we thankfully had the pool to ourselves, since my parents were both at work and Kelly was inside watching TV.

The pool temperature was just right for swimming. After we playfully splashed around for a while, Leah asked, "Remember when we used to pretend we were mermaids?"

"Yeah, that was fun." I smiled, recalling how happy we'd been while swimming with plastic rings around our ankles, imagining that our legs were long mermaid fins. For once, I had felt pretty as my long hair trailed behind me underwater, soft and silky to the touch. We'd played so blissfully then, but I felt no sense of bliss today.

"I'm glad you could come over, Leah," I said, fishing for something to say.

"Me too. I feel better today. I've been really sick lately."

"That's what your mom told my mom."

"Well anyway, how are things going with James?"

My mouth fell open in surprise. "Good!" I answered enthusiastically, feeling hopeful that she cared. But my enthusiasm died when I saw her grimace.

"Well, that's good, Court. I'm going out with someone."

After her nonchalant response, she splashed her way into the deep end.

"You are?"

I felt alarmed and sad. Leah and I used to share everything with each other. This sudden piece of news reminded me of the size of the growing wall between us.

"Who is it?" I grabbed a raft and followed her into the deep end.

"It's that girl I told you about, Angelica."

"A *girl*?"

The words escaped my mouth before I could filter them or stop them completely. Ideally, I would have acted as though I did not care. Yet now, I felt downright hurt. *I thought I was the only girl Leah would ever want to be with. She's the only one I could picture myself with. Sometimes I still wish we could kiss. And now she's actually dating a girl?*

"Yeah, she's really hot, too."

Leah dove under the water.

Why is she being so distant and curt? "Oh, well, I'm happy for you," I said when she came up.

Although I had committed to being with James, I had not been successful at "turning off" my attraction to Leah. I also could not stop the feelings that flooded my body whenever I saw a sexy woman on TV or in a movie.

"Hey Court, what do you think about having some Kool-Aid… you know, special Kool-Aid?"

I traced my hand in figure eights across the surface of the water, wondering how Leah would react to my answer. "Nah… I decided not to drink anymore."

"What? Why?" Indeed, her eyebrows tilted downward in irritation.

"I just got so tired of getting in trouble. I decided not to sneak around anymore."

"Is that why you can't kiss me anymore?"

Her fierce look pierced me like a knife. I sighed, feeling frustrated with Leah's lack of understanding. My body could not bear the discomfort of her disapproval. I just wanted her to be on the same page as me, but clearly that was an unrealistic fantasy.

Suddenly, my frustration turned to anger, as if a volcano had just erupted in my chest. Leah had *no idea* how difficult my recent decisions had been. I wanted to kick, scream, and yell, but instead I chose to stuff down my feelings. *Why can't she do the same? And why can't she do what I'm doing? It's a sin to "date" a girl.*

"Courtney, you don't know how to have fun anymore." Her tone was not only accusatory, but downright cruel.

"Oh Leah, I still have fun. It's just that now it's with… James."

Jeez, Courtney. She's already hurt. You didn't have to rub it in and make it worse.

"The best part is that I don't have to worry anymore about getting caught. My goal is to not get grounded for the rest of high school," I added, trying to sound chipper to blunt the impact of what I'd just said about James.

Leah sniffed. "Good luck with that, knowing your mom."

"What do you mean? What's wrong with my mom?" I asked, trying not to sound defensive. I could criticize my mom, but that didn't mean Leah could. Thankfully, Mom and I were getting along much better now that I was being a good girl and following her rules; she seemed more cheerful lately.

Leah raised an eyebrow.

"I want to be honest with her, Leah, and I just want to be a good person."

"Court, it's not honest when you can't tell your mom what you're really thinking. Just because she barks an order and you follow it, that doesn't mean you're being honest about what *you* want."

We looked at each other in silence, and anger and disappointment flooded the space between us. I decided that if Leah were going to jump on my case, I would jump right back. "Have you told your mom yet that you're dating a GIRL?"

"No, it's none of her business."

"You won't be able to marry her, you know."

Leah laughed. "Court, we've only been dating for a few weeks!"

I frowned as I visualized the horrific sight of Leah kissing another girl. Once again, we fell into silence. After swimming a few uncomfortable laps around the pool, finally, my defenses broke down, and my tone softened.

"I know you're not happy that I'm with James, but I miss you." I looked Leah directly in the eyes now.

"I miss you too, Court. Things will never be the same again." She sighed, and gave me a melancholy look, as if she were pleading with me to change my mind.

"I know."

My gaze drifted sadly to the water, and suddenly I noticed its coolness against my skin.

◎

For the remainder of the summer, Leah and I saw each other only occasionally, quite a contrast from the many summers we'd spent attached at the hip. Deep down, I was incredibly sad at the loss of my best friend. However, since I was growing skilled at tuning out my emotions, I focused on the positive—my new best friend James. His house provided a much-appreciated refuge where we had freedom and space to hang out alone. Whether cuddling, making out, or simply talking, our intimate interactions gave me something to focus on—well, other than exercise. We also spent a lot of time with his awesome parents and smart, beautiful sister.

Meanwhile, my plan to obey my mother was working beautifully. Now that I was being a "good girl," I delighted in the fact that Mom had let up on some of the rules. The more time James spent with my family, the more my parents adored him and felt like he was their son. The more Mom trusted me, the better I felt about myself. Being around her was far more enjoyable now, because I no longer had to worry about hiding things. Instead, I poured my energy into making her happy. We had fun doing mother-daughter things like shopping and going out to dinner. *If I can just keep being sweet like Mom wants, the rest of high school should be a breeze,* I often told myself.

Chapter 15

Craving the Crown

"Being thin does not address the emptiness that has no shape or weight or name… Spiritual hunger can never be solved on the physical level."
—Geneen Roth[xi]

Spring 1998

"Wow, Mom, there's so many colors. How do I choose?"

I felt overwhelmed by the kaleidoscope of prom dresses before us. I also felt thankful to be on another fun shopping outing with Mom. It had now been three years since I had given in to obeying her rules, and disconnecting from my own feelings had paid off. We now got along great!

"Well, Court, what kind of dress do you want this year?"

"I don't know, but this is my last prom, and I want to make it the best!" But as we sifted through the racks of dresses, the dreadful fear in the pit of my stomach told me I would probably pick the wrong one.

"What about this one?" Mom held up a pale purple dress with a velvet top and big satin skirt. The netting underneath made the skirt puff out like a princess dress, and the top's straps were adorned with flowers.

"Oooh, I love it!"

"I think James would love it, too"

My mind trailed off at the mention of his name. *James and I have had such a picture-perfect relationship. We've even made it through the past two years with him two hours away at college. Wow. High school is almost over!* Nervousness suddenly filled my veins.

"Mom, do you think I'll do okay with my graduation speech?"

"Don't be nervous, Court. You'll do great."

Mom held up a blue dress, and I shook my head at it. "I guess all my straight As and A+'s have paid off."

"They sure have! Co-Salutatorian of your class. I'm so proud of you!"

"Thanks, Mom."

"I'm also proud that you're nominated for prom queen this year!"

Embarrassment set in. "Oh Mom, I won't win," I said, anxious to remind her of reality.

"What do you mean?"

"I'm not one of the popular girls. I don't even know why I'm nominated."

"Courtney, you deserve it. You shouldn't doubt that you could win."

"Well, I know one nominee that definitely won't win."

"Oh? Why?" Mom asked, raising her eyebrows.

"Well, she's the only lesbian in our school, and she's making the whole thing into a joke. She's posting signs all over school that say 'Dana for prom queen.'"

"Is everyone else campaigning?"

"No," I shook my head.

"Well that seems like an unfair advantage to the rest of the girls."

"Yeah, the whole thing is weird if you ask me. I heard she's gonna wear a tuxedo to prom."

Mom's eyes widened with shock as we walked into the dressing room. As she arranged the dresses and began unzipping one for me to try on, I slipped off my jeans and T-shirt. Standing in front of the mirror in my bra and underwear, I admired the fruits of my labor. *Finally! My thighs and butt are slimmer.* I turned to look from all different angles, just to make sure I wasn't dreaming.

"Courtney, you're in a smaller dress size than you were last year."

"I know, isn't it great?"

"I guess so. You looked fine before. I just want you to be healthy."

"I am, Mom. I'm so glad I joined the women's gym. I was getting tired of all those step aerobics videos. Now, I'm doing all different classes. One of the instructors is mentoring me. I want to teach kickboxing someday!"

Just then, my happy bubble burst as I zoomed in on the reflection of my stomach. Looking at it from the side, I noticed that it still poofed out. *What will it take to get rid of that fat?* I wondered in disgust. Just like that, my self-esteem dropped through the floor.

As I slipped on fabrics of satin, lace and chiffon, dress after dress was "okay" or "not quite." I felt gross in most of them. Then we got to the pale purple one. I stepped into the big princess skirt and slid my arms through the flower straps. As Mom zipped up the back, for just a moment everything became still. It just felt right. Much to my satisfaction, the shape of the dress hid my fat stomach perfectly.

"This is it, Mom! Can we get this one?"

"It's a little more expensive than I was planning, but it's too beautiful to pass up. Sure, you can get it."

Immediately, my mood lightened again. "Thank you, Mom! You're the best! Now I *really* can't wait for prom!"

◎

"Wow, she looks like a princess!" Granny Long said as she walked up the path to our house.

The night of our final prom had finally arrived, and both my grandmothers were sweet enough to come see me off. Shortly after they arrived, James pulled up in his purple truck. He glowed in his tuxedo and matching purple cummerbund, and I felt like a real-life princess as my family took picture after picture of us until I told them we had to get going.

As we drove along, for a moment I stared out the window, wondering if Leah would enjoy her school's prom tonight. *I miss her*, I thought. *Things haven't been the same between us. I hope she's happy.*

The truck came to a stop. As James looked my way, his eyes twinkled. "Are you ready, beautiful?"

"Sure, handsome. Are you?"

"Yeah. Some of my college friends were teasing me about going to a high school prom, but they know how much I love you."

"Thank you for going with me. We'll have fun, I promise."

As we entered the banquet hall, we walked into a rainbow of colors, sights, and sound. I felt overwhelmed as I scanned the enormous room and saw how many of my classmates had already arrived. Although most people perceived me as outgoing, I often felt shy and nervous around others. I cared far too much about what they were thinking and what they thought of me. This seemed especially true tonight, as their opinions would determine whether I would become prom queen. Although I would never admit it to anyone else, my popularity and self-esteem depended on winning that crown.

"Hi!" Abby called as she approached us with her date following close behind. Seeing my best friend relieved and comforted me instantly.

"Hi!" I responded, giving her a loving hug. "Abby, you look beautiful!"

"So do you! I love your dress and hair!"

"Thanks!" Abby then hugged James and introduced us to Tony her tall, brown-haired, handsome new boyfriend. He had a warm, friendly face, and I could tell I would like him.

The rest of the night was filled with pictures, friends, and dancing. Yet, I had a drumroll of anxiety rumbling in my stomach the whole time as I anticipated the announcement of the prom king and queen. As James and I slow danced, I felt distant, though I was not sure why. He seemed a little distant, too. *Well, we don't see each other every day like we used to*, I thought. *Hopefully, we will reconnect this summer when he's home.*

After what seemed like an eternity, the music stopped and Ben, our class president, grabbed the microphone. He instructed us to gather around the stage, which my classmates and I obediently did. *I know I won't win*, I thought to myself, *but who knows… maybe there's a tiny chance. Maybe this will help me to finally feel good about myself!* James held my hand, and I held my breath as Ben announced the results.

"Prom king goes to Tom Gray!" Ben declared. The very handsome and athletic Tom made his way to the stage.

At this point, I felt lightheaded and weak from the anticipation.

"And prom queen goes to the one, the only… can I get a drumroll, please?"

My classmates obliged, some by rolling their tongues, others by tapping their hands on the backs of chairs.

"Prom Queen goes to—wait, are you sure you're ready?"

"Yes!" my classmates cried.

"Your Prom Queen is… Dana Thompson!"

I let out a deep breath of disappointment as I watched Dana walk to the stage, accompanied by whistles and loud cheers. Out of politeness, I maintained my composure. *Oh well, I didn't think I'd win, anyway.*

"Oh, I'm sorry, Court," Abby said.

"You should have won," James said.

"Thanks, you guys," I said, smiling on the outside yet wanting to cry on the inside. I had hoped so desperately that I could be good enough to win. *How stupid of me. I'm not popular. I'm not good enough, and I never will be.* "Hey, wait a minute, what happened to Dana's tuxedo? She was wearing it earlier, and it looked really good on her. Why did she change?" I asked, hoping to avert their attention from the disappointment, anger, and jealousy brewing inside me.

Dana was now wearing a bright blue satin dress. In all my years attending school with her, I had never seen her wearing anything feminine. Although days ago I had scoffed at the idea of her wearing a tuxedo to prom, it now made sense. In fact, I admired her bravery and out-of-the-box thinking. The shiny blue satin looked out of place and just… wrong. Suddenly, I felt angry on her behalf.

"I heard that Principal Murphy told her that she couldn't wear a tuxedo to dance with the prom king," Tony explained.

"That doesn't seem fair," I said. "If she wants to wear a tux, she should be able to. And why does she have to dance with Tom, anyway? She likes girls."

"It's school tradition, I guess," Tony answered.

"Something feels weird about this," I said. On one hand, it felt like a victory for Dana, since throughout high school she had been bullied for being gay. Now people were cheering for her. The 'joke' had turned into a true victory. However, it left a bittersweet taste, since she still had to fit into our high school's boxes.

"Do you mean it's weird that they turned the prom queen contest into a joke?" James asked. "Dana's not a queen. She's more like a boy."

"Hey, don't be mean about it," I said. "I wouldn't have won anyway."

"Well, you're the queen in my eyes," James said.

"Thanks, James," I said halfheartedly. "Oh well, let's just be happy for Dana and forget about it."

I certainly didn't feel like dancing anymore, but James and I danced to a few more songs, anyway. We then said goodbye to Abby and Tony and headed home. It had been a long evening filled with fun and disappointment. This night reminded me that life was never quite what I expected or wanted it to be. At this point, I did not even care that Mom would not allow me to attend the after-prom party. At least she was allowing James to sleep on our living room couch. I just wanted to go home, cuddle with him, and go to sleep.

Maybe the fairy tales were wrong after all, I thought later that night. *Maybe there is no happily ever after period of bliss. Or maybe I will find it in college. That'll be a whole different place for sure! But first I have to get through the last month of high school... including my graduation speech!*

I took a few deep breaths to calm my nerves, then fell fast asleep.

Chapter 16

Can't We Just Be Happy?

"We've come into this world to be role models of peace and bring light into the world. The only way to do that is to be happy." —Doreen Virtue[xii]

The shiny gold tassel tickled my cheek as it dangled from my cap. I reached for the braided fibers, just to insure that I was not dreaming. I then rested my hand on my leg, feeling the smoothness of the white satin gown. I hardly noticed the discomfort of the hard, plastic seat beneath me. Instead, my mind bounced quickly from thought to thought, feeling nervous, excited, and satisfied at the same time. After years of hard work, studying, and the drudgery of having to go to school every day, freedom was now just a few moments away.

The sound of trumpets and other band instruments echoed throughout the arena of the nearby college as I excitedly looked out at the crowd. A few thousand people had filled the seats to see their loved ones graduate from high school. I quickly spotted my family: Mom, Dad, Tracy, her fiancé, Kelly, Uncle Phil, my cousins, James, his parents and sister, Granny Long and Granny Bova. Unfortunately, my grandfather was too frail and sick to attend. Even so, he sent his love and support. I felt so grateful for my family and their presence at such a significant moment in my life.

Principal Murphy took the podium, said a few words of welcome, and then introduced our class president. After Ben spoke, a few other classmates took the podium, including the co-valedictorians and my co-salutatorian. I tried not to panic. My speech would be totally different from theirs. They would reflect on the past four years, sharing memories of teachers, sporting events, and interactions with friends. Mine would be more of a philosophical reflection that I hoped would help and inspire the people in the audience.

Should I have done it more like theirs? Is mine wrong? Oh well, I thought, *I can't change it now*. Even though I attempted to reassure myself, my mind still raced with fear that no one would like what I had to say.

"Now we welcome to the stage co-salutatorian, Courtney Long."

My legs trembled as I walked down the aisle, attempting to stand up tall and hold my head high. I climbed the stairs of the stage and took my place at the podium. After adjusting the microphone, I glanced out at the crowd. *So many people!* I thought. I took a deep breath, prayed for the best, and began sharing my words of wisdom.

"Life is like a butterfly… always moving and changing. If you don't appreciate the beauty in it, it'll be gone before you even realize it's here."

The sound of my voice echoing throughout the arena surprised me. I paused, allowing the audience to absorb the quote. I had dreamed it up one day while journaling outside and felt quite proud of it.

"This is the best piece of advice I could give to anyone. Make the best of each day and situation, and you will almost always be happy. This attitude has gotten me through thick and thin these last four years. This is what life's all about. It's a game of attitude."

I looked out at my classmates. I saw both Janelle and Abby smiling at me, which gave me a bit more courage.

"Now, here are some words of wisdom that I have learned over the past four years. Number one, count your blessings. Each day, take time to think of all the things you are thankful for. Don't judge people before you get to know them. Learn to love little things like butterflies. Get excited over something silly."

A visual popped into my mind of my friends and me playing hopscotch during gym class.

"Believe in yourself. Be brave. Be confident. Set goals for yourself, then pursue them. Take time to play in a field of dandelions. Be yourself. Remember that the only person you have to impress is you."

Suddenly I realized how calmly and confidently I was saying each word. In amazement, I understood that I had set aside my self-doubts to deliver a very important message, which I prayed would help those in the audience.

"Give everything in life your best effort. Be nice to everyone. Don't complain too much. Enjoy yourself. Love your life. And above all, be a happy person."

I then concluded by thanking my teachers, classmates, and family. Backing away from the podium and breathing in a tremendous sigh of relief, I heard the loud roar of applause. As I descended the stairs and made my way back to my seat, I felt even more relieved.

"That was great, Courtney!" Abby whispered from the seat next to me.

"Really? You think so? Thanks!" *I did it,* I rejoiced. *And thank God it's over!*

As the ceremony progressed, each row of classmates filed onto the stage to shake our principal's hand and receive their high school diploma. As my row began the procession, the enormity of the moment suddenly hit me. Through the last fourteen years of school, I had worked my butt off, both figuratively and literally. Now, I would be rewarded with a gold-embossed sheet of paper. However, it was not just any sheet of paper. In some sense, it was a golden ticket—a golden ticket to a better life, and hopefully, the life of my dreams!

I beamed as I received my diploma and felt my heart soar as I heard my family and friends cheer from the crowd. As I took my seat once more, reality settled in. In three months, I would leave everything I knew and go away to college. I would embark on this journey alone, as my friends would attend the same college as James. Before allowing the fear to set in, I decided to refocus on the excitement of *this* very moment. *I just graduated!*

As soon as the ceremony concluded, we graduates experienced a whirlwind of hugs, photos, and congratulations. I loved the excitement, yet looked forward to getting home to a smaller crowd. Mom was so proud that she was throwing me an ice cream sundae party back at the house. *I suppose one sundae won't hurt*, I thought. *It's not every day that I graduate. Now that school is over, I'll have even more time to exercise!*

I smiled as echoes of my speech rang through my mind. *'Life is all about attitude.' 'Just be happy.' If I follow my own advice, maybe the rest of my life can be just that simple!*

PART II:

Cocoon of Self-Discovery

Chapter 17

Sweet Freedom

"Every moment presents a wonderful new opportunity to
become more of who I am." —Louise L. Hay[xiii]

Autumn 1998

My final summer under my parents' roof passed quickly. I could hardly believe that in just a few short days, I would be a college student! I had been like a fish in a small aquarium, comfortable in my discomfort, because it was all I knew. Now, I sensed my whole world would open up as I entered the great, wide ocean.

What will this new world be like? I wondered. *What if I encounter bigger, scary fish? Will I be okay? Am I actually ready to make my own adult decisions?* During my final night at home with my parents, I confessed my feelings to my journal:

> *"I am so nervous about leaving. Nothing will ever be the same after tomorrow. I wonder if I will just spend the whole day crying. It's just that I'm scared. So so so scared."*
> —Journal, age 18, Tuesday, 9/1/98, 12:04 a.m.

I must have fought off those scary fish in my dreams, because I woke up feeling happy and excited to go. With my belongings packed into my car, I made the forty-five minute drive to school, with Mom and Dad following closely behind in their truck.

During the drive, my mind drifted off to James. My hopes for us reconnecting over the summer had been dashed. I often came home from my summer golf course job excited to see his truck in the driveway, but was quickly disheartened when I entered the house and saw that he was hanging out with my parents, not necessarily waiting for me. After saying "hello," I'd retreat to my room, hoping he'd join me. However, sometimes it took him an hour to do so. I wondered why I was no longer making him happy, but I did not have the guts to ask him. I also did not have the guts to admit to myself how unhappy I was in the relationship. He was the boy I was supposed to marry, after all, and I was committed to making our relationship work.

Upon entering the city surrounding my university, thoughts of James faded. Once I saw my new dorm building, my excitement quickly returned. My new roommate Emma had already settled in by the time we arrived. She was tall and thin with a cute, doll-like face framed by short, curly blond hair, and she seemed easygoing and friendly. We were soon laughing together, deciding that my butterfly decorations would perfectly match her moons and stars, which already hung from the ceiling and walls. Already I had a feeling that college was going to be a lot of fun.

Soon I saw a sight I had not expected—Mom crying as she said good-bye. She rarely showed vulnerability, and it touched me to see how much she loved me and would miss me. Now that Kelly had moved out of the house into her own apartment, Mom would return home to an empty nest. I had mixed feelings myself about being away from my parents. Even though Mom still made me furious sometimes, she had practically become my best friend. I would miss her and Dad, too. But I was also excited for the freedom that awaited me.

After several hugs and kisses, my parents left, and Emma and I headed down to the cafeteria for dinner. We claimed our places at the end of the line near the cafeteria entrance. Suddenly, the two girls in front of us spun around.

"Hi!" A bright, smiling face greeted us. "I'm Chelsea! This is my roommate, Tiffany."

"Hi, I'm Courtney." I enthusiastically shook their hands and Emma did the same.

Chelsea seemed sweet, outgoing, and caring. Her long, curly red hair fell all the way to her waist. Her roommate Tiffany was tall, blonde, quiet, and nice, but a bit uptight. As the four of us waited in line, I felt thankful to meet such warm, friendly people so soon after arriving. It had been a long and emotion-filled day, and the smell of food wafting from the room in front of us made my stomach growl.

"Hey, I heard there's a big fraternity party tonight," Emma announced. "Want to go?"

"Sure!" I answered. "It'd be good to meet some people and have fun now, since classes start in two days."

Like always, I planned for school to be my top priority. I needed to get good grades so I could someday have the career of my dreams… whatever that might be. However, I wanted to have fun, too. During dinner, my new friends and I chatted about our majors, classes, and of course boys. Each of them was single and hoped to find cute boys to dance with at tonight's party. I envied Emma and Chelsea's carefree natures and hoped their light, relaxed energy would rub off on me.

After a few fun fraternity parties to kick off the school year, classes began. I loved the flexibility of my new schedule. Gone were the endless hours of sitting in class day after day with the same thirty students. Now, the lecture halls felt like huge caves, and I was just one ant among hundreds. I could hide in that cave, and hiding made me feel safer. I didn't have to be the co-salutatorian anymore; now I could just be a number.

But not everything made me feel so safe. Almost every day, someone bombarded me with my least favorite question: "What are you majoring in?" I wanted to scream from the top of a mountain, "I don't know! Stop asking me!" Figuring out my major was already stressful enough. Instead, I politely smiled and said, "I'm not sure yet. I just know that I want to help people and be happy." I concentrated on the classes I was interested in, like psychology, Spanish, diversity and social justice and tried not to panic over my major by trusting that God had a plan for me. But sometimes, panic set in, anyway.

A few months into school, panic arrived on a very important day. During the summer, I had studied long and hard to receive a national certification as a group fitness instructor. Thankfully, the week before college started, I had passed the test! Now was my opportunity to make my dream come true and teach exercise classes at the university level. This was a pivotal moment for me, since I dreamed of someday opening my own gym where people could learn to love exercise as much as I did. First, however, I needed to get through an audition without my legs wobbling like a fool.

"Oh my gosh, I'm so nervous, Chelsea," I said when my friend poked her head into my dorm room to wish me good luck.

"You'll do fine!"

"What if I mess up?"

"Don't worry, Court. Just do your best!"

I took a deep breath. I must not have looked convinced, because Chelsea continued."You've been studying and training for this for months. Now it's time to go show off what you know!"

"Thanks for being such a good friend. You always say what I need to hear!" I gave her a big hug. When she left after saying some more words of encouragement, I laced up my tennis shoes, grabbed my water bottle and bag, and biked to our university's recreation building. The whole way there, I reviewed my routine. Step-knee up, step down, grapevine to the left, two jumping jacks. Step-knee up, step down, grapevine to the right, punch-punch.

I can hardly believe I got an audition. I know I'll mess up, but I have to get every move perfect. Otherwise, there will be hell to pay.

After locking my bike near the entrance, I shakily headed through the door and downstairs to the fitness office. The receptionist pointed me to a waiting area, where I sat on a hard blue chair and nervously flipped through a fitness magazine. Since I usually loved reading all the diet tips and tricks, I hoped this would calm my nerves while I awaited my potential new boss.

Still, I was too nervous to do more than scan the pages until a headline caught my eye: "Girls kissing girls." Intrigued, I buried myself in the article. It explained that some teenage girls feel attracted to other girls due to raging hormones. Once the hormones balance into adulthood, it stated, the attraction often goes away.

Maybe that explains what happened with me, I thought. *See, I didn't think I was bisexual.*

"Hi Courtney, I'm Sandy."

I looked up from the page at the thin figure with bright blue eyes and a gentle yet confident demeanor. I quickly closed the magazine and stood up, greeting her with a handshake.

"Are you ready?"

"Sure," I said, attempting a confident smile.

She guided me to a large open room where an aerobics step awaited me. I put on my headset microphone while taking deep breaths to remind myself I was okay. As the music played, I went through the steps one by one while instructing my imaginary students on how to follow me safely and effectively. Partway through the song, the music stopped.

"Okay, Courtney, that's enough. Thank you! You did a great job. I'll contact you in a few days with my answer."

I wanted to jump up and down with relief. Instead, I thanked her, ran outside to my bike, and cycled back to my dorm.

"Well, Court, how'd it go?" Chelsea asked when I peeked into her room.

"I didn't mess up!"

"That's great!" We high fived.

When Emma and Tiffany came in, we shared the good news with them. I changed my clothes, threw my books into my backpack, and we headed to the library.

"Hey guys, I kind of feel like sitting in the grass. Do you mind?" I asked when we got there.

"No, not at all," Chelsea answered. "We'll be inside."

I made myself comfortable in the lush, green grass just outside the library and wondered what it would be like to be an aerobics instructor, and if I could teach others to love exercise as much as I did. *Exercise helps with anxiety and depression*, I reasoned. *I don't know how I'd get through life without it.* I exercised whenever I felt uncomfortable, frustrated, scared, or needed a boost in self-esteem. I even exercised when I needed to make a decision. Inevitably, the answer would come during laps or a punch-kick sequence. Most importantly, I loved the power I felt— especially from kickboxing. With each punch and kick,

I felt strong, like I was the one in control of myself and no one else could hurt me or even come near me.

It's no wonder that I feel so irritable when I can't get my exercise in. For this reason, I had even started taking my kickboxing shoes on family vacations. I did not like the thought of disturbing people on the floor below, but I had to get my workout in. This usually meant waking up before my family and doing kickboxing in the dark next to their beds while they continued to sleep. Amazingly, I could get in an awesome workout, minus my usual grunting and "ka-pow" sounds.

Oh well, I thought. *At least I'm not as obsessed with losing weight anymore. Exercise is just something I do, no matter what! And now, hopefully I'll get paid for it!*

Although, I thought after a moment, *I don't like how panicked and freaked out I get about it.*

◎

"Hi, is this Courtney?" I recognized Sandy's voice on the other end of the phone.

"Yes," I said, trying to keep my voice even.

"I'd like to offer you a position teaching step aerobics and kickboxing. Do you need a day or two to think about it?"

"No, I know already. I would love to teach for you. Thank you so much! I'm so excited!"

"Great! Your classes will start next Tuesday. See you then."

We hung up the phone. After jumping up and down like a self-powered pogo stick, I immediately called my parents. As soon as Mom's picked up I said, "I'm so excited! I got the job!"

"Congratulations! I'm so proud of you. Dad's saying to tell you he's really proud of you, too."

"Tell him thanks!"

"Everything going okay so far?" I heard the concern in her voice.

"Yeah, yeah, it's good."

"Are you homesick?"

"No, Mom, I'm okay. Thanks, though."

Even though I wasn't in the room with her, I felt her energy shift, as though she was either suspicious or disappointed. "If you get homesick, just let me know. We're not too far. We can always come up for a visit."

"Thanks, I appreciate it," I said, resisting the guilt that wanted to spoil my celebration. *Maybe I should be homesick? I don't want to hurt Mom's feelings.* "I gotta go. I have a lot of homework to do. Talk to you later!"

The truth was, I could not let myself feel homesick. I loved the freedom of being in college, away from all my mother's rules. However, there was another piece of freedom I craved, and it had to do with James. In order to fully embrace this new chapter of my life, I sensed I needed to close a door on the previous one.

Chapter 18

Dreams Shattered

"If you want to live an authentic, meaningful life, you need to master the art of disappointing and upsetting others, hurting feelings, and living with the reality that some people just won't like you." —Cheryl Richardson[xiv]

"Ready for the concert?" James asked. He had just arrived in my dorm to take me with him to see one of his all-time favorite singers, Elton John.

"Yep." I tried my best to smile, but I knew it looked unenthusiastic and didn't reach my eyes. But James was practically jumping out of his skin with excitement, and I didn't want to spoil the concert. So for now, I covered up my turmoil and pain and tucked away the fact that the evening would end in sorrow.

Despite Elton's talent and pizzazz, I hardly paid attention to the concert. I was far too busy rehearsing the conversation I'd have with James when it was over. I questioned my decision, but I also knew that something had to change. The college experience had already taught me to go for what I wanted, and that did not include holding onto an unhappy relationship. I wondered if James still wanted to marry me anymore anyway. Regardless, I just needed some space to figure out who I was and who I wanted to be.

After the concert, James brought me back to my dorm room. Thankfully, Emma was out with friends. We sat down on the futon and reluctant dread washed over me.

"James, I need to talk to you."

"Okay. I noticed you were kind of quiet at the concert. Didn't you like it?"

"Yeah, it was great. Thanks again for taking me."

He nodded. "So what's up?"

I sighed. Although I knew where to end, I did not even know where to begin. Already, this was the most painful moment I had ever experienced.

"James, have you noticed that we've been kind of distant lately? Like, we're just not as close as we used to be?"

"Well sure, we live two hours apart. I've been at college for two years now, and you're just starting."

It feels different in other ways too, I thought. "But there's more to it. I've felt distant for a while now."

He gave me a puzzled look, and I sighed. "James, I'll just be honest. Sometimes it feels like we're more brother and sister than boyfriend and girlfriend."

"What are you saying, Court? Get to the point."

I took a deep breath and glanced downward. Looking him in the eyes and telling him the truth was far more difficult than I had imagined. And yet, I couldn't hold back anymore. The tears welled in my eyes and flooded my entire face. "James, I'm unhappy in our relationship. I have been for a little while now."

His eyes now welled up with tears, too.

I continued before losing my momentum. "I need to go in a different direction."

"What do you mean, like break up?"

I nodded and looked away. I could not bear to see the look of hurt and devastation on his face. It was worse than I had expected. I could not differentiate where his pain ended and mine began; I felt it all. As I looked into the distance, I could see all the dreams of our future together crumbling. I could not believe I was hurting him, my best friend and my knight in shining armor.

"Can't we try to work on things? Courtney, are you sure?" He asked after a while.

"James, I'm so sorry, but I can't. I know this is the right thing to do," I said through my tears, crying even harder now. "We've spent the last four years of our lives together. I don't know how I'm going to live without you, James. I'm sorry."

He stood up. I could see from his face that he was getting angry now.

"I gave up the last two years of college for you. I drove home so many weekends to see you. My friends were always telling me I was missing out on the best parts of college life. But I did it because I wanted to be with you. Now you start college and you're breaking up with me? I can't believe this."

He paced back and forth.

I had not realized the daggers in my heart could hurt any worse, yet the pain intensified.

I don't remember what happened that night. I don't even remember if we had a goodbye kiss. All I knew then was that James was no longer in my dorm room or in my life. I felt the most gut-wrenching pain and intense emptiness I had ever experienced. It was so unfair. I was supposed to marry him. This was not how I expected life to turn out at all. And on top of it all, I still loved him… so was I making the right choice?

My doubts swirl all around me as I cried myself to sleep.

◎

I dreaded breaking the news to my parents, but finally I realized that I couldn't put it off forever.

"What's wrong, Court? You sound down," Mom said after we exchanged hellos.

I tried to answer, but wasn't expecting a flood of tears instead of words. In no time at all, I was crying so hard I wasn't sure I could talk coherently.

"Mom, I have something to tell you. James and I broke up."

"What, he broke up with you?"

"No." I paused, hesitating to share the rest. Whatever her reaction was, it wouldn't be good and would hurt me just as much as James' had.

"Are you playing some kind of practical joke?"

"No, Mom. I just… my feelings have changed. I'm not in love with him anymore. I need to go in a different direction."

"Courtney, are you crazy? I don't even know what to say. Here's your father."

I had not expected her to acknowledge my pain nor to understand. Yet her words cut me deeply.

"Court what's going on?"

"Dad, I broke up with James. I know you won't be happy. I know you'll disapprove. But this is what I have to do."

"Courtney, of course we're not happy. We love James like he's our son."

"I know."

That was part of the problem, I thought. *He became more of my brother than my boyfriend.*

"Courtney, you know I'll support you no matter what. I will always respect your decisions, even if I don't like them. I love you!"

"Thanks, Dad. I love you, too."

Knowing that my dad would respect my decision even if he didn't understand it comforted me a little. I felt so thankful for his love. When he handed the phone back to Mom, she sounded calmer, as th she'd spent the minute we hadn't been speaking calming down.

"Courtney, stop crying. I know you'll worry about what everyone thinks, but you don't need to. It'll be okay."

I nearly sighed in relief when someone knocked on my door. I needed an escape from my parents' disappointment.

"Mom, someone's here. I've got to go."

We hung up and I opened the door on Chelsea's sweet face.

"Doing okay? How did it go last night?" She walked in and sat beside me on my bed.

"Well, I did it. I told him."

Tears again streamed down my face. I felt as if every cell of my body were filled with darkness.

"Court, I'm sorry, I know it's so hard." She hugged me. "Are you okay?"

"Yeah, but it just sucks."

"Yeah, breaking up sucks. Just remember that you weren't happy. And you deserve to be happy."

"I don't know about that. But I know it wasn't fair to stay with him when my heart wasn't fully there anymore."

I spent the next few days moving in and out of guilt and turmoil, questioning my decision, wanting to know that James was okay, and feeling frustrated over the lack of support I was receiving. It seemed like so many people—my family, James' family, and many of my high school friends—were disappointed in me for breaking up with James.

Why don't they understand? I wondered. *Why are some of them actually mad at me? It's my life, not theirs. Do they want me to stay in an unhappy relationship just to make them happy? I can't, and I won't.*

But I still felt guilty about it.

> *"James isn't doing too good. He e-mailed me and he's still really upset. I just feel like my whole world is going so crazy. And now it's finally up to <u>me</u>, everything. It's up to <u>me</u> to decide what is right for me. I will get through this. I have felt somewhat a sense of relief. In that I finally did something about this. I was strong, and I did it."*
> —Journal, age 18, Sunday, 9/20/98, 8:54 p.m.

Breaking up with James devastated me, but it also meant making a very brave decision to face the unknown without the comfort of my best friend and the person I had thought was my one true love. Thankfully, my sisters and new college friends understood and supported me. One dear friend from high school even sent me a supportive e-mail.

> "Courtney, you have just opened your wings, spread them, and are flying away from home. Shedding your cocoon and spreading your beautiful butterfly wings, attempting to be on your own. Look at you now, nothing is the same. You take care of yourself, of everything. You make sure that you are up, that you go to classes, that your homework is done, and that you are happy and such. Nothing will ever be the same again. This is a huge change in your life. Now that you are on your own, you need to get

131

into your groove, figure out what you like, what you want, and exactly who Courtney Lynn Long is. What do you want? What will make YOU happy?"

She was right, I thought as I read these words. But before I got too excited, I heard that familiar voice of doubt, shame, and anger. *What are you doing, Courtney? You ARE crazy to let go of James. He was the best thing that ever happened to you.*

I began to wonder where my wings really were and if they would ever come out so I could fly. I didn't know where I was heading, who I was, or who I wanted to be, but I did know one thing: my lack of success in making others happy left me feeling like a miserable failure.

Chapter 19

Looking for Me in All the Wrong Places

"No one man can, for any considerable time, wear one face to himself, and another to the multitude, without finally getting bewildered as to which is the true one." —Nathaniel Hawthorne[xv]

As the shock of the breakup dissipated over the next few weeks, I felt anxious to leave the past behind. I wanted to sprint into the pleasures and freedom of single life that awaited me, but ropes of fear and guilt held me back. I seemed to be walking in circles around my own feet. I looked everywhere for happiness and safety, but I couldn't seem to find it. Every weekend, I danced the nights away at fraternity parties. I flirted with boys, dancing as close as I could, longing for someone to take the pain away.

After a few months, I went on a couple of dates. Although some of the boys were cute, I felt nothing for them. I reached a state of panic when I realized there was no one around to save me from the emptiness and pain I felt deep inside. Even so, I kept searching. At the same time, I pushed my emotions down as deep as I could. Connecting with them was far too scary and dangerous. If I let loose the anger I had long kept at bay, I had no idea what would happen. I pictured myself running around screaming on a violent, destructive rampage if I gave in. What if I hurt someone? My perfectionist self would certainly not allow *that* to happen. Therefore, I kept it at bay, distracting myself through the only two "safe" activities I had: schoolwork and exercise.

As with everything else in my life, I took my new job as a group fitness instructor very seriously. Each morning, I woke up bright and early at 6:00. After eating a bowl of oatmeal, brushing my teeth, combing my hair back into a ponytail, and changing into workout clothes, I ran or biked to the recreation building. I taught several hard-core kickboxing and step aerobics classes per week at 7:00 a.m. and often hung around after to lift weights or run laps.

Just like an ice-cold drink on a hot day, the non-stop punching, kicking, grunting, jump roping, push-ups, sit-ups, squats, and knee lifts brought me an incredible sense of satisfaction. Once my thirst for a workout had been quenched, somehow I felt safer. At least for the rest of the day I did not have to hear that tormenting inner voice telling me how fat I was and how much I needed to exercise. As long as I had used up every ounce of energy, I could rest in the knowing that I had done all I could for the day.

My journal continued to be a place of comfort and escape.

> "My life revolves around exercise. I constantly work to perfect my punches and kicks. Teaching gives me so much energy. For one hour at a time, it is a complete break from everything. As an aerobics instructor, I feel on top of the world. I am so powerful. I can do anything. This is what makes me happy. What seems to give my life purpose and meaning—movement."
> —Journal, age 18, Tuesday, 1/19/99, 6:54 p.m.

My friends provided another source of comfort and distraction. No matter how anxious or depressed I felt when I was alone, I felt much calmer and lighter when I was with them.

"I think we should cut our hair," Chelsea said one day as she, Tiffany, Emma, and I had sat down in the crowded cafeteria for lunch.

"What kind of haircut?" Emma asked.

"Like really short hair… for me and Court."

"That sounds like fun, but I don't know if I'm daring enough," I said as I grabbed a strand of my long light brown hair. I looked at Chelsea's ultra-long curly, dark red hair. *Wow*, I thought. *That would be a huge change.*

"Oh Court, don't you know?" Tiffany asked. "That's the best thing you can do for yourself after a breakup—cut your hair. It's empowering!"

"Hmm…" I said with a mysterious smile.

A few weeks later, Chelsea's best friend from high school Tammi came to visit for the weekend. She happened to be a hairstylist—and quite a beautiful one with medium-length straight, shiny black hair, brown eyes, and gorgeous thick eyelashes. She hadn't been there long before we all decided to take the plunge.

"Are you girls ready?" Tammi asked, pulling shiny scissors out of her bag.

"Ready as I'll ever be!" Chelsea proclaimed.

"Me too," I chimed in. "But not too short. I don't want anyone to think I'm a lesbian."

Chelsea and Tammi giggled.

"Seriously, I'm going with my social justice class members to an LGBTQ Pride Rally next week. I totally support equal rights for LGBTQ people. I'm pretty sure other straight people will be there too, you know, as allies. But, I won't be wearing a button that says 'straight girl,' and well, you know how people can be."

"You mean how they judge other people on their looks without knowing what's inside?"

"Exactly."

I didn't dare tell Tammi or Chelsea that I long ago I had kissed a girl; they would have been horrified. But even though I'd tucked it away as deeply as I did my anger, my secret still haunted me occasionally. On my way to classes, I sometimes noticed a hot female walking by. Thankfully, a bright red light flashed in my mind then, instructing me to "stop."

"Court, just don't go wearing rainbows on your clothes, and you'll be fine," Tammi reassured me through her laughter.

I looked down at my rainbow-striped shoes in alarm. *I had better stop wearing these around campus,* I realized. *I love rainbows, but since they're a symbol for LGBTQ pride, I can't risk giving anyone the wrong idea.*

The three of us grabbed a chair from Chelsea's room and made our way to the community bathroom. Excitement permeated the air as Tammi cut Chelsea's hair. Long, dark red hairs fell to the bathroom floor like blossom petals from a tree. Chelsea squealed with delight.

"It looks so good!" I cried.

When it was my turn, I felt a sense of freedom and release as soon as I sat on the chair. I took one last glance at my waist-long wavy hair in the mirror behind my head before I gave Tammi the go-ahead. With each "swoosh" of her scissors, I felt lighter—physically and emotionally. Once the scissors had completed their task, Chelsea and I stood in front of the mirrors to look at Tammi's work. I was shocked yet thrilled by my ultra-short, sassy style. We both looked older and more confident. *Maybe things will make a turn for the better now*, I thought with a smile.

Unfortunately, my life had been mirroring the cold, wintery weather arrived outside. Determined to shake off my dark feelings, I made lists of things that made me happy, like music, butterflies, eating healthy food, spending time with my friends, writing in my journal, sunshine, and Spanish class. And yet, the feelings persisted. *I have every reason to be happy*, I thought. *So what's wrong with me?*

I was finally in college, which I had expected would be the "best time" of my life. I had tons of friends, a job that I loved, and I was finally running my own life just the way I wanted. However, once the initial high of starting college had worn off, I realized that I felt like a slave to my classes, homework, job, and friends, always trying to do my best and make everyone happy. Instead of feeling free and happy, I just felt drained and exhausted!

> "Happy Courtney went somewhere else, to some other school. I don't know if I forgot how to make myself happy, or if I just don't want to anymore. I have been very quiet lately. I feel so bad to worry my mom so much. I think I have a lot of depression."
> —Journal, age 18, Sunday 11/15/98, 5:02 p.m.

Bed became my favorite place, because I didn't have to do anything or be anyone there. I only regretted that I couldn't spend more time there. I was far too busy exercising and focusing on my achievements. Some days I just wanted to retreat and run away from life itself, but I would not let the depression slow me down.

"God has blessed me with the most wonderful family, awesome, caring friends, health and so on. But I am still not happy. Not the inner happiness I used to have when James and I were in love. I just can't find it in me. I'm not the happy Courtney Long that everyone used to know. I guess I just need to concentrate on school right now."
—Journal, age 18, Sunday, 1/3/99, 11:45 p.m.

◎

"How was your Christmas break, Court?" Chelsea asked enthusiastically. We had just returned to the university after a three week break spent at home with our families.

"It was okay. How was yours, Chelsea? What did you do?" I hoped my downtrodden demeanor would not put a damper on her upbeat mood.

"It was good. I saw friends, cooked, baked, and relaxed."

"Nice. That sounds like fun." I attempted to be cheerful, but I knew I wasn't really sounding that way.

But Chelsea pressed on. "Catch me up. What's new in your life? I really missed you."

I took a deep breath, quite nervous to answer her question. "I missed you too. Well, I told my mom that I've been depressed. She took me to our family doctor, and I got a low-dose antidepressant. Don't tell anyone that, okay? It's embarrassing."

"Court, it's nothing to be ashamed of. I've had depression, too."

Nothing to be ashamed of? Who is she kidding? If anyone knew, their positive perception of me would be destroyed—and that, I was convinced, would be worse than death itself. At least, it did comfort me a little to know that Chelsea had had depression too.

"Did the doctor suggest therapy?" Chelsea continued. "You know, my dad's a psychologist. He sees depressed patients all the time. Therapy is really helpful for it. I saw my dad's coworker for a little while, and it wasn't so bad."

I nodded my head as I listened to her. "No, he said I shouldn't need it, that it's probably something imbalanced in my brain."

137

At least he didn't lock me into a psych ward. I breathed a sigh of relief, remembering how nervous I'd been about that.

"Okay, so what else?"

"Well, just some other things. But I don't feel like talking about it. Tell me more about *your* break."

I did not feel like telling Chelsea how sad I was that my sister's boyfriend would soon move to Atlanta, which meant Kelly would move away with him. Also, I was still sad that our family dog had recently died and had just found out that my grandpa was terminally ill. *I do not need to bring anyone else down by sharing this stuff. I can get through it on my own,* I told myself as our conversation shifted to other things.

That night we dolled ourselves up for a party in a dorm-mate's room with makeup, hairspray, and sassy, sexy clothes. Despite my cute appearance, I felt like a mess inside. I just wanted an escape from all the sadness.

I remembered the rum Leah and I used to drink all those years ago, how it always seemed to make us feel great after just a few sips. *Maybe if I drink enough rum tonight, I can forget about everything, even just for a while.*

At the party, I held a bottle of rum up to my mouth and let the poisonous nectar flow down my throat, each drop simultaneously comforting and burning. All I remember after that was falling into a black void. When I had wanted to "forget about everything," I guess the universe took it literally.

My next moment of conscious awareness occurred at 7:00 a.m. the next day, when I woke up in on white sheets in a cold, sterile environment. I shook my head, assuming I was dreaming, but the voices of hospital staff reassured me I was not. Tiffany's face appeared, and I grasped her hand tightly, as though my life depended on it. My whole body started trembling as tears of panic poured down my face.

Once I had calmed down enough to breathe at a reasonable pace, Tiffany recounted the details of the previous night. Apparently, I had drunk so much that I could not hold myself up. As we walked to the fraternity party, I fell into the snow several times. A kind grad student had offered us a ride, but unfortunately, I vomited in her car. After a long, tumultuous evening at the party, my friends took me to the hospital, where the doctors pumped a saline solution through my veins to detoxify my blood. Thankfully, my caring friends had stayed by my side the entire night.

The doctor released me that morning, sending me with a fair warning and brochure on the dangers of binge drinking. Since I was underage, I breathed a deep sigh of relief that the campus police had not gotten involved. Thankfully, there were no academic or legal consequences—just a heavy dose of humiliation. I returned to the dorm to sleep for the remainder of the day.

Courtney, what did you do? I chastised myself as I lay in bed. *You totally lost control.* I was mortified and felt incredibly shaken and unsafe. Once again, my body had betrayed me. Or, maybe I betrayed *it. You need to promise to never drink too much again. You're so good at restricting your food intake... you can certainly do the same with alcohol.*

The following day, once Chelsea's hangover had worn off too, she and I sat down to talk. I appreciated her support, but I did not want her or anyone else to shame me. A few friends already had, not to mention the excellent job I had already done shaming myself.

"Court, why are you so depressed? What's been bothering you?"

I glanced down at my hands resting on my lap and twiddled my thumbs in discomfort. I remained silent, unsure what to say.

"Your family didn't talk about feelings much, did they?"

I thought for a moment. "No. We all knew when my mom was feeling something. But other than that, my family wasn't so into 'feelings.'" I put air quotes around the word with my fingers.

"Well, my family talked about feelings a lot. There's got to be something bothering you, Court."

"Probably, but I don't know what."

"You're not suicidal, are you?"

What's with all these questions? God, I feel like I'm being interrogated. "No, don't worry about that," I said instead. "I read a long time ago that you can't go to heaven if you commit suicide. I don't even know if I believe in heaven, but I'm not taking any chances."

"You should go to counseling services, anyway. They have free sessions for students."

"Oh really? At this point, I'm desperate. I'll call and make an appointment." Though also, I was desperate to get Chelsea off my back.

"Okay, good. Also, I know it's a touchy subject, but don't you think you're doing a lot of exercise?"

"No, not at all. In fact, I could be doing more." I hoped I wasn't being too angry or defensive. I did not want to be mean, especially not to Chelsea.

"Well, one day last week, you were at the gym for like three and a half hours."

"Yeah, I was. I took yoga, then taught kickboxing, then attended a karate class. What, are you keeping tabs on me?" Now I was livid. *How dare you criticize me?* I thought. *I know way more about exercise than you do!*

"Court, I'm worried about you."

"I have a lot of energy. My body just really likes to exercise."

"How do you have *that* much energy? It's like you push yourself beyond human limits. I just don't understand."

Since most of my exercise was driven by all the anger I kept bottled up, I had plenty of fuel. I had disconnected from the intense sensations in my body long ago. It was as though my consciousness was a white cloud hovering just above my head. The cloud would not dare go into my body for fear of unbearable emotional and physical pain. Therefore, I could not detect when my body felt tired, or when it felt hungry or full. I could not *feel* much at all. However, I could easily *think* and be immersed in obsessive thoughts. I did not know how to explain any of this to Chelsea. Unfortunately, I did not even understand it myself.

"Court, please just make sure you're eating enough."

"Yeah, I am. Don't worry, Chelsea."

I reached for my box of Lucky Charms cereal to pour on top of my bowl of vanilla yogurt. *Chelsea's a good friend,* I thought, *but she needs to mind her own business.* After she left, I turned to my journal.

140

"This whole alcohol incident made me realize that I was not taking very good care of myself. I am always so damn worried about what others think and so careful not to make them upset. I worry myself to the point of sickness. I had been getting dizzy in classes, like I might pass out. I knew I was doing it to myself, but it still wouldn't stop. I am putting too much pressure on myself. Chelsea is exactly what I needed... someone to help me through this depression."

—Journal, age 18, Tuesday, 1/19/99, 11:07 p.m.

Fear ran through my veins and controlled my life. Fear that I would gain weight. Fear that I would miss a workout. Fear that I wouldn't turn in an assignment on time. Fear that others would discover I really didn't have it all together after all. Fear that if I told anyone my true feelings, they would reject and abandon me.

Even though my body couldn't tell when it was hungry, *I* was hungry. Hungry for love. Hungry for connection. Hungry to be myself. And in my hunger for love and acceptance, I exercised more. I ate less. No matter what I did, nothing seemed to fill the emptiness I felt deep inside.

◎

After years of fearing that I had a psychological problem, my nightmare had come true. Within the following week, I attended my first appointment at the university counseling center. Scared and ashamed, I sneaked up to the third floor of the student union to the counseling office, praying that no one would notice me. Once inside the carpeted, comfortable-looking room, my anxiety quickly dissipated. Soon, a warm, nurturing therapist greeted me.

My therapist Rebecca had shoulder-length curly, brown hair, glasses, and a pear-shaped body. I could not believe how comfortable I felt with her. Once safely inside her office, we talked about all the changes happening in my life. I confessed that I didn't know why I was depressed, and she listened closely as I tried to figure it out.

"I put a lot of pressure on myself. My whole future lies ahead of me, and it's scary. After college, where will I live? What will I do? Will I have a husband and kids? I feel like I should know all the answers right now. And what if I make a bad decision? So many questions are always spinning through my mind. It's like the noise inside my head never stops."

I felt anxious as I explained the crazy thoughts in my head, and braced for Rebecca's judgment and the dreadful psychological evaluation she would give me.

"Courtney, there are no 'have tos' or 'shoulds.' That's an old cognitive thinking trap that many people have. The truth is that many options would be great, and you should pursue whichever ones *feel* the best to you. You can be a painter, a landscaper, a college professor, or whatever you want. And thankfully, you have plenty of time to decide."

Her kindness and insight immediately put me at ease. As I took a deep breath, I released a layer of fear. *Maybe she won't judge me after all,* I thought.

"Rebecca, another thing that bothers me is that I always feel more serious than other people. It seems like all my friends want to do is go out, party, and hook up with guys. I'm just not into that anymore."

"That's understandable."

"I like going out, but not all the time. I'd rather get a good night's sleep. My friends even started calling me 'grandma.' I just feel different than them." I wondered if Rebecca could hear the sadness in my voice.

"Courtney, how does that make you feel?"

"I don't know, kind of down."

Rebecca handed me a chart with several cartoon faces showing a variety of facial expressions.

"This is an emotions chart. Do any of those feelings resonate?"

As I studied the chart, my stomach twisted in knots of nervousness. *I don't know the answer. What if I look like an idiot? What if she gets mad?* "Rebecca, I'm sorry, but I just don't know," I said at last. "Usually, I either feel happy or depressed. And if I'm not happy, I beat myself up."

"Tell me more about the depression. What's it like?"

I thought for a few moments. "Well, I know life has to have meaning. I just don't know what it is. I want to know why we're on Earth and what this place is all about."

"Do you have spiritual or religious beliefs?"

"I used to. But where I'm from, everyone was Christian. Here, some of my new friends are Buddhist and Jewish. Christianity can't be the only right way. I don't feel like going to church anymore. I guess I'm not sure what I believe."

Rebecca nodded, her expression compassionate. It seemed like she actually cared and wanted to help me.

"The only thing I really like is working out. But I can't teach aerobics the rest of my life. I have to be successful and do something educated, or my parents would be so upset."

"What would happen if your parents were upset with you?"

"I would feel sick to my stomach with guilt. Actually, I feel guilty all the time, like I'm always walking on eggshells or waiting for something bad to happen."

Rebecca looked at the clock. "Courtney, we're done for today, but I have a test I'd like you to take. It will evaluate you for an eating disorder. Based on a few things you've said, I think it's worth checking out. You can sit in the lobby to complete it, and we'll review the results next week. Is that okay with you?"

"Sure, I guess so." But deep down, I was irritated. *How insulting. I don't have an eating disorder. Oh well, if it's what she wants, I'll just take this silly test.*

Still, the session was great. Much less terrifying than I'd feared it would be. As I left the counseling center, a long-lost spark of hope returned to my step.

◎

The following week's appointment revealed no surprises. Just like I had guessed, the test had come back negative. Technically, I did not have an eating disorder. I was relieved. I would rather have died than cut back on exercise!

But I wasn't quite out of the woods yet. According to the results, I had several "thought patterns" similar to people with eating disorders. Rebecca said that she could help me work through some of these dysfunctional patterns, like perfectionism and black or white thinking. The free sessions were limited to six, however, so she told me about another therapist in town who I could see for longer-term treatment.

How messed up does she think I am? I wondered. But I was beginning to appreciate my therapy sessions and the insights they provided. I felt a sense of relief at sorting through my thoughts and feelings within the safety and support that Rebecca provided. Sharing my fears aloud seemed to take some of their power away and helped me feel calmer. It still helped to confess my fears to my journal as well.

> *"I think that I love food too much. I always think about eating, and anytime something feels "off," I assume I'm just hungry. Kelly has hypoglycemia, and growing up, anytime she was crabby, Mom told her to eat a snack. That helped her a ton! I seem to think that eating a snack will solve everything for me too, yet it never does. Sometimes I just feel sad, angry or upset, not necessarily hungry. So then why do I fantasize about food all day long? I feel like I am gaining weight because of this. Sometimes I get really sad all the sudden... like now, when I feel so alone. I just wish I could be happy."*
> —Journal, age 19, Wednesday, 2/3/99, 1:04 p.m.

Chelsea poked her head into my dorm room, interrupting my journal writing. "Wanna go eat?"

Maybe next time I should find a more private place to journal, I thought. But instead of feeling annoyed at Chelsea, I blamed myself for not having been in that better spot. "Oh no, I um, actually already ate at one of the other dorms."

I was lying. I did not feel like eating with her or anyone else. After she left my dorm room, I would just eat some baby carrots to tide me over until dinner.

"Okay, well, we haven't had a meal together in a while. Do you want to eat dinner with Tiff, Emma, and I tonight?"

"I'm not sure. Can I let you know later?"

Chelsea frowned. "Court, are you okay?"

"Yeah, I'm good. I just have a lot of studying to do."

Her expression was suspicious, but I did not care. Since starting at the university, it was becoming easier to eat alone, and better for me to do so in general. I needed to focus on my food to make sure I savored and managed each bite, and conversation with others was far too distracting. Anyway, I felt embarrassed about eating miniscule bites and picking my food apart to avoid unwanted ingredients, like removing everything but the vegetables from our dorm's strange version of chicken fried rice. I obsessed over having the right amount of vegetables, as little fat as possible, and nothing that would upset my stomach, even though I had a stomachache every day now, anyway. *Probably from stress*, I imagined.

I could not risk the pain of hearing my friends' criticism about how much or little I ate. From all the exercising, I had a high metabolism, so even though I restricted my food intake, I still ate more than the average person. I hated when other people commented on my food, which seemed to happen quite often; I criticized myself enough as it was. Worse, as soon as I finished eating, the turmoil only escalated. *I shouldn't have eaten that. What was I thinking? I ate too much. My stomach feels bloated. I'm gonna have to work out more tomorrow. Why do I feel so fat?*

I often felt trapped within the prison walls of my own mind.

Chapter 20

Who Am I?

"True salvation is fulfillment, peace, life in all its fullness. It is to be who you are, to feel within you the good that has no opposite, the joy of Being that depends on nothing outside itself." —Eckhart Tolle[xvi]

January 23, 2012

The rain continued to pour down as Sarah and Courtney refilled their drinks.

"Courtney, you took the best part out of the chicken fried rice—the chicken and rice!" Sarah teased as she sipped her coffee.

"I had a feeling you'd say that. Speak for yourself!" Courtney waved her hand, playfully dismissing Sarah's comment. "Now that I'm 'healthy,' I would eat all of it. But the veggies are still the best part!" She winked.

"Let's just agree to disagree, shall we?" Sarah said with a smile. "So how was the rest of college?"

"A lot of fun, actually."

Sarah raised her eyebrows, her expression disbelieving. "Even though you were depressed?"

"Well, the antidepressant kicked in and helped a lot. It kind of numbed me. Sometimes I wanted to cry, but I couldn't. It felt like the tears were there, but they just wouldn't fall out. Anyway, it helped me set aside some of the worries and have some fun too."

"Like doing what? More drinking?" Sarah asked wryly.

Courtney smiled proudly and sat up straighter. "Nope. Alcohol-free fun, actually."

"Oooh. How did that come about?"

"Well, the next few years, Chelsea, Emma, Tiffany, and I rented a house with a few other girls. Even though they were still drinking a lot, I decided to cut way back. Actually, I cut back on spending time with them too. I just felt myself changing inside, like I was becoming more of who I wanted to be. And I didn't want to do things just to fit in anymore. After that, drinking felt empty to me."

"Yeah, I know what you mean. Wouldn't it be cool if we could just be ourselves and have fun without it?"

"Yes!" Courtney nodded her head firmly. "Once I withdrew from my friends, I got pretty lonesome. But thankfully, toward the end of undergrad, I went to this intercultural leadership retreat during spring break and made a bunch of new friends from all different countries. We hung out back at school too, and we'd take turns making traditional meals from each of our cultures. Our conversations were so meaningful that I *did* have more fun without alcohol. When I was with them, I forgot about all my problems. I even ate their foods without worrying too much about calories."

"Oooh la la!" Sarah laughed. "Seriously, that sounds awesome! Especially the food part."

Courtney smiled. "I had such a weird relationship with food, like I feared it and worshipped it at the same time. I'd sit in classes and fantasize about my next snack or meal. Whenever I felt uncomfortable or didn't want to face what was right in front of me, I escaped by thinking about food."

"But then when you ate, you'd beat yourself up for it, right?"

"Right. It sucked. But I guess the obsession served a purpose. It kept me distracted from all the pain and anger I had buried inside. I guess really, I feared facing *that* far more than I feared food or gaining weight. And that's saying a lot, because I was *terrified* of being fat."

"Wow, it's so interesting. Did you like to cook too? I've heard that some people with eating disorders love cooking for others, but don't eat much themselves."

"Oooh, I never heard that before," Courtney said thoughtfully. "Actually, I *did* get really interested in cooking. I bought tons of low fat cookbooks and printed tons of recipes off the Internet. I loved making them for my new international friends."

"Did you eat with them?"

"Yeah, and good thing, because it was delicious!" Courtney winked. "But I kept it to small portions."

"Like how small? Like the recommended portions on food boxes?" Sarah rolled her eyes. "Sometimes those seem ridiculously tiny, at least compared to what *I* eat."

Courtney scoffed. "Yeah, I know what you mean. I used to freak out if I ate more than it said to, like I was a bad person or would get in *huge* trouble. Now I realize that those recommended portions are *suggestions*, not *rules*. They don't apply to everyone or every situation."

"They don't?" Sarah's eyes were wide with surprise.

"No way! We all need different amounts of food, based on our metabolism, weight, activity level—you know, that kind of stuff."

Sarah exhaled loudly. "That's a relief! I always beat myself up over that."

"I think the best thing is to eat intuitively."

Sarah leaned back and studied her with interest. "What does that mean?"

"You know, just listening to what your body wants to eat—the types of food and amount. Sometimes we're hungrier than other times. And eating for fuel, not as a distraction from your feelings. If we actually listened to our bodies, our bodies would generally ask us to eat healthy, energizing foods. And then if we want few cookies, we eat them—without guilt and without needing to eat the whole box." Courtney giggled.

"But I have no idea what my body wants. How come?"

"Maybe because for so long, we've been told all these rules about what to eat. You know, thinking foods are 'good' or 'bad,' which makes our inner rebel want to eat the 'bad' ones even more. No food is all good or all bad. That kind of thinking just leads people who are prone to eating disorders to start cutting out the 'bad" foods."

"Wow. That intense, huh?"

Courtney nodded. "That's right. Just like no diet or way of eating works for everyone. We all have different chemistry, and it's up to us to eat whichever foods feel best for *our* body. Not just what a diet book tells us."

"Don't you think that following a bunch of strict diet rules just sets us up for failure anyway? I've tried so many diets, and I can never follow them. I just end up feeling worse about myself."

Courtney nodded. "I know what you mean. Anyway, food is for fuel, not for judgment."

"Oooh, I never thought of that!"

"Yeah, food is supposed to make us feel good. You know, energized. It's not supposed to be just another way we beat ourselves up."

Sarah smiled. "I like this intuitive eating!"

"Me too. It's awesome to have the freedom to eat what I feel like eating. I trust my appetite now and honor what my body needs. That's what I call A-M-A-Z-I-N-G." Courtney laughed.

"It sounds like you're totally in touch with your body now."

"Yeah, can you believe it? Most of my life, I had no clue when I was truly hungry or full. I just ate when it was 'time' to eat, just like when I was a kid. Even though I was at college and could eat whenever I wanted, I was terrified to break the rules. You know, my old 12:00 p.m. lunchtime, 3:00–4:00 p.m. snack time and 5:30 p.m. dinnertime. If I missed a meal or snack, I got really anxious."

Sarah pursed her lips. "It's so ironic, Courtney. You hated your mom's rules, so I would think you'd break free of any and all rules when you got to college."

"Yeah, I wish." Courtney chuckled ruefully. "Instead, I made my own eating rules. Ironically, though, mine were even stricter than my mom's had been." She sighed. "In college, my big thing was yogurt. I could not eat an entire six ounce container in one sitting. I wrapped the lid with plastic wrap and ate the next serving the following day. Sometimes one yogurt would last three to four servings."

"Oh my gosh! Didn't Chelsea ever say anything to you about it?"

"No. She was really into her new boyfriend, and I think she just gave up on worrying about me."

"I'm sure you saw other people eating 'normal' portions. What did you think about that?"

"Actually, I just judged them. But not aloud. Just in my head. One of my other roommates ate a whole yogurt in front of me once, and I told myself she didn't have much self-discipline."

"Wow, Courtney. Didn't your body fight back? Like weren't there any consequences to not eating enough? Oh, and exercising so much?"

Courtney looked down in regret. "Yeah, well, now in my thirties, I'm having issues with my back and hips. Basically, some of my muscles fused together over all the years. I always stretched, but apparently not enough for all the wear and tear on my body. It's become a real problem for my posture, and it hurts!"

"Yikes."

Courtney sighed. "When I exercised so much, I never thought there'd be consequences. In college, my period disappeared. That kind of worried me, but I also felt grateful for a break from cramps and bleeding. I was freezing cold all the time and had tons of stomachaches. Oh, and insomnia on and off. But otherwise, somehow my body kept going."

"Didn't people comment on your weight?"

"Yeah, all time! And I loved it. I thrived on the attention. People commented on my strong arms and tiny body. They praised me for being so thin, not realizing what was going on behind the scenes."

A stern look came over Sarah's face. "But you weren't willing to admit that you had an eating disorder."

"Admit that I was less than perfect?" Courtney shook her head empathetically. "Unh-uh, no thank you. I was way too freaked out about what other people would think."

"But they never suspected? I mean, eating disorders are really serious conditions though, aren't they? So you'd think more people would worry about them."

"Yes, very serious. Anorexia has the highest mortality rate of any mental health condition out there.[xvii] Bulimia and Binge Eating Disorder are really serious too. Also Body Dysmorphic Disorder."

"What's that?"

"It's when someone obsesses over a certain body part that they feel is defective. They can get really afraid of being rejected because of it.

Sometimes to the point of severe depression. I've heard that a lot of transgender people struggle with that, actually."

"Yeah, that makes sense. I'm sure trans people are prone to body image issues. They were born into the wrong body, after all."

"Exactly," Courtney nodded. She then sighed. "I've met people who had to be hospitalized because of their eating disorders. And others who have had heart attacks, kidney failure, and multiple knee surgeries—all of them in their mid-twenties."

Sarah's eyes grew wide. "I thought eating disorders were serious, but I didn't realize they could be *that* serious."

Courtney nodded. "When a body doesn't get enough rest or nutrition, it starts to break down in a lot of awful ways. It's sad, isn't it?"

"Yeah, and scary. I get everything you're saying, Courtney, but I *still* can't believe no one knew about yours. I mean, you were so thin and ate so little."

"Well, I still ate a decent amount overall, because I had such a high metabolism from all the exercise. I was thin in college, but muscular too, and I didn't look sick or anything. That didn't happen until later."

Sarah raised her eyebrows.

"You know, Sarah, I bet people just assumed I was healthy and fit. I think a lot more people have eating disorders and body image issues than we realize. They hide because of all the shame, or maybe they're not even aware of what's going on. You can't tell from someone's weight, because people with eating disorders can be any shape or size."

"Really?"

"Yeah. I've heard that anywhere from ten to twenty-four million people in the US have a serious, life-threatening eating disorder.[xviii] Isn't that *wild*?"

"Whoa! Well, and not to mention all the people who just hate their bodies."

"Yeah, exactly! Even if you don't have an eating disorder, there are still unhealthy behaviors you can have about food that can hurt you."

Sarah nodded. "I want to learn more about the warning signs of eating disorders, you know? Just in case I know anyone else with one."

"That's a great idea. I appreciate you, Sarah!"

Sarah blushed.

"Courtney, you were still in therapy, weren't you? So you had help for all this, right?"

"Nope. After my six sessions with Rebecca, she recommended a local therapist off campus. But I didn't think I needed to go."

Sarah raised an eyebrow.

"The eating disorder test in college was negative, remember?" Courtney said.

"Yeah. Weird how that happened," Sarah mused. "So what did you do?"

"Well, I just dealt with things on my own."

"Or, you mean, *didn't* deal with things."

Courtney chuckled a bit darkly and nodded as if confessing. "Yeah, I guess that's a better way to put it! Finally, four years later, toward the end of grad school, I had struggled enough that I went back to therapy. I looked up the eating disorder therapist Rebecca had recommended, Amy Pershing."

"And then you finally started addressing the eating disorder?"

"Well, sort of, but I was still in total denial. I admitted I had eating disorder thought patterns, but I still wasn't willing to accept the label of an 'eating disorder.' Or tell someone about my food and exercise behaviors. I clung to them and kept them secret, because I felt they were all I had. The only way I could control my world."

"Well, I'm sure Amy suspected more was going on, don't you think?"

"Yeah, for sure. My denial was okay temporarily, though, because food and exercise were just symptoms of something deeper, anyway. Amy helped me with that deeper stuff."

"Sounds like digging for buried treasure!" Sarah laughed.

"Ha, sure, I guess so. It felt like we were peeling layers off an artichoke, actually, and the authentic Courtney was inside just waiting to be discovered. But first I had to remove all those layers of shame and fear."

"So what was Amy like? It sounds like you liked her."

"Oh my gosh, I loved her! She was so warm and kind. Great sense of humor. I loved her hair too—long, straight reddish-brown—and beautiful, caring eyes. At first, she seemed to understand me far better than I understood myself!"

"Really?"

"Yeah. I had no clue what my feelings were. Thankfully, Amy taught me how to tune into them. I realized that a lot of the fear I carried was not even mine; it belonged to my mom. Remember when I said that when I was a kid, my mom got upset when my sisters or I disagreed or had a different opinion from her?"

Sarah nodded.

Courtney continued: "I was so enmeshed with her that I seriously thought her beliefs were mine. The more I explored with Amy, I realized my beliefs and opinions were very different from my mom's. In one session, I imagined holding a big ball of fears and beliefs and handing it back to my mom. It was so cool!"

Sarah smiled. "It sounds amazing, like you were learning to be your own person. Figuring out who *you* were, not who you thought your mom wanted you to be."

"Yes!" Courtney smiled. "Therapy was awesome. I started learning about boundaries there too. I felt so empowered, like there was finally a sense of hope!"

"I'm so happy to hear that. I was wondering what the turning point would be!"

"Wait a minute though, Sarah. I was already jumping ahead to grad school. Let me backtrack just a little to the end of undergrad. I wouldn't want to leave out a very important detail. A very handsome one, actually." Courtney winked as she took a sip of her tea.

Chapter 21

Anyone Up for Adventure?

"Everything will line up perfectly when knowing and living the truth becomes more important than looking good." —Alan Cohen[xix]

December 2001

College students hustled into the coffee shop, anxious to purchase their java and espressos, which would undoubtedly get them through late-night studying for final exams. I had just sat down to meet my friend Nathan. For much of college, we had thoroughly enjoyed invigorating philosophical discussions about religion, politics, the inner workings of the human mind, and sometimes more mundane topics, like our majors.

"How's college treating you?" Nathan asked.

I looked at the well-dressed, handsome man sitting before me. He had dark brown hair, brown eyes, and cute dimples. And thanks to his awesome sense of humor, our discussions inevitably included jokes and playfulness.

"It's good! I still don't know what I want to do with my life. But at least I finally decided on a major—psychology."

"Oh yeah? How did you decide?"

"Well… I think the power of our mind is fascinating. And you know, how our mind, body, emotions and spirit are all connected. My cousin Leah gets sick a lot. The doctors have given her different diagnoses, but they can never put their finger on exactly what's going on. It makes me wonder if her emotions and thoughts are affecting her health. I just want to help people, you know, to feel better."

"That's great. I'm happy for you!. And at least you haven't signed your life away to law school, like me."

We laughed.

"So, been back home lately?"

"Not in a while," I said. "My parents come visit every now and then. What about you?"

Nathan's hometown was two hours from mine and very similar in culture and demographics. He shook his head. "I'm due for a visit."

Nathan and I had met in a cultural studies class. He often sat next to me and cracked jokes every chance he got. I appreciated his presence, which had added lightness, sweetness, and warmth to my life, including my twenty-first birthday party and many other gatherings. I would miss him next year when he left for law school.

"I saw you teaching through the window of the rec building the other day. You looked fierce."

"What do you mean?" I asked, hoping I had not looked stupid.

"You know, all those punches and kicks. I'd better stay away from you!"

I breathed a sigh of relief, and we both laughed again. *I wish I felt that strong all the time!*

"How are law school applications going?" I asked.

"Well, it looks like I'll be heading to Columbia University in NYC."

"Oh my gosh! That's huge. Congratulations!"

I felt so excited for him. After a thorough and fulfilling discussion, we got up to leave. As we walked through the door, a colorful flyer stopped me in my tracks. It read: "Women's Empowerment Day. Come discover your magnificence!"

I pointed at it. "This sounds interesting."

"Who's putting it on?"

I scanned to the bottom of the flyer. "Hmm… two life coaches."

"Life coach? What's that?"

"I don't know. I've never heard of it."

However, a feeling in my gut told me I needed to find out.

◎

Within days, I registered for the Women's Empowerment Day. I had no idea what the event would entail nor why I felt so drawn to it.

On the day of the event, women of all ages, colors, and sizes filled the room. Thankfully, I did not recognize anyone as I took a seat at a circular table, avoiding the glances of the few women who already occupied it Today, like many days, I preferred to go unseen, under the radar. If no one noticed me, they could not possibly judge me. Despite my insecurities, I excitedly hoped the day would deliver just the spark of hope I longed for.

At the front of the room stood two confident, professionally dressed women. As the event began, the brunette in black slacks and a lime-green shirt introduced herself as Sherrie, while the blonde in a sassy orange dress introduced herself as Nancy. They explained that as life coaches, they saw people's potential, rather than their flaws.

Oooh, I love that, I thought. And just like that, my interest piqued.

Today, the women explained, they would guide us through empowering activities so that we too could connect with our greatest potential and vision for our ideal life. Goosebumps of anticipation tingled up and down my arms.

"We believe that our thoughts create our reality," Sherrie began. "If we focus on our self-doubts and all the things we do 'wrong,'" she said, making air quotes with her hands, "then we will just keep feeling worse and worse about ourselves.

"Ever notice that if you expect the glass to be half empty, it is? If you expect your day to be rotten, that's what you receive. What if you wake up saying that you'll have an awesome day? Then the glass is half full, right? It's the same with how we feel about ourselves. We're not victims of other people's opinions of us. *We* get to choose how to feel about ourselves."

"Low self-esteem block us from our dreams!" Nancy chimed in. "If we wallow in our self-doubts, then how can we possibly be successful? How can we possibly make a positive difference in this world?"

I looked around the room and saw several women nodding. Others had smiles on their faces, which mirrored the smile I felt inside my whole body.

"What about all the things you do 'right'?" Sherrie asked. "What about your strengths? Every day, there are reasons to celebrate yourself and feel good about yourself. Do you even know what your strengths are? What makes you special?" She paused as she too glanced around the room, observing the blank looks on most of our faces.

"Today you will discover them!" Nancy continued with a smile as radiant as her bright orange dress. "By focusing more attention on your strengths, you will feel better about yourself. If our thoughts create our reality, let's keep our thoughts really positive—about ourselves and others. Heck, about life! We receive what we ask for. It's like saying, 'Universe, I want a really awesome life. And I affirm that I have that really awesome life right now.'"

"Yes, exactly!" Sherrie continued. "Let's affirm how strong we are. How intelligent. How successful. Let's affirm that we deserve to have our dreams come true! The more empowered we are, the more likely we are to make this world a better place. We believe every woman is brilliant, strong, and deserves to be empowered. Let's inspire others by being successful, strong women ourselves."

Wow, I feel amazing already! I thought. It felt like I had stepped into a colorful new reality filled with positive energy and endless possibilities. I felt excited and encouraged as Nancy walked around delivering packets of handouts.

As the day progressed, Sherrie and Nancy discussed more empowering concepts and guided us through uplifting, insightful activities. I realized that my strengths include being open-minded and adventurous. Exploring these strengths and discussing how we could utilize them in our careers felt like crawling out of a deep hole and climbing up a beautiful mountain, then standing at the top victorious.

Suddenly, the whole world became still and quiet as something huge occurred to me. *Sherrie and Nancy are doing exactly what I want to do. I want to empower other people to shift their thinking from self-doubts to strengths, to see how incredible they are!* I had no idea how, where, or when it would happen, but I wondered: *was I born to be a life coach?*

◎

January 2004

After successfully graduating with my bachelors degree, I decided to remain at the same university for my graduate studies. Becoming a life coach seemed like an impossible dream, since I had no idea where or how to get trained in it. Therefore, in my desire for social justice and empowering others, I decided to go a more practical route—social work. Thankfully, my university's social work program included counseling classes with an empowerment twist, which reminded me of life coaching.

During this time, Nathan and I kept in touch via email and saw each other whenever he returned home from law school for the holidays. After visiting his family, he would make the two-hour drive to my hometown to visit me. Although my world was still very gray and bleak, Nathan showed up in just the right moments, to deliver rays of yellow sunshine.

One early January afternoon when we met for coffee, I couldn't help but think that we sounded like two bubbly characters in a comic book, cracking jokes and laughing hysterically. We laughed all the way to the front door of my parents' house, where he came in to meet them.

Not two seconds after he left and the door closed, the flood of observations and questions began.

"He's so nice," Mom said. "And very cute too!"

"Did you say he's studying to be a lawyer?" Dad asked. I could almost see his ears perking up. "Have you ever considered dating him?"

"You guys… Nathan's my friend." But the truth was, I had never thought of him in that light.

"I think he likes you," Mom said. "Hey, you haven't dated anyone in a while."

"Yeah, I've just been focused on getting through the rest of grad school," I said before excusing myself to go downstairs and exercise.

Surprisingly, shortly after his visit to my parents' house, Nathan and I began e-mailing each other far more regularly than ever before—every day, in fact. As I read his words, I sensed he was just as excited about graduating as I was.

"E-mailing Nathan again?" Tiffany asked with a huge grin. We were sharing a small apartment now.

"Yes, how did you know?" I had heard of intuition, but this surprised me.

Tiffany grinned at me. "Oh Courtney, anyone can see that you're falling in love. Your whole face lights up when you talk about him!"

"Really?" I wondered if my whole face was lighting up right then.

"Yes, really. I wonder if he'll send you anything for Valentine's Day."

"I don't know. Do you think he likes me?"

"From the things you've told me? *Yes!*"

Soon enough, Valentine's Day arrived. Several times during my social work internship that day, I checked my e-mail and voicemail. Tiffany was right; if Nathan had feelings for me, surely he would reach out today. However, by 5:00 p.m, I still had not heard from him.

Oh well, I didn't think he liked me. Maybe I'll just send him a quick e-card later, anyway, I thought as I headed home.

However, as soon as I arrived home and sat down, the doorbell rang. As Tiffany was in her bedroom, I announced that I'd answer it.

I opened the door on a short, rosy-cheeked woman. "Delivery for Courtney Long," she said.

"That's me! Oooh, flowers?"

"You got it!"

I thanked her, gave a tip, and said goodbye as Tiffany emerged from her room.

"Oooh, I wonder who they're from!" she teased.

"Probably my parents," I laughed. Then, with a pair of scissors, I cut back the green netting, revealing a beautiful bouquet of red, white, and pink tulips.

"Open the card! I can hardly stand it!"

"Okay, okay!" I peeled back the cover of the card, and found the sweetest note I'd ever read.

"Happy Valentine's Day, Courtney. These flowers may be beautiful, but not nearly as beautiful as you. Love, Nathan"

"Ahhhh! Woo-hoo!" I shouted as I jumped up and down.

"I'm so excited for you!" Tiffany cried as she jumped right along with me.

My heart fluttered. *Can it be? Nathan likes me?* Suddenly, life seemed overflowing with sunshine. After a long phone conversation that evening and several more over the next few weeks, romance was definitely in the air. My body buzzed with so much elation that I hardly slept for days. Nathan confessed he was having difficulties sleeping, too.

We could not wait until the next holiday to see each another. I needed to know how it would feel to kiss and embrace him. Thankfully, a few weeks later, Nathan drove ten hours from his university to visit me for the weekend. Tiffany made a point of visiting her parents that weekend so we'd have the whole apartment to ourselves.

I greeted him at the door, wrapping him a big, loving hug. When we separated, he gently cupped the side of my face in his hand. He then pulled me close and gently pressed his lips to mine. *I can't believe Nathan is actually kissing me!* I thought as fireworks exploded up and down my spine.

I showed him into the candlelit apartment, where we quickly became more acquainted with each another's lips as soft, sensual music played in the background. Eventually, I poured us glasses of wine, and we sat down for a romantic dinner. Our conversation was just as delightful as before, only now it had the added bonus of romance.

After dinner, we sat on the couch talking and kissing even more.

"Courtney, I do believe I have fallen in love with you," Nathan said. "No, I *know* that I've fallen in love with you."

My whole body tingled with exhilaration as I whispered, very quietly but certainly, "I do believe I have fallen in love with you too, Nathan."

Nathan had recently landed a job in Phoenix, Arizona. Although I had never travelled there, my adventurous side ached for some excitement. Perhaps it was early in our relationship for me to pick up and move across the country with him; however, we had now known each other for six years, and my heart knew what it wanted.

"Courtney, there's something I've been wanting to talk to you about," he said after we'd kissed some more.

"Okay, sure." I was excited to hear what he had to say.

"Well, you know I'm moving to Phoenix in a few months for work. I wish I could be more flexible and make more of a sacrifice. I don't expect you to move there. I don't want to pressure you. I want you to do what's best for you."

"It's okay, Nathan. I'll be graduating soon, and I'm ready for a big change. I've been in Michigan my whole life!"

"Yeah, I know what you mean."

"There's a whole world out there. As much as I love my family, it'd be nice to be on my own completely and really figure out who I am and what I want."

"Really? So you wouldn't mind moving to Phoenix?"

The excitement in Nathan's voice was contagious. I grinned and beckoned him closer, raising my eyebrows. "Can I tell you a secret?"

He nodded, looking a bit bemused.

"I've already been searching for job openings there."

His eyes opened wide and the corners of his lips turned upward in delight. I smiled too, thrilled that my news had made him so happy.

That night, sleep did not come easy. As I lay beside Nathan, my thoughts bounced back and forth like a ball at a ping-pong match. I felt giddy with excitement and of shaky with anxiety as I thought about it all.

I'm moving across the country!

Chapter 22

Just One More Workout, Then I'll Be Acceptable

"Every single one of us matters—tremendously. Our very existence affects countless people in countless ways… our internal experiences affect the whole of life more than we could ever imagine." —Daily OM[xx]

Autumn 2004

On the day I graduated from my masters program, I felt like dancing across the stage. Finally, after twenty long years of classes, homework, exams, and papers, I was finished! Nathan had sweetly driven in for my graduation and party, allowing my sisters, grandma, uncle, and cousins to meet him before we moved away. I attended his graduation as well and met his mom and brothers, who warmly welcomed me to the family.

Nathan bought a house in Arizona and moved there early in the summer to study for the bar exam. Meanwhile, I spent one last summer at home with my parents. Although I had been away at college the last six years, this truly was the last time I would live under their roof. Some moments were nostalgic and even surreal. Others felt unbearable, especially as I witnessed how much they argued nowadays. I could hardly wait to be on my way to join Nathan.

Soon enough I was driving across the country by myself, dreaming about my bright future in sunshiny Phoenix. I had said my goodbyes to my family and made several phone calls along way, especially to Mom and Granny Long, who both needed reassurance that I was okay.

When I made the turn into Phoenix, the beauty and lushness of the Sonoran Desert shocked me. I had imagined that it would look like a brown piece of construction paper, plain and flat. Instead, it had so many textures and colors: rocky mountains, prickly green cacti, succulent desert plants, flowers in every color, and even palm trees!

Nathan greeted me warmly as I stepped out of the car. After a long summer and many days apart, our bodies were ready to reconnect. We deserved this beautiful, love-filled reunion and filled it with plenty of time laughing and "playing" in bed.

During the next few weeks, we began exploring the local botanical garden and hiking in the desert mountains. Hiking calmed and nourished my soul. Compared to the vast size of the mountains, my problems seemed ant-sized. I gratefully allowed Mother Nature to absorb and recycle the negativity and fear I carried. Each time I went, I left the mountains feeling lighter and refreshed.

Some days it felt to me like Nathan and I were playing house as we cooked, cleaned, and took care of each another. Except this was not pretend; this was real adult life! Our relationship continued to blossom, and everything in my life seemed to be flowing in perfect harmony.

Thankfully, I had gotten a social work job quite easily at a local non-profit organization that served senior citizens and young adults with disabilities and traumatic brain injuries. I was responsible for social work duties *and* the management of one of the nonprofit's large day treatment centers.

"How was your day at work?" Nathan asked me one evening shortly after I started my job.

We stood in the kitchen making dinner together: a healthy chicken and veggie stir-fry. *If it were up to him, he would be eating peanut butter chocolate candy for dinner*, I thought fondly. *It's a good thing he has me to show him healthy nutrition!*

"It was good. I got to meet the directors from our other facilities," I said as I continued tending to the pan.

"Anyone your age?"

I looked up just long enough to catch Nathan's mischievous smile.

"Ha! No, definitely older. I hope people respect me, being in my twenties and a manager." I paused. "There was woman who intrigued me. Her name is Kasey."

"Oh yeah? What was intriguing about her?"

I loved Nathan's careful listening skills. He was truly a dream come true. "She seemed mysterious…. really quiet and standoffish. But when she spoke, I could tell she's really passionate about helping the clients. She definitely has a caring heart."

I reflected for a moment. Honestly, I felt puzzled about why she had intrigued me so much.

"Courtney, I really admire the work you do. At least you know that you're making a difference in someone's life every day."

"Yeah, that's true. I adore my clients and their families. Although I can already tell this is not what I want to do for the rest of my life." Even after all this time and studying, I felt like I was called to do something meaningful, but I still wasn't sure what.

Nathan must have sensed the sadness and fear in my voice, because he stepped in closer and hugged me tightly. "Don't worry, you'll figure it out. Maybe someday I will, too."

We laughed. I smiled at him, silently thanking him for bringing so much joy and love into my life.

◎

Now that schoolwork no longer required my constant attention, I had plenty of free time in the early mornings and after work. This translated to plenty of time to exercise, which I now did just about every day. Soon enough I had found a gym where I could teach step aerobics. Whether it was Pilates, kickboxing, hiking, lifting weights, boot camps, or just walking outside in the beautiful Arizona scenery, I loved having so much time to move my body.

I certainly had more motivation to exercise than the common person, yet I did not know how to listen to my body, nor how to stop. One particular morning offered a prime example of that. After crawling out of bed, I had quickly changed my clothes and started my exercise routine. Devastatingly, partway through the boot camp video, I felt terrible menstrual cramps. When Nathan got out of the shower, he found me weeping as I tried to go through my workout.

"Courtney, what's wrong? Why are you crying?"

"Oh, just cramps," I said as casually, hoping Nathan would tune me out and just focus on getting ready for work.

"Are you sure you're okay? You can hardly stand up straight. Why don't you just stop exercising?"

"*I can't!*"

The firmness of my voice surprised me. I was sure he wouldn't understand. To not be able to exercise would be equivalent to death by the guillotine. How could I tell him that I couldn't bear the risk of gaining weight, or even worse, feeling out of control?

Tears slid down my face. The cramping had worsened to the point that I was now lying in the fetal position on the floor. But the tears had originated not from the pain of menstrual cramps, but from the emotional pain of not being able to complete my workout. *What does this say about me? What kind of person am I who can't even finish a workout? I know something dreadful is going to happen.*

Nathan sat down next to me and put a hand on my shoulder in an attempt to comfort me. "Courtney, I've never seen someone so dedicated to exercise as you. I think you'll be okay missing one workout."

What does he *know?* I angrily thought through my tears. *He thinks I'm such a good person. If only he knew the truth.*

◎

Summer 2006

Over the next two years, I found my work as a director and social worker fulfilling, yet challenging. I worked far more hours than I wanted to and faced tons of stress. Thankfully, I had gone out with to dinner a few times with some of the directors, including Kasey. It helped to hear their tips on coping, but the stress overwhelmed me constantly.

Is this how the "real world" has to be? I constantly wondered. I had craved the freedom to do adult things my whole life, especially meaningful work. Now here I was, supposedly living "the American dream" and having to see a chiropractor for all the pain in my neck and shoulders. Something seemed off.

One day at our weekly directors' meeting, I caught a glimpse of hope. Kasey announced that a long-standing employee had quit, and she was now in desperate need of a social worker to fill the position. *Hmm,* I thought. *Her site is much closer to home. Being a social worker instead of a director would be much less stress. Then again, it's also a pay cut.* As our meeting transitioned to the next topic, I decided to think about the idea more later.

As the meeting concluded, I was surprised and suddenly a little nervous to see Kasey approaching me.

"Do you have plans this weekend? My partner and I are having a party. We wanted to invite you and your fiancé."

"Oh, thanks! Just so you know, he's not my fiancé, just my boyfriend." I felt a strong need to correct her statement. Even so, over the past two years my relationship with Nathan had strengthened. Besides both of us working way too much, we seemed happier than ever. I secretly hoped that wedding bells would be in our near future.

Kasey gave me a quizzical, surprised look. Bypassing further explanation, I answered her original question. "I'm afraid we already have plans. We're going to a party at one of the law partner's homes."

"Nathan sure is wining and dining you, huh?"

Wow, I never noticed how beautiful her smile is. I laughed. "Yeah, it's been pretty fun. I like getting all dressed up. Please tell your partner I said thanks, though. What's your partner's name?" I had a feeling Kasey might have a same-sex partner, but I did not want to assume.

"Her name is Monica."

So she is gay, after all. I was happy that Kasey felt comfortable enough to tell me. She seemed so introverted that I wondered how publically out she was. "Monica," I repeated. "I'd love to hang out with you both sometime, so definitely ask again."

"We will. Have fun at your party!" She gathered the rest of her papers and headed out the doorway.

During my drive home, my mind started racing. *It's funny how people just assume that Nathan and I are engaged. Actually, I've been meaning to talk to him about marriage. I'm definitely in love with him. If he proposes, I would be so happy to say yes. I hope it happens soon!*

Suddenly a deep, fast-paced voice on the radio interrupted my thoughts. "Do people often come to you for advice? Do you find yourself encouraging people to be the best they can be? Become a life coach today at the Southwest Institute of Healing Arts in Tempe, Arizona."

"Life coaching program? In the Phoenix area? Oh my gosh!" I said aloud. If I hadn't been driving, I would certainly have been jumping up and down! I turned the music up loud and danced along to it from my seat the rest of the way home, where I greeted my handsome boyfriend with a kiss.

"How was your day, Nathan?"

"Boring!" he laughed. "I spent hours reading legal documents trying to find one fact for my client. I almost fell asleep ten times! How about yours?"

"Good! I found out there's a life coaching program in town."

"Oh really?"

"*Yes!* Remember when we saw that flyer in Michigan a few years ago?"

"Oh yeah. Did you ever go to that conference?"

"Actually, I did. It was so empowered that I felt like I could do anything. This is what I want to do for other people. This is exactly what I was born to do... to be a life coach. I just didn't know how it could happen. But now I see!"

"Courtney, didn't you just finish school?" It was a good thing Nathan was smiling when he said this; otherwise, I would have taken that as criticism and felt guilty.

"Yeah, yeah... that's enough out of you!" I playfully gave him a little push. "The other good news is that Kasey invited us to a party at her and her partner's house. We can't go because it's this weekend. But since I haven't made many friends here yet, I was really excited to be invited."

"Wait a minute, back up. Partner? That's pretty vague." Nathan was obviously fishing for more information.

"Her girlfriend."

"Kasey's the mysterious one?"

"Yeah, but I'm getting to know her a little more, and she seems really down-to-earth." I had a bounce in my step as I pulled some veggies out of the freezer. "Does peanut butter pasta sound okay tonight?"

"Yum, my favorite! Well, I look forward to meeting her sometime. That's funny, because today at work people were talking about gay marriage."

"Oh yeah?" My ears perking up. *Perfect! Here's my opening to find out how he feels about getting married.* "I think gay couples should be able to get married if they want to."

"Sure, I agree. Everyone should have equal rights. But they're kind of lucky. They don't have to worry about marriage."

"What?" I felt the hairs on my back stand up. My stomach clenched in dread of what I sensed was coming.

"You know, marriages don't usually last. It's kind of like signing your life away. A lot of times when people get married, the relationship falls apart."

I felt my heart sink to my stomach.

"Oh… so where does that leave you? Does that mean you never want to get married?"

"I don't think so. It's just a legal arrangement, anyway." He certainly knew what he wanted… or rather, what he *didn't* want.

I turned to the stove, trying to hide my tears, but a river flowed from each eye. I cried silently for the next few moments.

"What about you?"

I took a deep breath, calmed myself down, and wiped my eyes with my sleeve, pretending there was something in them.

"Um, well… I always wanted to get married. I was one of those little girls who dreamed about wearing the white wedding gown, carrying the flowers, choosing my bridesmaids, all that stuff. To me it just means 'happily ever after' and that you're committed to each another."

"You can be committed to each other without having to get married, though. Look, I'm not saying I'd never get married. I'm just not the type of person who rushes into anything. I'd want to be sure first."

My heart sank even further. *This is so not the answer I was hoping for.*

Thankfully, Nathan and I conjured up other discussion topics during the remainder of dinner. Despite the lightness of our conversation, I could not ignore the pit of sorrow and anxiety in the bottom of my stomach. While half-listening to Nathan, I planned my escape. Although I had already exercised that morning, suddenly I felt fat and a strong need to do some more. It was Nathan's turn to do the dishes that night, so I gave him a kiss and scooted outside for a hot, vigorous walk under the summer sunset. As usual, the sky was breathtaking, covered with streaks of purples, reds, and oranges as if the universe was painting. But even amid nature's beauty, I could not help but feel rejected.

Nathan said he doesn't want to get married. He said he'd want to be sure. Does that mean he's not sure about us? What's wrong with me? Why aren't I good enough for him? I would die if Nathan knew how much I had hoped he would propose. I guess that dream is out the window. Despite my efforts to stop them, a few more strong-willed tears snuck out of my eyes. They intermingled with the sweat dripping from my forehead and found an escape route down my cheek, thus cleansing my body of unwanted energy and unneeded dreams.

Suddenly, a familiar stream of thoughts pounded their way through my mind. *You're fat, bloated, and disgusting. Time to lose more weight. Eating less and exercising more will fill this emptiness inside.*

Obediently, I quickened my pace and was soon jogging toward the remainder of purple streaks in the sky.

Chapter 23

Being of Light

"Inside of you is a light that can never be extinguished or soiled—it's pure and clear, and its embers are stoked by love." —Doreen Virtue[xxi]

Summer 2006

"Supposed to's" filled my life. Over the last twenty-six years, I had become professionally skilled at following what I was *supposed* to do. I had just finished social work school, and I thought I was *supposed* to be a social worker, even though my heart was nudging me toward life coaching. My mom had started talking about moving to Phoenix. I thought I was *supposed* to be happy about that. I thought I was *supposed* to be there for my clients and employees, even though the stress now prevented me from enjoying my job. I thought good girls were supposed to make everyone else happy.

But what will make me *happy?* I often wondered. This theme seemed to permeate my life. I ached to burst out of the "supposed to" bubble and do what I actually *wanted* to do. But first, I needed to figure out what that was.

That Saturday evening, I excitedly hurried to our closet to doll myself up for Nathan's lawyer party. For once in my life, I could not wait to show off my body. Good thing I had purchased a new shiny, satin turquoise dress, since my other dresses were now far too big. In fact, weight seemed to be falling off me now, which felt like a miracle. Although I often fantasized about being this thin, I had never dreamed it could actually happen!

I slipped on the tiny dress, stepped into my open-toed stilettos, and chose sparkly earrings to match. After styling my hair and sealing it with grape-scented hairspray, I pulled out my make-up bag. Blush, eye shadow, eyeliner, mascara… with each color I added to my face, I smiled. *Finally, I'm thin enough!*

"Painting yourself again, huh?"

Nathan had just walked in from the other room. He loved teasing me about being a girl.

"Yes, I am," I answered proudly. After applying my mascara, I put my makeup bag away and stood back to glance at the finished product in the mirror.

"Wow, you look incredible! How'd I get so lucky to have such a beautiful and sexy girlfriend?"

I thanked him and beamed. Nathan had never commented on my weight, but I had a feeling that if I were going to keep him, I needed to be as thin as possible. I took great satisfaction in eating just a little less than my body wanted, in putting my fork down just a few bites before I was full. *Who wants to be full, anyway?* I reasoned. *That would only make my stomach look more bloated.* If I was still hungry after dinner, I occasionally allowed myself the treat of sucking the juice out of a grapefruit—but not without an annoying side effect of guilt.

Nathan left the room to iron his shirt. I turned sideways in the mirror and frowned. *Why does my stomach still poof out?* I wondered with disgust. I unsuccessfully attempted to suck it in. I then thought of my coworkers' recent comments. They noted my weight and asked if I was okay. *How annoyingly rude.* In fact, a coworker even suggested that I eat a few donuts. If he only knew how insensitive his off-hand comment had been.

They seem to think I am sick or something. Oh well, what do they know? I finally look the way I've always wanted to. I don't care what anyone else thinks. Yet the truth was that I did care… very much.

That evening at the party, my mind drifted as Nathan schmoozed with his colleagues. The surface-level conversation at these parties did nothing for me, and I had other things on my mind. *I should transfer to Kasey's site for the social worker position. It'd be much less stress. Then I could do the life coaching program in the evenings and eventually start my own business.* On our way home, I told Nathan of my tentative plan, and thankfully, he seemed very excited for me.

Towards the end of the following Monday workday, a familiar face peeked in my doorway.

"Are you busy?"

"Of course, Navee. I'm buried under work. But please come in and talk to me."

Navee stood about five feet and three inches, no taller than me. With her Native American and Mexican heritage, she had beautiful thick black hair and deep, mesmerizing chocolate-brown eyes. I could hardly believe she was sixty years old. Her calm, spiritual nature had certainly slowed down the aging process, as her face was smooth, wrinkle-free, and glowing with peace.

I grew to love my daily visits from Navee. She came every day after work to pick up my coworker Josie, who was her roommate. From our very first meeting two years ago, Navee felt like family, as though I had always known her. Each day she always had something thoughtful to tell me.

"How are you today?" she asked as she moved to my desk.

"Stressed as always. There's endless work and fires to put out."

"Remember who you are, Courtney. You are Light. You are nobody's shadow. You are the light of the Holy Spirit."

I stopped shuffling papers and felt a wave of calm wash over my whole body. I felt the truth of what she said. However, I resisted the term "Holy Spirit," since it reminded me of the religious dogma I'd heard my whole life. I motioned to Navee to sit down next to me, then asked her to explain what she meant by "the Holy Spirit."

"The energy which flows through all things. Nothing more, nothing less."

"You mean like the energy of love?"

"Yes, Courtney. Some people call it God. Others call it Universe. Some say Spirit. That's it! This world is made of energy. Scientists know it. So do we."

"I like that. I don't think God is some figure in the sky waiting to punish us, even though that is what I learned. God is just energy… the energy of love. God is in each of us."

"I'm so grateful you understand me!" Navee bounced with excitement like a little kid. "We are made of energy. We are light.

Light is who we are. In fact, Courtney, many of those religious teachings are misunderstood. People are not sinners. No, they have simply forgotten their own light. It's not, 'Forgive them Father, for they don't know what they do.' Instead, we say, 'Forgive them, for they don't know *who they are.'*"

Oh my gosh, that is deep! I felt layers of shame lifting from my shoulders. The more I listened, the better I started to feel about myself. A newfound hope allowed me to consider the possibility that maybe I was not such a horrible person after all. Navee and I had soon formed quite a bond; we seemed to understand each another. I was so grateful to learn her teachings, and she was so grateful that someone understood her!

Two months later, I transferred to the social worker position at Kasey's site, and soon after, Navee began volunteering there. I was so grateful to learn from her and excited about the new adventure that lay ahead of me—becoming a Transformational Life Coach.

Life seemed to be turning around, a fact which I excitedly shared with my journal:

> "I have come SO far. Remember those days when I'd sit and write in my journal back in college? Remember how I felt so worried and so depressed? Well, things are changing now. I feel settled in my life, with my boyfriend, where I live, and my job. Also, I have been learning to let go of things. Learning what's important and what's not. Realizing how wonderful my life is and how little I truly have to be afraid of.
>
> From Navee, I have been learning that my physical body comes second. First, I am a spiritual being. First, I am Spirit. Only then comes in my physical body. Her messages resonate so deeply within me.
>
> So while it's not easy to just let go of all the fear, the deeper truth is that I'm OK. No matter what happens, no matter what decisions I make or actions I take, I will be

OK. I will continue to love the people around me, and love
is what matters most, after all.''

    —Journal, age 26, Monday, 8/14/06, 1:48 p.m.

Chapter 24

Fasten Your Seatbelt

"In understanding ourselves, we come to understand the world. In allowing ourselves to heal, we become the healers of the world."
—Marianne Williamson[xxii]

Autumn 2006

The moment I first walked into the Southwest Institute of Healing Arts (SWIHA), I felt a sense of comfort, as if I just had arrived "home." Walking through the hallways revealed beautiful paintings of angels, om symbols, and positive affirmations written in every rainbow chakra color. I also saw an eclectic mix of warm, smiling faces, including women in long, flowing skirts, men with long hair, and some with their hair styled in locs (also known as dreadlocks). People from all walks of life and backgrounds joined here to learn healing modalities like hypnotherapy, massage, or Reiki energy healing with the ultimate goal of making a positive difference in this world. I eagerly followed my new classmates through the doorway of the life coaching classroom and took a seat.

"Fasten your seatbelts," our instructor Richard said.

"Why?" we asked.

"You are about to embark on a rollercoaster ride of personal exploration, awareness, and transformation."

Richard spoke with an intensity and strength that commanded me to listen to his every word. Framed underneath his stylish dark brown hair, his handsome face and big blue eyes showed depth, power, and sensitivity. He explained that when he teaches, he is a vessel for Spirit. I had sensed this already.

"Your lives will never be the same. With the self-awareness you will gain in this class, the behaviors and relationships that no longer serve you will automatically be released from your lives."

Silence permeated the room as my fellow students and I absorbed his words. *I didn't realize I'd need a seatbelt*, I laughed to myself. I had no idea what this all would mean for me and for my life, yet here I was. There must be a reason I was in this Life Coaching program at this very moment, I thought. I had felt guided by something to attend this school. And within just the first few moments, I realized that this would help me not only professionally, but personally. *Thank you, Universe!* Even though I felt a little scared, I committed to letting go of whatever I no longer needed in my life.

Richard continued: "During the Life Coaching program, you will go through major transformation. It's like being in the cocoon for a while before becoming the butterfly. It's time to go within and discover yourself. Discover your gifts and strengths. Embrace your shadows, the parts of yourself you wish you could hide from, like addictions or dysfunction. Embrace the totality of your existence as both a human and a spiritual being."

A student with curly brown hair raised his hand. "But Richard, I thought we were here to learn how to coach other people, not to work on ourselves."

Richard flashed a smile, as though he had been waiting for someone to ask. "We heal ourselves first. Then, we support others in their healing. In order to be effective practitioners, we must clear away the blocks that stand in the way of our greatness."

Suddenly, I remembered something from long ago. Without hesitating, I felt my hand dart into the air.

"Yes, Courtney?" Richard said, reading my nametag.

"Did you know that the caterpillar sheds its skin, just like the snake?" Some of my classmates nodded their heads while others looked surprised. "It does this like four or five times before even entering the cocoon. It's fascinating how every part of the butterfly's life shows change and transformation."

A smile came over me. *I hadn't thought of that since first grade.*

"Thank you for sharing." Richard paused for a moment, and we all waited in silence. I sensed a profound statement arising within him that he would deliver with a bang.

"What are the skins each of you needs to shed in preparation for this journey? Please close your eyes, connect with your inner wisdom, and ask which behaviors or beliefs it's time to let go of."

I had just closed my eyes and taken a deep breath when I heard Richard's voice again. "Yes, Ashley?"

"What do you mean by 'inner wisdom'? When I close my eyes, all I hear is a stream of loud, random thoughts."

"Good question, Ashley. Okay, everybody, open your eyes for a second."

I did so, feeling relieved. I had wondered this, too.

"Where do your decisions come from?" Richard asked us.

Huh?

He apparently noticed the blank looks on our faces. "When you're deciding what color of sweater to buy or where to spend your money, how do you decide?"

A fellow student raised his hand. "I go with the most logical choice… the one that makes the most sense."

"So you decide from your head," Richard stated.

"Well, yeah. Isn't that the only place we think from?"

"Think again. Have you ever made a decision from your emotions, even though logic told you to do otherwise?"

"Yeah, like going back to an ex, even though he wasn't good for me," a female classmate shared.

"Where did that decision come from?" Richard asked.

"I guess my heart," she said.

I observed the interaction, enjoying watching the puzzle pieces falling into place.

"Okay, so the heart is definitely a better place to make decisions from than the head. The head can trip us up, because the ego is all about fear. It can keep us stuck. The heart, however, gets us more into the essence of who we are. But even the heart can get us in trouble sometimes, when we stay with someone we know is not good for us just because we love them."

I heard a collective "ooooh" from the classroom, as thought we had thought of similar situations in own lives.

"So then where do you suggest we make our decisions from?" another student asked.

"Down here." Richard placed his hand on his stomach. "Your gut or inner knowing. It never lies to you. It is the seat of your inner wisdom and all the answers you need to know. Have you ever met someone and knew instantly whether or not you could trust them?"

Each of us nodded.

"Have you ever gotten a gentle nudge to do something even though you didn't fully understand it? Like coming here to life coaching, for instance? How many of you know exactly why you are here?"

Only three out of twenty students raised their hands.

"Exactly. Answering the calling to be a life coach means answering the calling of Spirit, or Universe, or God, whatever you choose to call it. To be most powerful and effective in this world, to show up for Spirit the way we are called to do, we must make our decisions from our inner knowing."

He then guided us to again close our eyes, take some deep breaths, and place our hands on our stomachs. He asked us again which layers or skins we needed to shed in order to enter the cocoon of self-discovery. Immediately I heard the answer within my mind: "self-doubt, fear, and shame."

My eyes nearly flew open in shock. *These answers have been there all along? I have my own internal guidance system? All I have to do is get quiet enough to hear it? But I've been relying on other people's opinions and guidance for so long. Does this mean I can actually learn to trust myself?*

After our weekend class, I journaled about the messages I had received.

During the introductory Life Coaching class, not only did I learn how to be a Life Coach, I also experienced tremendous internal growth. I learned that I am beautiful, and that it is OK and actually good for me to celebrate the loving, accepting, spiritual, open-minded person I am.

> I have to remember that ultimately, God is in control, not me. I will go with the flow of the Universe. I am a Being of Light. And that is all I have to focus on. Letting Light flow through me. Not making things so complicated, and not being so caught in my mind.
>
> After these activities, I feel so strong. I have never before felt so at peace, so capable. So worthwhile, so valued. I am beginning to value myself, even to love myself. I have found meaning in my life and my purpose... to help others see that they are Light! To see it, feel it and then express it. I know what I am here to do now. And that feels AMAZING!"
>
> —Journal, age 26, Sunday, 9/17/06, 8:32 p.m.

As my life coaching training progressed over the next few months, I found myself on an incredible path of growth and discovery. I loved how we practiced the coaching protocols with fellow classmates. We simultaneously received tons of coaching while also learning to empower others.

I often was in awe of my classmates. They were like cups of love, overflowing and eager to share the love they contained. As they coached me, they placed their fearful egos to the side and looked at me through the eyes of unconditional love. I healed through love. I healed through their compassion, understanding, and validation. These souls energetically held my hand while I looked within. My self-confidence soared, and I was empowered to start validating, loving, and supporting myself. I realized I was on a divine path. Instead of being on earth by accident, alone and separate from everyone else, I understood that I was here for a purpose. Part of that purpose involved connecting more deeply with others, in order to give and receive love. I realized that I was not alone! In fact, I never had been.

In other moments, fear set in. I sometimes found myself wondering, *Who am I to be a life coach? I don't have all the answers.* Then I realized I didn't need to. I just needed to love. All I needed to do was surround people with so much love and acceptance that they could hear their inner wisdom and discover their own answers. I was here to help them discover who they were. But in order to do that, I knew that I needed to first understand who I was. I had a lot of old patterns to clear away before I was fully ready to help others clear away theirs. I needed to stop feeling like a victim before I could fully step into my power.

Chapter 25

Don't I Know You From Somewhere?

"The first thing we need to do is recognize and trust our own Inner Nature, and not lose sight of it." —Benjamin Hoff[xxiii]

The following Saturday morning, after kissing Nathan goodbye, I excitedly hurried to the center where I worked. Navee was hosting a small class to share her teachings. As on most days in Phoenix, the sun shined brightly. Even if it hadn't, I would have felt surrounded by sunshine from my excitement. Upon walking into the building, I beamed even brighter at the sight of Kasey greeting me in the lobby. We said good morning and exchanged a short, yet friendly hug.

"How are you?" she asked warmly.

"Great! How about you?"

"Excited to hear what Navee has to say."

I smiled all the way up to my eyes. "Me too."

"It's kind of strange to be here without all the clients!" Kasey said as we walked into the activity room. Here we chose seats next to the other attendees. Even though the room temperature was a bit cold, I felt plenty of warmth from all the loving hearts present.

I sat down as Kasey went to the kitchen to prepare coffee for everyone. I had decided that working with Kasey was like wearing an old, cozy sweatshirt. In her presence, I felt such a sense of familiarity and comfort, as if I had known her forever. I admired her calmness, confidence, and loving heart. I had never met someone who treated everyone equally. Regardless whether she was interacting with a staff member, client, or client's family, Kasey treated everyone with the utmost respect and consideration. She didn't care how someone looked, what abilities they had or did not have, or whether or not they could speak clearly. I admired her amazing ability to sense people's souls beneath their outer shells.

Kasey returned with the coffee and sat down next to me. "I have to admit, Courtney, I was looking forward to seeing you today."

I responded with a huge grin. "Something seems different about you today, Kasey."

"What, that I'm actually relaxed?"

We giggled.

"I guess, but there's something else. I can't quite put my finger on it. You know, when I transferred to your site, I had no idea I would be learning about spirituality with you. It's kind of funny."

Just then, Navee walked to the front of the room to prepare her teaching materials. She glanced at each of us, greeting us warmly with her eyes. For the few seconds that my eyes locked with hers, it felt like time stopped. Even after she looked away, I could still feel the love and warmth that had radiated from her eyes. *It feels like she can see right through me. Like she sees beyond my self-doubts and personality. I wonder if she senses my soul.*

I glanced at Kasey. *She looks at me the same way,* I realized. It was now three years from the day I first met her, and she still intrigued me.

"I have something for you."

As Navee continued preparing, Kasey quietly presented me with a book and a small brown box.

"What is it?"

"You'll see. Open it!"

Her smile warmed my heart.

I looked down at the colorful book and flipped through the pages.

"Louise Hay? I think I've heard of her."

"She's like the queen of positive affirmations. This book completely changed the way I thought about life. It will really open you up."

"Wow, thank you! I need stuff like this."

After feeling spiritually lost for years, I was thrilled to find teachings that resonated with me, and always hungry to learn more. I could not wait to dive into this book. I set it aside and slowly opened the brown box. Inside was a tiny, delicate white butterfly ornament.

"Did you know that I like butterflies?" I tilted my head sideways and gave her a playfully suspicious look.

"No, I just thought you might like this." She laughed as she looked deeply into my eyes.

For a moment, the thoughts that usually buzzed through my head stilled. In fact, *everything* felt completely still, as though in this moment nothing mattered. At the same time, everything mattered, and I felt connected to it all. As I stared into Kasey's chocolate-brown eyes, I felt connected to her, connected to myself, and connected to all of life. *Something very interesting is going on here*, I thought. *I'm not sure what it is, but I love it!*

Soon Navee began teaching. I scribbled notes vigorously, absorbing every word she uttered. Her face lit up like a child's, excited and animated. As she shared each concept, I could imagine her skipping and playfully bouncing around.

"Did you know that we have misunderstood the meaning of the word 'sin'?"

Upon observing our looks of uncertainty, Navee continued: "In the Spanish language, the word 'sin' means 'without.' In Latin, it means 'disconnect.' 'Sin' means to be without connection to your spiritual source… to be disconnected from God, which means to be disconnected from your own light."

The other attendees breathed this in silently.

"It's okay to make mistakes. God does not punish us for them," Navee said.

"We're the ones who punish ourselves," another attendee chimed in.

Boy do I relate to that, I thought.

"Yes!" Navee said excitedly. "Everything is a learning experience. Why should we punish ourselves? Let's stop that and be sweeter to ourselves. All we must do is learn the lesson and move on."

"So you don't believe in 'sin'?" the attendee asked.

Navee chuckled. "The only 'sin' is when we forget who we are." She then practically jumped up and down with glee. "Isn't that a relief?" She raised an eyebrow. "Remember who you are... light!"

Whenever Navee said this, I felt as if the angels had descended from the heavens singing the sweetest, most glorious music of truth and love. However, once the music dissipated, another experience took over.

I raised my hand. "Navee, it feels so good when you say that we are light. I believe it, but when I get home, I forget. It's like my mind takes over and tells me I'm still too fat, not smart enough, and so many other annoying and upsetting things. Why does that happen?"

"Does anyone relate?"

In unison, all attendees raised their hands. Navee giggled. "Oh, that's just your ego, Courtney. We all have one, and it doesn't like you knowing the truth of who you are. And that's okay. We'll just tell the ego we still love it, anyway."

What a funny concept, I thought. *Send love to my ego?* I didn't quite understand, but I hoped Navee would tell me more later.

"I'm sorry to say we're about out of time for today," Navee announced.

I couldn't help but feel sad at the announcement. When I was with Navee, I felt a sense of hope and peace as if everything really was as okay as she said. This was a new sensation for me, and I liked it. I felt increasingly thankful for Navee, Kasey, and their beautiful presences in my life.

As we said our goodbyes and exchanged hugs, Kasey presented me with an interesting opportunity. "Do you want to hike after work Monday?"

"Ooh, I would love to!" I said, surprised that she had asked.

As I walked out the door and headed home, my mind and body felt so light, as if I really was walking up there with the angels. I did not even care that I had agreed to spend the rest of the day watching boring football with Nathan. At least I could journal at the same time.

"I am realizing what is most important. It's not exercising, food, or worrying about gaining weight. It's the

186

spiritual energy flowing through my body. Staying connected to my source, my loving spirit. When I can focus on this, I am at peace. In fact, I am on the verge of a really big change. I just have to be open to it. I want to let go of my past patterns of thought.

Courtney...open up, let this change come. Open up to this beautiful light. Let it happen. Let the energy & beauty flow through you."

—Journal, age 26, Saturday, 9/23/06, 2:33 p.m.

◎

The joyfully, light feeling carried me through the rest of the weekend, all the way to my hike with Kasey late Monday afternoon. After a full day's work, a refreshing break sounded delightful. She and I laced up our hiking boots and spent the rest of the day hiking up and down the peaks of South Mountain. Most of the time, she led the way and I followed closely behind, though occasionally, the trail widened enough for us to hike side by side.

"So what's the deal with you and Nathan? You're not engaged?" she asked during one of these times.

"No, he doesn't want to get married." As I looked out toward the horizon, I wondered how much to share with her. I carried enough worry inside; I did not need to burden her with it. At the same time, something about her made me feel safe sharing. Being surrounded by these beautiful mountains made me feel safe, too.

"Well, what about you, Courtney? How do you feel about marriage?"

"I thought I wanted to get married, but I guess it doesn't matter that much. I love Nathan, and our relationship is really easy and fun. I'm really happy."

Who am I trying to convince? I wondered. *Kasey or myself?* I decided to change the subject. "What about you and Monica?"

"What do you mean? What about us?"

I was taken aback by Kasey's short, defensive tone. "Sorry, should I not have asked?"

"No, it's okay, sorry. Go ahead."

"I just wondered if you guys ever had a commitment ceremony. You both wear rings, right?"

I felt nervous, unsure where Kasey's frustration was coming from. I looked down at the rocks beneath my feet and hoped I hadn't said anything wrong.

"No, we haven't. Actually, we're pretty much on the verge of breaking up." With a kick, Kasey sent a rock spinning through the air.

"Oh, I didn't realize that. I'm really sorry, Kasey." My body suddenly felt heavy with sadness for her. I had met Monica a few times, and she seemed like such a sweet person. The two of them had seemed so good for each another.

"Don't worry about it. It's for the better."

"Even so, I imagine it's really hard. Kasey, are you sure you're okay?"

"I will be. Look, can we talk about something else?"

"Sorry. We can." But I could tell she was not okay. Still, the tone of our conversation became light and joyful once again as we started to chat about work and Navee's latest class.

"Courtney, were you religious when you were growing up? You don't strike me as the religious type."

My face wrinkled in perplexity. "That's funny you should ask, Kasey. I'm not sure what the 'religious type' is."

"Well, I was raised strict Catholic. It drives me crazy when people believe something just because they're told to, without keeping an open mind to other possibilities."

"How open-minded of you!" I teased, bumping her with my elbow. "You know what I think is interesting? So many of us were *told* what to believe instead of being encouraged to *discover* what we believe. That's why I like life coaching so much. I ask empowering questions so people can go within and connect with *their* truth… not someone else's."

Kasey nodded and smiled.

"So yes," I continued, "I was baptized Catholic, but when I was ten, my family switched to a Lutheran church. It seemed like everyone in my town was Christian, and I didn't know about other religions. In college, some of my friends practiced Buddhism and Judaism. I realized then that my religion couldn't possibly be the only ticket to heaven, I guess you could say. I felt really disillusioned, and I stopped going to church altogether."

"I know what you mean. There was a point when I started questioning, too. I started wondering if heaven even existed. I didn't want to live my whole life in fear of not getting there."

"Good point! What if heaven isn't a place or destination at all? What if it's a state of mind?"

"Yeah, we definitely create our own internal heaven or hell with our thoughts," she said.

"And if you're living in fear, you're creating your own hell in hopes of getting to heaven."

We both laughed at the irony. It felt so comforting to talk to someone who "got it" and who got me so well, too.

"So what happened after you stopped going to church?"

"Well, I wanted to believe in something. I was on a big quest to figure out what. I read tons of books and found things I liked about each religion."

"Did you practice any of them?"

"No, I'm kind of making up my own thing."

"Me, too. It's empowering, isn't it?"

I nodded. We hiked along in silence for a few minutes. The sun was setting, and a golden wave of calmness washed over our surroundings, calming and soothing the cacti, bunny rabbits, hummingbirds, and us. I admired how the golden spines of the cholla cacti glowed in the soft sunlight.

After a while, Kasey broke the silence: "Courtney, we should hike again. This feels really good."

"Yes, for sure. And thanks for talking about this stuff with me. It means so much to me to have someone to share it with."

"Me, too!"

If you only knew how much…

"It's kind of like we're spiritual study partners," she reflected.

Thanks to the sunset, the remainder of our hike glowed with a magical hue. As we reached the parking lot and wrapped up our conversation, we gasped as we spotted two coyotes trotting by.

"We're never alone," Kasey pointed out.

"I guess not!"

I laughed as I leaned in to hug Kasey goodbye. I hesitated to let go. Her presence comforted me, as did her hugs. But finally I did let go and, with a last glance at her beautiful-chocolate brown eyes, reluctantly got into my car. As I pulled away and headed home, I wondered, *Why do I feel so full when I'm with her?*

That evening, dinner conversation with Nathan seemed dry and boring. Neither of us had much to share. After dinner, he went into the office to answer some e-mails, and I went outside and wrote in my journal.

> "Nathan doesn't want to discuss spirituality too much. He's so into his football and blackjack. That's fine. I can get the spirituality part from Kasey and other friends. Except for one tiny problem... I'm starting to feel attracted to Kasey.
>
> She is so beautiful and strong... assertive. She speaks up for herself and goes after what she wants. I admire that. I love sharing books with her... and music... and sandwiches during our lunch breaks at work. I'm starting to feel this intense magnetic pull to her. I need to talk with her, spend time with her, and just be near her... as much as possible. Actually, my stomach does flip-flops when she's near. Oh dear... what am I getting myself into?"
>
> —Journal, age 26, Monday, 9/25/06, 7:54 p.m.

Chapter 26

Confessions

"Love should come before logic ... Only then will man come to understand the meaning of life." —Fyodor Dostoevsky

The dark clouds that had loomed overhead most of my life were drifting away. The sunshine in my mind as of late felt exhilarating! Through the life coaching program, my spiritual exploration, and now my blossoming friendship with Kasey, I felt empowered to stop worrying about what everyone else thought and just be me. Finally, I started understanding who I was—not who I thought I needed to be. Life was grabbing me by the arms and lifting me up above the clouds, out of the depression I had felt most of my life.

During the next few weeks, Kasey and I shared a few more hikes after work. One sunny morning after one of these hikes, she walked into my office as she usually did to share some quiet social time before the clients arrived. Today, however, Kasey seemed a little nervous as she sat on the edge of the table.

"Can I ask you something?"

"Is it a work question? It's still early, and I don't know how well my brain is functioning yet." I laughed.

"No, it's a personal question."

Now my interest piqued. *Why does she seem so nervous?* "Okay, Kasey, go ahead."

"I want to ask you if something is true… something I've been hearing."

"Like a rumor?" Her nervousness was contagious. My stomach began to ache.

"Sort of."

Kasey looked down. She was normally so confident, and I had never seen her act this shy! I wanted to calm and soothe her. Whatever it was, I wanted her to know that it would be okay.

"Navee keeps telling me that you love me."

Huh? What? I quickly leaned back in my seat and started channeling my own nervousness into talking, quickly and a lot. "Well, Navee is intuitive. Of course I love you. And I love working with you. Thank you for treating me like I'm your equal. I appreciate that so much."

My cover-up was failing miserably, and I knew it. Disappointment covered Kasey's face as she stared at me blankly. Determined to make it better, I wracked my brain for something to say.

"Kasey, it's been awesome to get to know you better. I love our time together."

"Okay, but Navee keeps saying you love me deeply... and that you always have."

As Kasey shifted in her seat, sitting up a little taller, I stared at her in puzzlement. *I cannot jeopardize my relationship with Nathan. She does not need to know the full truth.*

"Never mind Courtney, I guess I'm just reading something more into it than is there. Don't worry about it." She quickly stood up to leave, reminding me of a funnel cloud, ready to destroy whatever was in her path.

"Kasey, wait! Maybe Navee is right!" The words escaped my mouth before I could think.

She stopped in mid-stride to the door and turned back to me. We looked at each other for a few moments, then she walked back to the table and again sat down. I breathed deeply, still unsure of what to say next.

Thankfully, she spoke first. "Courtney, I'm your boss, and this is totally inappropriate of me to say... But I'm attracted to you. Like *really* attracted. And the more I get to know you, I see what a caring, compassionate, giving, loving person you are. Your light shines so brightly, and..." She trailed off and looked away.

My mouth dropped open. *Kasey is attracted to me? She's so strong and confident. What does she see in me?* I did not have time to understand… it was all happening so fast. My stomach fluttered nervously—or was it excitedly?

"Kasey, you're beautiful and so attractive."

Did I really just say that? Thoughts jumped through my mind like salmon in a river. For days now, I had sensed tension between us, not from stress or frustration, but from chemistry. Physical tension. I wanted to be close to her. Each morning, I looked forward to the beauty of her smile. I adored hearing her laugh, sharing lunch with her, discussing spiritual books, and of course, our hikes. And now, she actually confirmed out loud that she felt the same? My body shuddered, releasing a wave of excitement.

"Kasey…" Overloaded with emotion, words failed me.

"I know this is totally inappropriate. We work together. And Monica and I just broke up this past weekend."

"Really? You said it would be for the best, but I'm so sorry!" As I looked at her in sympathy, I couldn't help wondering what this meant. Although Kasey was now free, I was not.

"Courtney, whatever this means, I don't want it to be awkward between us."

"No, don't worry about it. It won't be." And yet, I couldn't help wondering whether I was attempting to reassure her or myself.

"Kasey, do you still want to hike after work?"

"As long as you're still up for it. As long as I haven't made an ass of myself."

"No, everything's fine. Let's hike!"

Explosions of energy filled my stomach. I wasn't sure how to process the conversation, but I tried to maintain my chipper demeanor the rest of the day. However, attempting to concentrate on work was pointless. I sighed as I thought back to my teenage years. The 'tiny' detail about being attracted to females that I had tucked away with all of my other emotions had resurfaced at last. Apparently, my attempt to wish away my sexual orientation had failed miserably.

I can't believe that I'm attracted to a woman after all these years. And she's attracted to me! What am I getting myself into?

I pictured myself walking across a rickety, unstable bridge over murky, crocodile-filled waters. *Why don't I just stay on the land where it's safe...with Nathan?* Instead, I felt suspended in some weird in-between space, unsure how to proceed.

I need to tell Kasey that we can't act on this, I resolved. *I'm happy with Nathan, and there's no way I would ever leave him. But I don't want to upset her. I can't. She's my boss. What if upsetting her means losing my job?*

As the workday ended and Kasey and I drove in separate cars to the hiking trail, I attempted to set aside the shame and fear. *If I just pretend everything's okay, maybe it will be. Optimism usually works, right?*

Indeed, it did... at least temporarily. Our hike was pleasant and filled with beauty as usual, thanks to my stellar ability to push aside discomfort. I laughed at the irony, because the past several weeks of life coach training had taught me to embrace the discomfort, because it indicated that I was growing and changing. Richard had told us that even positive changes can be uncomfortable. Instead of feeling or acknowledging the discomfort, however, I still insisted on pushing it away. As Kasey and I hiked, instead I focused my attention on the sweetness of her words.

"Courtney, I know you worry about your weight. Though, you know what? When I'm with you, I see beyond your body. It's like I see your soul first... *then*, I see your body."

"Really? Kasey, how do you see my soul?"

"I don't know, but I can just... sense it. It's this energy of love and joy emanating out of you. And your soul is so beautiful that it makes your body even more beautiful."

Her words were better than the most delectable sweet nothings whispered in my ear. They caused my whole body to beam brightly, to feel as if it were overflowing with sweetness, love, and joy. Not only was spending time with Kasey good for healing my soul, apparently, it was good for the healing of my body image, too! I had never felt so seen and understood on a deep, unspoken soul level. My whole life, I had hidden from people. Now, somehow, Kasey could see me—not just my outer shell or personality, but the real me underneath.

After our hike, I drove home with a bag of mixed emotions. As if it were a real thing resting on the passenger seat, the bag was open and spilling out worries. *Can I really have dinner with Nathan, just pretending the conversation with Kasey didn't happen this morning? I'm definitely not going to tell him. I don't want to give him anything to worry about. Anyhow, that discussion with Kasey will go no further. But what if Nathan somehow senses what happened today? I didn't cheat on him, but it feels like I did.*

Upon arriving home, I tried to put these worries back into the bag, determined to choose a different emotion for the rest of the evening. Upon seeing Nathan's handsome smile, I allowed the joy to pop out of my bag and onto my face.

"Hi, Nathan. I'm so happy to see you!"

I wrapped my arms around him for a big hug. He hugged me back, but not before I noted his confused expression.

"Um, aren't you always happy to see me?"

I nodded, winking at him. After three years together, he still found ways to make me laugh. I could tell from the mischievous look on his face that he was in one of his playful moods tonight.

"Good hike with Kasey today, huh?"

"Yeah, it was great!"

"You know, we should hike again sometime soon. We haven't gone in forever."

"Oh, sure! That sounds great." But just like that, those worries were flying out of the bag again. Did I really want to hike with him? After these awesome, magical, intimate hikes with Kasey, how could hiking with Nathan compare?

After a rather uneventful evening, Nathan went to bed slightly before me. I climbed into bed next to him, soothed by the sound of his gentle snores, and quietly scribbled a few things in my journal.

"I feel really hungry for something... and I'm not sure what. Is it food? I don't think so. In fact, I need a break from needing food. From obsessing and thinking about it all the time. It's tiring. Though it's kind of funny, since when I eat, I don't let myself eat enough to feel satisfied.

195

Is it love that I hunger for? Is it connection? Whatever
it is, do I deserve it? Will I accept it if it shows up?"
—Journal, age 26, Wednesday, 10/11/96, 10:44 p.m.

After tucking my pen and journal safely under the bed, I lay down and cuddled into the covers. I tried to empty the worries from my bag and fill it with joyful gratitude instead. *How amazing to be loved by a woman as beautiful as Kasey. Navee was right! It feels like I've always loved her.*

As my head rested peacefully on the pillow, a brilliant idea suddenly occurred to me. *Love is abundant! Why can't I love Kasey and Nathan? Loving her doesn't mean I love Nathan any less. In fact, what if love multiplies? What if feeling Kasey's love opens my heart wider and allows me to love Nathan even more? Maybe I don't have to say 'no' to her. Maybe I can just do what feels the best... love!*

My whole body smiled with relief as I drifted off to sleep.

◎

The next morning .at work, I buried myself in client paperwork. The faster I worked, the less emotional discord I had to feel. After a few tedious hours of writing progress notes, I looked up at a very welcome sight— Navee was peering into my office.

"Do you have a moment?"

"Sure," I said, putting my pen down on the desk.

Navee's intuition had sensed my attraction to Kasey before I had fully admitted it to myself. I wondered if she knew about our recent hikes. I suddenly felt a bit anxious, fearful that she might not approve.

"Courtney, how's your mum?"

I felt relieved. *At least she's not asking about Kasey.*

"Oh, she's as feisty as ever. She just drives me crazy sometimes."

Navee chuckled.

At this point, my parents had taken a leap and bought a second home in Phoenix. Mom missed me and was growing tired of cold Michigan winters, so she settled into their new Phoenix house. Dad remained in Michigan to work one more year, after which he planned to join my mom for winters in Phoenix and summers in Michigan. They probably needed a break from one another anyway, as they now seemed to argue every time I was around them. After deciding to move to Phoenix, Mom seemed lighter and happier than ever.

I wished I could say the same for me. On one hand, I would enjoy having a family member around, especially for holidays. On the other hand, the timing was awful. Here I was, trying to become my own person without the influence of Mom's needs or opinions, and suddenly she just *had* to be close to me.

Oh well, I'll just have to set some boundaries, I had reassured myself before her move. *I don't need to see her every day.* Even so, I felt guilty and mean for even thinking this.

Of course, setting those boundaries was another story. Upon arriving, Mom did not know anyone in the city besides Nathan and me, and she ached for something to do. Without even thinking, one day I blurted out, "You should volunteer at my work!" Really, sometimes, I was *far* too eager to help. Finally, I was more aware of my feelings and needs, but still found myself pushing them aside if it meant helping someone else—especially my mom. As much as I wanted to be my own person, winning her approval still meant the world to me.

Soon after I made the suggestion, Mom took me up on it. Much to my surprise, however, at my work she transformed before my eyes. Her kindness shined forth as she interacted with our clients, who had mental illnesses, dementia, speech impediments, and several other disabilities. I had never seen her giggle so much and glow so brightly as she did when she was volunteering. Seeing my mom having so much fun warmed my soul! She also got along great with Kasey and Navee. In fact, Mom and Navee grew quite fond of each other, and spent quite a bit of time together on the days their volunteer shifts overlapped.

"Remember, Courtney," Navee told me one day. "You came through her, but you are not of her. You are light. So is she. In fact, she is one of your greatest teachers."

"Greatest teacher?" I couldn't hide my confusion. "Navee, what do you mean?" *Sometimes Navee says the weirdest things,* I thought. Still, before I totally disregarded her statement, I wanted to hear more.

"The people who challenge us the most are here to teach us. And we are here to teach them."

"Oh. I never thought of it like that." Still, I was skeptical.

"On a soul level, before you came here, you chose your mom and dad."

"Navee, are you *sure*?"

She grabbed her belly as she laughed wholeheartedly. "Yes! Each of us chose just the right parents to help with our soul's learning. Courtney, there are no mistakes."

I sat still for a moment, noticing how calm and at peace my gut felt. *Perhaps what she's saying is true. It feels true.*

"Courtney," she continued, "you're far more powerful than you realize. Forgive your mom. She is beautiful, and she's done the best she can. I know she hurts your feelings sometimes. Let her get angry and have her temper tantrums. It does not need to affect you."

"But it does affect me. Very strongly."

"Then you have not yet learned your own power. It's time for you to stand up for yourself. Be who you came here to be."

I felt tears swell in my eyes, but I dared not release them. I turned away, hoping Navee would not notice. *Be me?* I reflected. *I'm afraid to. If Navee only knew what I go through every day inside.*

I turned to look at the framed picture on my desk, recently taken at the "senior" prom that my coworkers and I had created for our clients one day at work. Wearing the same pale purple princess dress I had worn nine years prior, I stood between two people I loved dearly. To my right stood handsome, smiling Nathan, who had come to volunteer that day, dressed in a fancy tuxedo. My heart lowered in my chest with worry as I looked at him. As my eyes drifted to the person on my left, I felt a surge of hope and promise. Beautiful Kasey's eyes glimmered, as though she was quietly whispering, *"Courtney, it's going to be okay."*

Chapter 27

A Magical Hike

"The authentic self is soul made visible." —Sarah Ban Breathnachxxiv

A month passed, during which Kasey and I developed even more of an emotional bond. What an honor that Kasey wanted to be near me so much, I thought. Never before had I wanted to spend so much time with someone. *Maybe it's because I don't have to pretend around her,* I often told myself. Being with her felt easy, effortless, and peaceful, as though I could let go of my façade, relax, and finally just *be.*

> "She is in my thoughts all the time. I feel so connected to her, almost like I am falling in love with her. I think I am. I see so much depth when I look at her eyes. So much of her loving, beautiful spirit. So much of her light. It is right there for me to see, through her beautiful eyes. She is so soft, gentle, protective and caring. This woman has so much love in her heart."
> —Journal, age 26, Thursday, 11/9/06, 9:05 p.m.

Maybe we can just be close emotionally and spiritually, I attempted to reassure myself. *That's not cheating, right?* However, each day my longing to connect with her physically intensified. *How can I keep denying it?*

Because you're in a relationship with Nathan, that's why, my inner voice shot back. Instantly, guilt overtook me.

> "When contemplating what's happening with Kasey, and the feelings I am having toward her, and the beautiful relationship we are developing, I think my ego is getting in

the way, wondering if I should be having these feelings, especially physical attraction.

But then, I am using my head and ego instead of using my spirit. If I listen to my spirit, I will act on these feelings no problem. Because they are natural, and beautiful. I love her so much, and I just want to have another way to express to her my love for her. When we hug, it is the most amazing inner experience I have ever felt. Sparks, fireworks, warmth, energy, tingling, all over. She is of a very beautiful energy vibration, very loving and beautiful, spiritually grounded energy. Even when my hand brushes hers, or our arms brush against one another. The feeling is amazing, indescribable. I wonder what it would be like to kiss her. To touch her, to hold her. To kiss her and to make love to her. I think it would be the most amazing physical sensation available."
—Journal, age 26, Saturday, 11/12/06, 9:26 a.m.

Fully aware of the dangers in the water, I kept walking further and further across the rickety, unstable bridge. However, despite the guilt, fear, and inner turmoil, I followed my heart. Maybe, I hoped, my heart could create a bubble of protection around us and we could forget everything else, like the reality of the fact that I was in another relationship.

However, I had a feeling that whatever awaited me at the end of this bridge would feel more "right" than anything I had ever experienced, that all this turmoil would be worth it.

One afternoon, Kasey and I went for another hike. However, this hike was unlike any other we'd taken together. The summer heat had finally passed, and we could now get through a whole hike without losing a pound of sweat! As Kasey took the lead along the narrow trails, I followed just behind and shared how guilty I felt about not spending more time with my mom.

"Kasey, I'm listening to my inner voice more, but sometimes I just feel like such a bad person."

The negative thoughts funneling through my mind had distracted me so much; I didn't notice Kasey had stopped dead in her tracks until I bumped right into her.

"Courtney, listen."

She spoke firmly as she turned and placed her hands on my shoulders. She gently rocked me back and forth, attempting to shake some sense into me, or perhaps shake the doubts and fears out of me.

"I don't want to hear you say that. You're not a bad person. You never were, and you can't be. All you need to do is be Courtney. Just be her, because she is beautiful inside and out. She is nothing but light and love."

I stared deeply into her beautiful, chocolate-brown eyes. *All you need to do is be Courtney. Just be her...* Her words echoed through my mind again and again. For a moment, I lost all sense of time, space, and thought. And then, tears welled in my eyes.

Could what she just said be true? Is it possible I could let go of all these self-doubts and just be me?

We looked into each other's eyes a moment longer and then turned to resume hiking. As I felt the firmness of the dirt and rocks underneath my feet, I thought, *the earth is supporting me, just as Kasey does.* The sun was starting to set now, and the familiar yellow glow came over the mountain, cacti, and desert flowers.

"Thank you, Kasey. I'm working on all this," I said as we continued. "It's just that I have all these old negative thoughts that keep me from remembering my light. Isn't it amazing that we can change our thoughts and beliefs? I had no idea."

"Yeah, it's wild! Most people don't realize that just because we have a thought doesn't mean we have to believe it."

"Ha! I saw a quote the other day that said, 'Don't believe every thought you think!'"

Kasey laughed quietly. "It makes sense, though. It's kind of like a computer. When we were little kids, we were programmed with all these beliefs—our parents', society's, religion's. We thought our beliefs were true, because it was all we knew."

"Yeah, like me thinking it was wrong to kiss a girl."

"What?" Kasey glanced back at me, her eyes wide in shock.

I bit my lip and gulped. *Well, here goes.* "When I was a teenager, my cousin and I kissed. I got scared, so I told her we had to stop."

"Courtney, why didn't you tell me this sooner?"

Despite my nervousness, I took a deep breath. *Time to be honest.* "I don't know, Kasey. I guess I didn't want to add fuel to the fire. I think you know by now that I would love to kiss you. I would love to be close to you."

But I can't cheat on Nathan.

"I know you're in a tough situation. I know you love Nathan. But Courtney, I'm crazy for you. But I don't want to pressure you."

"I know, Kasey."

"I want you to be strong and stop worrying about what everyone else thinks. I want you to see the beauty I see when I look at you."

The area around my heart tingled with a feeling of deep peace. *I think I'm addicted to the way Kasey makes me feel. It's tantalizing. Is it possible to be loved this much?* Already, the love between Kasey and me was more profound than I have ever dreamed love could be.

"Kasey, I appreciate you more than I can say. I'm so glad you showed up in my life. Ever since I met you, life feels magical!"

"It *is* magical, Courtney. Thank you for brightening my world. I haven't laughed this much my whole life!"

Suddenly, she stopped walking and turned to look at me. My body melted at the sight of her mesmerizing eyes. Then, she pointed to a large formation of rocks at the side of the trail.

"Let's sit down for a moment."

Feeling both excited and nervous, I followed her. I would have followed her anywhere, even to the moon and back. Although I felt closer and closer to her every day lately, today felt different… somehow even more special and magical.

When we sat down on the rocks, she reached for my hand, and electrifying sparks of energy zoomed from my fingers directly to my heart. *This is all just from the touch of her hand?* I wondered in disbelief. She looked me in the eyes and spoke, her voice soft and sweet. "Courtney, I love you. And the fact that *you* love *me*… it blows my mind."

"Oh Kasey, don't be silly. You're amazing! I love you so much."

I placed my hand over her heart, connecting us even more deeply. I ached to kiss her, to know the depths of our love on the physical level. The warmth and beauty of her eyes overtook me, and being this close to her sent me into another realm, one of passionate sensation and divine love, where I forgot all the human "rules," including all the reasons I usually held back from connecting with her physically. In fact, I forgot that anything or anyone else existed. Nothing mattered beside this very moment and the intense, timeless, sacred love between us.

The magnetic energy brought our faces closer together, forehead to forehead, nose to nose. My heart pounded. For a moment, I reached for her face. My body tingled as my hand melted into the softness of her skin. All we needed now was a way for my heart to join with hers.

The setting sun shined all around us, as though it was blessing our romantic encounter. Then, like a butterfly delicately landing on a flower, her lips touched mine. Our kiss was sweet nectar to my hungry soul.

We separated briefly, and I looked at her as love coursed through me. She looked more beautiful than ever, as though she had just shared with me the essence of her soul. Leaning in, we kissed some more… and some more, and some more. Her lips were tantalizing.

When the sunlight had dissipated completely, we stood silently and finished the last mile of our hike. I floated along so freely that I hardly remembered a step. I vaguely remembered saying our goodbyes in the parking lot, followed by a loving embrace and another sweet, soft kiss.

Despite how "right" my kiss with Kasey had felt, reality sunk in as I drove home. I had just officially cheated on my boyfriend.

What were you thinking, stupid idiot?
He would be crushed if he found out.

Well, I'll just make sure that he doesn't.

How can you look him in the eyes? You pretend
to be so sweet, but you're just a liar and a cheater.
You don't deserve Nathan. You don't deserve anyone.

But I want to be loved.

Are you sure you deserve it?

"Leave me alone!" I screamed. I was so tired of tormenting myself.

I'm just trying to figure out what I want, okay?

You mean figure out WHO you want.
Do you really want to come out, Courtney?
Do you really want to be a lesbian?
Do you know what that would mean?

Well, yeah, it sounds kinda scary, and I don't
know how my family would react. But if
I'm in love with Kasey, it'd be worth it.

Are you sure?
Your life with Nathan is so simple and happy.
Are you sure you want to give it up?

Upon arriving home, I *did* have a difficult time looking Nathan in the eye. It felt strange to kiss him after I had just kissed her; therefore, I kept the affection to a minimum. After dinner, thankfully he went into the office to play blackjack on his laptop. I needed some space to wallow in my guilt. Sitting outside on a lounge chair, I looked up to the stars, praying for some guidance:

Universe, I've gotten myself into a hopeless situation. What am I supposed to do? I sighed as my mind drifted back to the first life coaching class. *Richard said that the behaviors and relationships that no longer serve us would fall away. What does that mean for me? I don't want to lie anymore to anyone, especially not to myself. Will you help me be honest? Will you help me be strong enough to be me?*

Chapter 28

Seismic Activity

"The cave you fear to enter holds the treasure you seek."
—Joseph Campbell

Spring 2007

Up until this point, my life had seemed calm, pleasant, and stable on the outside. The ups and downs happened internally, unbeknown to anyone. My family's life seemed good and uneventful, too. My parents had been together for forty-three years, and other than a few arguments here or there (during the summer I'd lived at home before moving to Arizona, for example), they seemed to be relatively happy together.

At least, that's what I thought.

Usually, a period of odd stillness precedes any storm, earthquake, or eruption. Those in tune with their intuition sense this, stock up on food or supplies, and seek shelter. Although I had no idea if any storms were coming, I found myself busy stocking up on love and seeking shelter in Kasey's arms.

Connecting with Kasey physically had catapulted me into a whole new world. Over the next few months, whenever we kissed or touched, I felt a sense of wholeness unlike I had ever felt. It was ironic that Nathan did not want to marry me, I thought, because Kasey and I connected so deeply that it felt like we had already said "I do." The marriage of our bodies, minds, emotions, and spirits nourished us and elevated our existence to levels of love I had only dreamed of until then.

I thought back to what Richard had taught my classmates and me about the head, heart, and inner knowing. My relationship with Nathan was amazing at the head level. It was fun, playful, and so loving. My heart certainly loved and adored him. Yet my inner knowing was guiding me toward Kasey. Only she nourished me on the deep soul level. I knew there was no turning back now; I had to be with her. I didn't know how, but my happiness and survival depended on it.

A few months after our first kiss, Kasey invited me over for a magical night at her house. I wanted to be as honest with Nathan as I could, so I told him I would be sleeping over. He did not bat an eyelash. After wishing me a fun night, he headed to the casino, and I headed to Kasey's place on the other side of town. I felt grateful, yet annoyed at his lack of concern.

After we shared several kisses, Kasey said, "Courtney, I don't want you to feel pressured, but I have something for you."

I gave her a light-hearted suspicious glance. She smiled back and placed within my hands a wooden ornament of two Chinese girls smiling out from underneath a brown roof. One was dressed in blue, the other in red.

"It reminded me of us." Kasey blushed.

"Oh, Kasey, I love it. Thank you!"

I looked at the roof above the girls' heads. *Will this someday be Kasey and me... in our own home together?* In what was now becoming a regular occurrence, butterflies were migrating through my stomach.

After a fabulous meal of eggplant parmesan, she reached for my hand and guided me outside to the back patio. The vivid, almost-full moon and thousands of gorgeous, twinkling stars illuminated the entire sky. We stood staring up at nature's bounty as Kasey snuggled up behind me, and wrapped her arms around me.

"Kasey, do you know what your touch does to me?" I whispered.

"No, tell me." She kissed me neck.

"It takes me to this incredible place. It's like I feel calm and excited at the same time."

"I like when you're excited."

I flashed her a flirty smile. "You know, it's like you send me into orbit. And want to know the best part?"

"What?" she asked before kissing my neck even more passionately.

"You're right there in orbit with me."

I spun around and pressed my lips against hers. Upon impact, satisfaction spread through my body like hot molten lava. At some point, we made our way to the double chaise lounge chair and lay down. Underneath the moon and stars, our clothes left us, and our bodies knew exactly what to do.

Indeed, we had gone into orbit, where time, space, and fear do not exist. As we lovingly explored each other's bodies, we entered a place where all that mattered was this very moment, wrapped up in the sensation of wholeness and pure, divine love.

After hours of escalating excitement and passionate release, we lay still in each other's arms, peaceful and content.

"Kasey, what comes over me when I make love to you? I had no idea I could feel such intense passion. And what comes over you?"

"It's amazing, isn't it? I've never experienced anything like it." I smiled, grateful for the confirmation that she had been right there with me.

"You are so damn beautiful, Kasey! Your body, spirit, and this loving energy that comes from within you. I'm so glad your body expresses it so beautifully, and that I'm the one who gets to receive it."

We lay still for a few moments. I thought back to the first time we had made love. I had known that making love to a woman would be different from making love to a man, and worried that I would not know how to do it. But thankfully, my body had instinctively known what to do. Somehow, it felt natural and familiar.

"Courtney, what am I supposed to do with you?"

Although Kasey's tone was playful, I took her question very seriously.

"Do you really want me to answer?"

"Of course, beautiful."

I answered slowly, whispering into her ear. "Be with me every day. Spend time with me every day. Make love to me every day. Talk to me every day, because I love talking to you. Meditate with me. Love me, and let me love you. Help me to grow and learn, and let me help you to grow and learn." As I spoke these words, I felt they were coming directly from my heart, my spirit, and my entire being without any hesitation. This is what my heart and soul wanted, I finally realized. I wanted to be with Kasey.

◎

Whenever Kasey and I were together, our love temporarily veiled my guilt. However, in moments alone or with Nathan, no veil could protect me from the heavy, mud-like feeling of shame and self-hatred. Lying on the couch after work just before Nathan came home one day, the ping-pong match within my mind resumed.

You're such a liar and slut. You said you weren't going to compromise your relationship with Nathan, but you did.

I wasn't thinking. I didn't mean to fall in love with Kasey. But I'm glad I did. Her love is healing to me.

Who cares about your healing? How can you be so cruel to Nathan?

Well, he knows I'm close to Kasey. He sees how much time we spend together. He sees me texting her every night. He doesn't care.

Yeah, but stupid, he doesn't know just how close you and Kasey are.

He told me that he's happy I have someone to spend time with, since he works so much.

Don't you wonder why he's not jealous?

208

Don't you wonder if he even cares?

> *Yeah, it makes me angry. Why doesn't he pick*
> *up on things intuitively like Navee and Kasey?*
> *Instead, he remains clueless.*

You can't blame him, though, Courtney.
You're the one gambling with your relationship.

In the midst of my inner turmoil, thank God I had my journal console me.

> "I am so terrified of someone finding out that we are together, especially Nathan. He would never forgive me. Will I ever forgive myself? I hate living a lie. The sneaking and dishonesty is draining every ounce of my energy. Something needs to change.
>
> God, why can't I have them both? They both bring different energy to my life. Nathan reminds me to be light and playful, and Kasey supports me spiritually and emotionally. For the first time in my life, I'm finally starting to get in touch with my emotions.
>
> I would love to have both a boyfriend and a girlfriend. But I don't know, do people do that? Sadly, there's no way I could. Nathan and Kasey would <u>not</u> be okay with an open or multi-partner relationship. I don't know if I could handle that either. It sounds like a lot of work. I need to make a choice. But how?
>
> I have never felt the passion and connection that I feel with Kasey. And for the first time in my life, I feel so attached to someone. I know my soul belongs with her, and I think I want to be with her exclusively. But I love Nathan and I don't want to let him go.

I don't want to be scared. What is meant to be will be. God would not have placed this beautiful human being in front of me if I weren't supposed to love and support her. I am tired of listening to others' opinions. When will I start relying on my own?"

—Journal, age 27, Friday, 3/30/07, 5:12 p.m.

◎

My life and my family's lives had seemed so calm for so many years. Now, I sensed pending storms and earthquakes left and right. I could no longer pretend that everything was okay. My attraction to Kasey elated and excited me, but I was terrified of the decisions that lay ahead.

So far, I hadn't told anyone about my attraction to Kasey. I was ashamed, scared, and worried about being judged both for having sex with a woman and cheating on my boyfriend. The guilt was eating me alive. At the same time, I knew holding this all in was no longer an option. I needed to confide in someone... someone who would love me no matter what. I had no idea how he would react, especially to the fact that I was in love with a woman. He accepted homosexuality in general, but would the rules of the game be different when it came to his own daughter? I prayed for the best as I grabbed my cell phone and headed out the door for a walk around the neighborhood.

I breathed a sigh of relief when he picked up. "Hi Dad, it's me. Can I talk to you?"

"Sure, Court, I'm glad you called. Actually, there's something I need to tell you."

Curiosity overrode my urgency. "Okay Dad, go ahead. Mine can wait."

"Court, bear with me. This isn't easy for me to say."

The unusual seriousness of his tone made me gasp. Although I'd called seeking comfort, I was about to experience the first in a series of earthquakes.

"Court, I know you've noticed your mom and me arguing a lot lately. I've been trying to stand up for myself for the first time in my life."

"I'm proud of you, Dad."

"Thanks. I hate to say this, but I am asking your mom for a divorce."

The street was calm and quiet, but I felt the earth shake beneath my feet just the same. *Noooo! Not my parents. Everyone else's parents get divorced, but not mine.* Hearing these words from my father's lips was devastating. *What does this mean for our family? Do we still have a family? What does this mean for Mom?* Quickly, I pushed my feelings aside so I could reassure Dad.

"Dad, you've always told me that you'd support me no matter what. Well, I support you, too. I know this will be a huge change for all of us, but we'll get through it. I want you to be happy."

"Thank you, Court. That means so much to me." I sensed tears of relief streaming down his face. "This is the hardest decision I've ever had to make. I love your mom. I want her to be happy, too." This time his voice shook, making the tears even more evident.

"She'll be okay, Dad."

But that was a lie. I knew Mom would be devastated. I fought down the urge to sigh. *They say God only brings what you can handle. Our family must be damn strong.*

"Yes, let's hope. We can talk more about this later, Court. What did you want to talk about?"

My heart raced. *Do I tell him now?* I wanted to say, "Dad, I have some big news for you, too." However, the timing no longer seemed right. Yes, I decided. Coming out would have to wait. We had already experience enough seismic activity for one day.

"Don't worry about it, Dad. I'll tell you another time."

"Are you sure, Court? I'd like to hear."

"Well, let me just ask you this. If you were in love with two different people, how would you choose between them?"

"Uh-oh, does this mean you and Nathan are having troubles?"

"Kind of. I'm so lost and confused, and I don't know what to do."

My face contorted, and I felt my own tears start. I just wanted Dad to make it all better, even though unfortunately, he couldn't.

"Well, what's going on?"

"I don't feel like explaining right now. But basically, I love both of these people, and I'm trying to decide which one needs me most."

"Court, I don't think that's the best way to decide here. Don't worry about what they need. What do *you* want?"

"I don't know." I didn't lie to be mean or to deceive him. I lied to him because I was lying to myself. I did know the answer; I was just scared.

"Well, listen to your heart, Court. The answer will come to you, just like mine did."

I appreciated Dad's attempt to reassure me, but I felt more worried than ever now. If my answer would result in an earthquake like my dad's, I might have to consider whether I should listen to it. Who wanted to cause so much hurt and devastation?

"Dad, why can't life just be easy?"

"I don't know, Court. Maybe the hard stuff is what makes life worthwhile, especially when we come out on the other side. Keep your chin up, okay? Looks like we're all going through some big changes."

Yeah, if he only knew just how big.

After we hung up, I sighed and stared at the sun as it set behind the outline of the nearby mountain range. *I know the other side is out there,* I thought. *I'm just not sure I will get there.*

Chapter 29

The Strength of Surrender

"The most courageous way to move through life is by choosing to find the good in every moment. The moment of complete darkness is the beginning of life." —Dr. Darren R. Weissman[xxv]

When Dad told my mother he wanted a divorce, it felt as if all hell broke loose. Mom was livid and made sure that my sisters and I knew it. I felt concerned about her, compassion for her devastation, yet also frustration at her insistence that we ought to take her side. There were no sides to take. I loved both of my parents. All the emotions flying around quickly depleted my energy.

If the appearance of our calm, happy family had fallen through the fault line after Dad's announcement, it was buried beneath a pile of rocks, when I learned that my parents had considered divorce twenty-four years ago, after my mom caught my dad having an affair. I had always placed my dad on a pedestal of perfection, so this was a huge blow.

He cheated on my mom? He's not perfect? They'd been unhappy in their marriage? Why had they kept this from me? I often asked myself as my heart sunk in my chest. My whole family's existence suddenly seemed inauthentic.

Unfortunately, the news of my parents' divorce delivered only the first shock wave in a series of unexpected earthquakes that suddenly erupted through my life. With varying degrees of magnitude, each quake shook the very foundation of my existence. After a while, I just wanted to hide from it all.

In fact, many afternoons after work, I did hide. I cuddled up in bed underneath the covers, both for emotional protection and from my body's utter exhaustion. With all the stress and shame in my life of

213

late, I was unconsciously punishing myself more than ever. I ate less and exercised more. However, frustratingly, my body weight was now so low I only had the strength and stamina to do a third of my usual kickboxing routine. Although my body was thinner than ever, I had never felt so heavy.

One April afternoon, I sat in bed journaling while huddling in blankets and a comforter for warmth. With very little body fat, my internal temperature gauge seemed permanently set at "frigid." No matter how many clothes I wore this spring, I felt uncomfortably chilled to the bone and longed for the Phoenix summer's heat. As I burrowed in the blankets, I reflected on the decisions ahead of me. I knew what I needed to do, but I was terrified of the repercussions. As I braced myself for the next earthquake, thoughts bounced back and forth in my mind.

*Do I really want to leave everything
I've ever known to be with a woman?*

*Yeah, stupid, do you really want to come
out? What if your family hates you for it?*

*I'm nervous about their reactions, but if Kasey
and I are together, I refuse to live with her in the closet.*

*Well, you'll still have to be secretive at work.
Unless you want to lose your job, that is.*

*That's true. Our company has a nepotism policy
and no protection clause for LGBTQ employees.
Technically, I could be fired for being bisexual.
Oh well, it's a risk I'm willing to take.*

*What if you lose all your friends? After all your
stupid worries about people thinking you were
a lesbian because of your short haircut, now
you want to admit that you're into women?
You're ridiculous.*

214

Well, the way it is now… and hiding and being secretive is ripping me apart. I can't stand to look at Nathan, knowing that I'm deceiving him. I love him.

But you don't mind having sex with him, even though you're also having sex with someone else.

Yes, I do mind. It feels terrible. It's not the right thing to do.

See, I told you a long time ago that you're a slut. By the way, I thought you were so happy with him. What changed?

I guess I didn't realize how much love and nourishment I needed on a deep soul level until I met Kasey. Leave me alone now, okay?

The constant self-criticism was draining me even more. *Why won't my mind ever be quiet? WIll I ever find peace?* There was now a huge fault line in my love life, dividing me between my love for a man and love for a woman.

I turned to my journal.

"It's complicated for me. I will be leaving a heterosexual life and admitting to people (to my loved ones, friends and society) that I am bisexual. And many won't understand that and immediately label me a lesbian. In some ways, maybe that will be to my benefit, because it will help explain to people why I would leave such a wonderful man, such a wonderful relationship, to be with someone else. They will blame my sexuality."
—Journal, age 27, Tuesday, 4/17/07, 5:02 p.m.

215

Suddenly, the noise of the garage door opening stopped my pen in mid-stroke. Panic shot sparks through my body. I hurriedly closed my journal and tossed it under the bed.

"Hey Court, I'm home!" Nathan called from the garage.

"I'm in bed…" I tried to muster up energy to say it loudly enough for him to hear, but sensed I had failed.

"Court, are you here?" Nathan was in the living room now.

"I'm in here." My voice seemed so weak.

He now walked into our bedroom and saw my weakened state. "Are you okay? You've been so tired lately."

"Yeah, I just have a lot on my mind. And I'm upset about my parents' divorce."

He opened the blinds to let in some sunlight. I preferred the darkness.

"I'm sorry about that. Divorce sucks. See, I told you it's easier not to get married in the first place."

He laughed but quickly saw that I did not. At this point, Nathan and I had agreed to disagree on the marriage issue. He gave me a kiss and a loving look. "I'm going for a run. I'd invite you, but I don't think you have the energy, huh?"

"No, but you go and enjoy."

After changed his clothes, lacing up his sneakers, and leaving, I returned to my contemplation.

How can I break his heart? I wondered in despair. *I want to be with Kasey, but I will miss Nathan so much. I'm such a horrible bitch. I can't live this way anymore. Should I give up? Or should I take the risk to be me?*

I suddenly felt an annoying itch on my back. As I scratched it, I wondered, *Why does my back feel so pokey?* It took me a second to realize that my ribs now protruded through my skin. *I don't remember being this bony before. That's not healthy, is it?* I panicked, sensing another earthquake about to erupt.

The itch reminded me of another annoyance. Not only had my coworkers expressed concern about my weight, now my sister Kelly had, too. She had recently visited my mom and me in Phoenix, and during our usual shopping trip to the mall, I needed several breaks to sit and rest due to my physical frailty. Kelly had practically freaked out with concern.

But I look better than ever, I thought. *I'm finally thin. I don't get what her problem is.* On the other hand, though, I did "get" it. I felt my body breaking down more every day.

> "My body is exhausted. I'm in bed meditating and praying. I'm also resting my body, which is HUGE for me. I never rest. Resting feels like death to me.
>
> Navee is right. I am too beautiful for this darkness and negative energy. I am too beautiful to give in and be broken down. I have too much to give. Too much to do in this lifetime. Navee says I am a Lightworker, you know, that I'm here to share love and light, to make this world a better place. How can I do that when I feel this drained?"
> —Journal, age 27, Tuesday, 4/17/07, 5:55 p.m.

I had reached my breaking point, the darkest moment of my life. I had to make a choice to live or to die.

Courtney, you are slowly killing yourself.
Are you going to continue being half-alive,
letting everyone else make the decisions
for you, while your weight drops even lower?

> *I don't want to. I want to live.*

Well, then you have to take the risk to
actually start living. It's time to be authentic
and tell people who you really are.
Anorexia is deadly, you know.

> *What do you mean? I don't have anorexia.*
> *Remember the test results in college?*

That's enough, Courtney. Stop fooling yourself.
When you look in the mirror, you're not seeing

217

yourself accurately. You have an eating disorder.
You need help.

Do you really expect me to admit that
I'm not perfect? Admit that I'm falling apart?
Admit that I need help? Are you crazy?
That would be the end of me. The end of
life as I know it. What if people stop loving me?

What if you could learn to love yourself?

Suddenly, everything became quiet.

That was it. That was what I needed… to love myself. I wanted to, but how could I? I had hurt people I loved. I had been dishonest, and not only to Nathan. I had been dishonest most of my life. I had hidden my true feelings. I had hidden the authentic Courtney.

How could I forgive myself? How could I love myself when I was still not even sure who I was? Could I give up the need to be liked and the endless striving for approval and acceptance? Could I learn to love my flaws and imperfections?

I needed help, but that would mean creating cracks in the walls I had built around myself so that someone could peek in. That sounded not only scary, but deadly. However, in my heart I knew I couldn't go on this way. In an effort to have control over my weight and my life, I had lost all control of my body, heart, and mind. The bullying energy of an eating disorder was controlling me. In this moment, the darkest of my life, I knew I had to fully discover my inner light and claim back my power.

It's okay, Courtney. Just admit it. I heard the voice of my inner wisdom encouraging and consoling me. I broke down and sobbed, pounding my fists on the bed with all the strength I could muster.

"No!" I yelled through my hot tears. "I don't want it to be true, but it is."

Unleashing my anger gave an unusual strength to my body. Hot angry blood rushed through my veins and sought outlet through my fists, which now pounded the bed harder. Climbing onto all fours, I punched the comforter, mattress, everything I could get my hands on.

At some point, fists were no longer enough. I hurled pillows across the room, then hopped off the bed and jumped forcefully up and down on the carpeted floor, kicking the air, crying hysterically, and screaming in pure terror. The intense fire burning within me needed an outlet. It was hungry for destruction, and up until now, I realized in sorrow, my object of destruction had been myself.

"No, no, no, no, no!" I screamed, scanning the room for something to throw. I spotted a candleholder on the dresser, grabbed it, and forcefully arced it across the room and into the wall. I grunted as it shattered, hurling multiple shards of shattering glass flying through the air.

*What is happening to me? I've never done
this before. Am I a complete freak?
Should I be locked up in the psych ward?*

*This is what they call anger, Courtney.
Rage, in fact. Stop fooling yourself.
You've expressed it for years... internally.*

I took a few deep breaths, aware of their shaky unevenness. I felt like I had just been in a fight! Though my heart was still pounding, I felt it slow a little. My energy reserves exhausted, I crashed down to the floor like a ragdoll.

"Is this what you wanted, God? For me to destroy something else beside myself? Fine, I'll admit it. I have an eating disorder! What more do you want from me?"

All I heard in return was silence.

Instead of feeling frustrated with the lack of a response, I suddenly felt a deep peace in my heart.

It's going to be okay, Courtney. Time to destroy the rules by which you've been running your life. Time to create a new way of being. You can do this. It's going to be scary as hell, but God will help you through it. So will Kasey.

I felt a deep understanding that this moment of complete darkness was now turning into light. I was making the *choice* to turn it into light.

"God, I know you're there. All right, I surrender. I am done trying to control, worrying that things won't work out as they are supposed to. I'm asking you to take over from here. Show me whatever is for my highest good."

Just then, I heard the front door creak open. Nathan had returned home from his run. I hurriedly gathered the pillows strewn all over the floor and climbed back into bed, quickly brainstorming a believable explanation for the broken candleholder. For now, I needed to rest. Once I had gained some strength back, I knew what I needed to do.

Chapter 30

The Uniting of Souls

"The spiritual food required by my mind and body is a constant flow of love. I love myself in myriad ways." —Louise L. Hay[xxvi]

A few days later at work, I had just finished up a meeting with a client when Navee walked into my office.

"Courtney, what's going on?" Navee asked with concern in her eyes. "You haven't seemed like yourself."

"I've been sick with a bad cold, actually. I feel so weak and tired, and my throat feels like it's been rubbed raw with sandpaper."

"You're not speaking your truth. That's why."

"That's why my throat hurts?"

Navee nodded. She and I both knew the source of my turmoil ran far deeper than a cold. "Courtney, the mind, body, and spirit are intimately connected. C'mon. Let's go to Kasey's office."

I followed her next door to Kasey's office and felt somewhat relieved that it was empty. *Kasey must be in the activity room with the clients*, I thought. I just needed a few minutes to collect myself before seeing her. In the meantime, Navee and I sat down in Kasey's chairs to talk. Until this point, it had been impossible for me to cry in front of anyone, to be anything less than strong. I felt terrified of what she would think and say, but I couldn't hold it in any longer. I burst into tears.

"Navee, I'm not happy."

Navee stared into my eyes. "I know."

"I want to be with her. I want to be with Kasey."

I looked both ways in fear of punishment. This was the first time I was saying it out loud... to anyone!

"You've wanted to be with her a long time, haven't you?"

I nodded. *Does she think I'm crazy?* I wondered. However, the look of love and compassion on her face said it all. She understood.

"I can't be with Nathan anymore. I love him, and I don't want to hurt him."

After several more tears, silence washed over me. Then unexpectedly, my voice strengthened. "Navee, my soul belongs with Kasey. The way I feel about her is the strongest, most passionate feeling I have ever experienced."

Navee seemed to know exactly what I needed to hear. "You are coming together to teach and learn from one another. You two are so similar in the spiritual realm. In the physical realm, you are very different, and you balance each other perfectly. Be patient. You will be together in perfect timing. In the spiritual realm, you have already united as one."

I breathed a sigh of relief. Navee was right. Kasey and I were already connected spiritually. In order to become a couple in the physical world, there was still much work to do, like accepting my bisexuality, breaking up with Nathan, and coming out to my family and friends, none of which would be easy tasks. However, in this moment, I felt confident that I could handle them.

Navee's voice brought me back to the room. "Oh, I can just see your mom now, parading around saying 'I told you so.'"

I tilted my head and looked at her. "How did you know? My mom asked me a few weeks ago what was going on with Kasey and me."

"She notices things, you know, your mom. She's very perceptive… intuitive in her own way."

"Yeah, well, she laid into me about it. She told me it would be a mistake to leave Nathan. And she's worried I would face discrimination if I were with a woman. She said she thinks this is why I've been sick lately, because Kasey is in love with me and I'm not admitting to myself that I'm in love with her."

"Your mom loves you, Courtney. She just has very strong opinions, and she wants to protect you from harm."

"You mean protect me from Kasey." Sparks of fiery anger shot up through my arms. Sometimes I wondered if Mom loved me or just liked controlling me. "It's my happiness, not hers. My decision, not hers. I felt guilty enough when I broke up with my high school boyfriend James because my mom was so upset with me. I'm not going to feel that again."

"Is the little ladybug Courtney Long putting her foot down?" Navee chuckled.

I smiled half-heartedly. I was growing tired of always being the sweet, soft one. It was time for me to step into my power.

"Do not worry about your mom. She will never fully understand the deep connection you and Kasey share. Courtney, you must listen to the voice of your soul."

I breathed in Navee's statement. *That's exactly what I'm doing*, I thought. *Listening to my inner wisdom... my soul*!

Just then, Kasey came into the office. She looked between Navee and me. Without uttering a word, I could tell she was asking why I had tears streaming down my face and what was going on.

"Kasey, I told her."

"That you love me?"

"Yes, and that I want to be with you, Kasey."

The sweetest smile came over her and melted both of us.

"Ladies, let's say a prayer," Navee said.

The three of us stood in the center of Kasey's office, holding hands in a circle. All my stress and fear melted away at the touch of Kasey's hand. As Navee prayed words of eloquence, beauty, and inspiration, I sensed peaceful warmth filling our circle and pulsating through my arms and hands.

"Remember that you are light. And light is all there is. You come together to teach others how to *be* love. Your love inspires others to be themselves!"

Although I did not fully understand how that would happen, somehow my soul knew it to be true. I felt a deep gratitude for Navee. Not only had she understood, she had blessed our union. As we held hands, I sensed the individual lights in our hearts beaming out into the center of the circle, intermingling, and becoming one beautiful light. This light transformed my fears into hope. *Okay, Spirit. You've gotten me this far. Now get me through the next steps!*

Chapter 31

Mom, There's Something I Need to Tell You

"Change happens when the discomfort of the familiar outweighs the fear of the unknown." –Anne Parker[xxvii]

May 2007

Reluctantly, I pulled my car into my mother's driveway. After parking and unbuckling my seatbelt, I rehearsed my lines. A bead of sweat dripped from my forehead, and I noticed hot moisture on my usually cold hands. I had no way of knowing how Mom would react to my news, so, as usual, I braced myself for the worst.

Since the divorce, she'd been so emotionally volatile that I knew I had to confirm her suspicions before she leaked the news to Nathan. With a deep breath and shaky legs, I walked through the entryway to the living room and found Mom knitting in her brown leather recliner.

"Hi Mom. I need to talk to you, okay?"

She nodded. I hugged her apprehensively then sat down on the couch.

"I know what you're going to say, Courtney… that you're in love with Kasey."

The look on her face was blank and matter-of-fact. Who would have guessed that *she* would be the one to drop the bomb! The boldness and negativity of her tone insulted me.

"Mom! You say Kasey's name like it's a bad word."

"Well, Courtney, I'm not surprised, the way you two practically sit on *top* of each another. I was wondering when you would finally tell me."

Tears welled up in my eyes, though I blinked them back down. Suddenly, I felt guilty for not telling Mom sooner. Embarrassment turned my cheeks hot, like a teenager caught breaking the rules. But I pushed on. "Mom, I love her. Are you disappointed?"

"Because you're in love with a woman? No, not at all! Of course I accept you for that."

As I breathed a sigh of relief, the tension in my shoulders melted away. *She accepts me!* I felt like celebrating. However, I let my guard down too soon.

"I'm upset about Nathan. Courtney, I adore him. You may be breaking up with him, but that doesn't mean I have to."

"That's weird, Mom." I leaned back.

Defensive, angry energy ran through my veins. *Why does she always have to make it about her? Doesn't she care about my feelings? Is this her version of being supportive, or is she trying to shame me? I don't get it.*

"Courtney, I feel sorry for Nathan. You *deceived* him, just like your father deceived me after forty-three years together!"

Geez, thanks Mom, for laying it on thicker. I already feel bad enough. Despite the painful churning of guilt in my stomach, I defended myself. "Mom, it's not the same thing at all. Kasey and I haven't cheated." I lied about that fact, protecting myself from even harsher judgment.

To dodge her look of suspicion, I quickly changed the subject: "Anyway, I'm sorry about the divorce. I know you're really upset."

"Well, Courtney, aren't *you* upset about the divorce, too?" She raised her eyebrows.

My gut instantaneously tightened with fear. I felt intimidated, just like I had as a child. If I didn't say "yes," I sensed I would be in huge trouble. Yet the truth was, now that the news had settled in, I felt okay about the divorce. Sure, I was sad, but I was also excited for my parents. I sensed that a better life lie ahead for both of them, free of fighting and trying to control each another. However, to prevent Mom's pending rampage of hurt and anger, I left out the details and said what I needed to say. "Yeah, of course I'm upset, Mom. But I also trust that it will be better for you both in the long run."

Her eyebrows bent in fury as words of attack darted from her mouth: "Courtney, how could it be *better*?" she barked condescendingly. "My whole life was just *ripped* up from under me! You have *no* idea what it's like to lose the love of your life."

I sighed, clueless about what to say to that. It was clear that Mom did not want to hear my perspective. She just wanted me to agree with her, and just like usual, if I didn't, all hell broke loose. After a moment of sitting quietly while she huffed and puffed, breathing heavy with fury, I chose to change the subject. "Well, Mom, thank you for accepting my sexual orientation. It means so much to me."

Thankfully, her tone now softened: "I've always told you that I would love you no matter what. You are my daughter! I only want what makes you happy. Anyway, a person's sexuality is their business and only a small part of who they are."

After smiling at her, we sat quietly for a moment, breathing in all the change.

"Courtney, are you sure you and Kasey aren't just friends?" Mom asked after a while, apparently still clinging to one last hope.

"Yes, Mom, I'm sure. I feel attracted to her, and the feelings are mutual." I folded my hands in my lap.

"Well, I didn't think it would last with Nathan, anyway. Every time I get attached to someone you love, you end up breaking up with them. Maybe this explains why your relationships with guys have never lasted more than four years, since you're a lesbian."

Immediately, I jumped to my own defense, eager to correct her statement: "Mom, I'm bisexual. I like men, women, and all genders, actually. I've known since I was a teenager. I was just too scared to tell anyone."

She sat up tall with an air of superiority. "Well, I don't believe in bisexuality. I think people are either one or the other, gay or straight. I guess we know which one you are now."

Inside I was flaming with anger. I had no idea how to respectfully express that or to stand up for myself, so I got up and walked away to cool down in the bathroom.

Who is she to tell me what my sexual orientation is? I thought. *How* dare *she think that she knows more about it than me. Oh well, I don't have the energy to deal with her. I have enough worries on my mind.* I paced back and forth across the bathroom floor.

Soon enough, guilt settled in. Although Mom had just hurt my feelings, I felt bad for getting angry with her. *Don't forget, Courtney,* I added. *Overall, she is being supportive, to the best of her ability.* My chest deflated as I sighed. *At least she accepts me.*

After regaining my composure, I reentered the living room, sat down, and thanked Mom once again. Much to my surprise, she apologized for questioning if Kasey and I were just friends. She confessed that she didn't want me to face discrimination, now that I would be "out" in a judgmental world. I hugged her warmly. Despite the ups and downs of our relationship, at least she loved me.

◎

The next few days, as I prepared myself to break up with Nathan, I did not know who would be more heartbroken, him or me. He was the best boyfriend I had ever had. At the same time, I felt I did not deserve him. *Maybe that is part of the reason I need to let him go,* I reasoned. *So he can be with someone he deserves. Not someone who has cheated on him. Not someone who let herself fall in love with a woman when she was supposed to be committed to him.* My heart and emotions were a mess of turmoil, guilt, and anger. Yet, I also felt excitement. The sooner I broke up with him, the sooner Kasey and I could begin our official life together.

The following Wednesday, as soon as Nathan got home from work, I told him we needed to talk. He seemed to sense my seriousness. We sat down, and I told him that I needed to leave our relationship because my feelings had changed and we were not on the same spiritual path. I explained that something deep within me was telling me I needed to go. I dared not tell him the full truth, because I did not want to hurt his feelings even more. I also could not risk admitting to him that I was not "perfect" and that I had been hurting him behind his back for months.

At first, Nathan took it quite well... or at least pretended to. To me, it seemed as though he had been expecting this. There were tears.

There was graciousness. I could tell that Nathan did not understand, and as I heard the words escaping my mouth, I wasn't fully sure that I did, either.

He allowed me to stay with him a few more days as I packed and started moving my belongings to my mom's house. He also offered to take me out to one last fancy dinner together, which I happily agreed to. He said a toast of gratitude for all the time we had together. It was beautiful and momentous. I could not believe how giving and loving this man was.

The day I was to leave, he asked if I was sure I needed to go. With tears in my eyes, I replied, "Yes." As we said our final goodbye, feeling my lips upon his one last time broke my heart into even smaller pieces. I was scared to depart from someone with whom I had found safety, comfort and countless moments of joy. I hoped I was not making a huge mistake, as my mom had implied.

Once settled into my mom's, Kasey seemed ready to celebrate our newfound freedom together. I was too, but first I had some major grieving to do. A great deal of healing and self-forgiveness awaited me. At some moments, fear overtook me. My soul knew I belonged with Kasey, but my mind still questioned my choice. I had left everything I had ever known and entered into totally new territory. *Will I like this new territory? Will I be accepted there? Can I truly learn to accept myself?*

> "I have left my relationship, after 3 ½ years, the best boyfriend I have ever had in my entire life. I have left him because I have found my soul mate. The person with whom I connect on the deepest, most beautiful, even spiritual level I have ever felt. She helps to raise the vibrational energy of my entire being. She is beautiful."
> —Journal, age 27, Tuesday, 5/22/07, 3:34 p.m.

A few months after our breakup, Nathan asked if he could take me to dinner again. Here, I made a very courageous decision to tell him more of the truth—that I had feelings for Kasey and was planning to date her. He did not take it very well, highlighting her character flaws and cautioning me against being with her. I know he was heartbroken, and so was I.

As I moved through the next few months of work, life coaching school, and adjusting to my new relationship with Kasey, I was grateful, empowered, excited, and in other moments, unsure of myself. Thankfully, whenever I told my SWIHA classmates I was bisexual, no one batted an eyelash. Some even chimed in, "Me, too!"

My weary heart was relieved. The secret I had kept buried for years was now being received with warmth, compassion, and in some moments, even celebration! Realizing how many other bisexual people are out there helped me feel a bit more confident.

However, I still struggled with guilt over hurting Nathan and doubts about being in an intimate relationship with a woman. My body dealt with these doubts through sore throats, headaches, and insomnia—waking in the middle of the night with an anxiously racing heart. Clearly, I was in love with Kasey and meant to be with her. However, I still struggled to let Nathan go. Plus, after being with men my whole life, I still wondered if I would be happy being with a woman long term. When I found myself in the midst of fearful, racing thoughts, I tried to console myself.

> "I'm scared. Yet, I need to let go and trust. I know God is taking care of me. I know God has led me to Kasey for a reason. For sooooo many reasons....I love all these lessons I am learning. It is time to go with LOVE instead of fear. To be fearless and loveful. Plus, instead of worrying, I'd rather enjoy the gift the Universe has given me... Kasey.
>
> Every time I kiss her, I go to an indescribably beautiful world. I have never seen someone so filled with love and beauty. Her physical body is beautiful, her skin so soft. Her eyelashes so pretty. Her eyes so intense. And her soul is so beautiful. Incredible. Thank you, God!"
>
> —Journal, age 27, Tuesday, 8/2/07, 4:48 p.m.

PART III:

Love Cocoon

Chapter 32

One Step at a Time

"Embracing yourself as you are is the first step and the last step. You must be who you are... The Universe has made you like that."
—Sri Bhagavan

January 23, 2012

The raindrops continued their playful dance, making pitter-patter sounds on the coffee shop windows. Coupled with the crashing, cymbal-like sound of thunder, nature was creating quite an orchestra. Just on the horizon, bright bolts of lightning electrified the clouds, illuminating the sky for all to see, as if the clouds could no longer hide in the dark shadows of the sky.

"Courtney, I'm so happy for you," Sarah said. "You were honest about your sexual orientation. You had the courage to break up with Nathan. You trusted your gut—for what sounds like the first time in your life. That's amazing!"

Courtney beamed with pride. "Thanks, Sarah! Yeah, it took courage. It was the most exhausting time of my life, but also the most worthwhile. But, I wasn't fully authentic yet."

Sarah frowned. "Huh? What do you mean? I just assumed this is where your journey ended. After all, it sounds like you became authentic and free when you came out."

Courtney couldn't help but chuckle fondly. "Yeah, I can see why you'd think that, but it wasn't as easy as that. I still had a ton of inner work to do. Do you remember the story about the caterpillar my teacher taught me?"

Sarah pursed her lips in thought. "The part about shedding layers?" she finally asked.

"Yes! I had shed the skin I put around my sexual orientation, but didn't have my butterfly wings quite yet. I had a few more to go—like my people-pleasing skin."

Sarah nodded enthusiastically. "Oh, believe me, I get that. I worry way too much about hurting others' feelings too."

Courtney paused as she thought her next reply over carefully. "Sarah, it's good to be caring, but not if it means neglecting ourselves or hiding our truth to make someone else happy. That's not fair to anyone. Know what I mean?"

Sarah nodded as she sipped her coffee. "Yeah. I totally sacrifice my own needs if it means making someone else happy. It makes me feel good to help other people, you know?"

Courtney nodded.

"But when I overdo it, I get resentful... well, and sometimes depressed. It's so hard to find that balance. How did you do that?" Sarah gave Courtney a pleading look.

Courtney paused as she pondered the question. "Well, I'm still working on it, but I realized that I deserve to be happy too! And if I hide my needs from others, then I'm not being completely honest."

"But what if you speak your truth and someone's feelings end up hurt?"

"Oooh, that's such a good question. Well, I don't like hurting other people's feelings, but now I realize that they can handle it."

"Huh?"

"Okay, here's the affirmation that helped me: 'I am 100 percent responsible for my own needs and happiness. Others are 100 percent responsible for their own needs and happiness.' People are capable of handling their feelings. Hurt feelings suck, yes, but we get through them. Know what I mean?"

"Sort of."

"Well, the more I was willing to feel my own pain and deal with my own stuff, the more willing I was to let other people handle their own pain. I don't need to 'rescue' them from it. What if jumping in and saving the day would block them from their own growth or lessons? If I try to stop their pain, they might just have to repeat the lesson again in another situation. Or what if going through a tough situation means that something good is waiting for them just around the corner?"

"Okay, I'm a little confused. You're saying that sometimes it's good for people to have hurt feelings?"

"Yes! If they're willing to learn and grow from them." Courtney tapped her finger against the table thoughtfully as she formed her next words. "You know that old saying 'When one door closes, another one opens'? That's what happened with Nathan. Even though I felt so guilty for breaking up with him, a few years later, he moved somewhere that I would never have moved and found a new job that he loves. That wouldn't have happened if I hadn't broken up with him. See what I mean?"

"Did that help you with the guilt?"

"Yes, but I still wish I had been totally honest with him earlier on. I know I didn't want to hurt his feelings, but I think withholding the truth from him hurt him worse, you know? I kept kicking myself for that."

"Yeah, I guess sometimes the truth hurts. But sometimes, withholding it becomes a lie, and lies hurt even worse. Who knows, Courtney, maybe he and Kasey would have been okay with an open relationship. At least it would have been good to let them choose."

"I agree, Sarah. In the future, I just want to be totally honest with people about my feelings. No more hiding."

Courtney stared out the window, her expression suddenly disheartened. "I have to remember that I did the best I could at the time, with the tools, resources, and knowledge I had. I needed to forgive myself for so many things… like being imperfect, hurting myself, my dishonesty with Nathan, my lack of authenticity, everything."

"There's no point in regretting things. What's important is that we learn from our mistakes and do it differently the next time, right?" Sarah asked.

Courtney's expression brightened as she glanced back at her friend. "That's right. But there's even more to it. To be truly authentic, you have to face people who may not realize that you have needs too, because you've been dedicated to pleasing them. They can be totally surprised when you actually start speaking up for yourself. For me, the hardest person I needed to face was the one I feared the most—my mom."

"Yeah, what happened with your mom?"

"Well, the more I expressed my authentic self over the next few years, the more we argued. At some point, we stopped talking for a whole year. It was so hard, but I needed to spend that time with me. I needed to go into my cocoon and figure out who I was and how to express myself without having to worry what other people thought."

"Oh, I see. You mean your *love cocoon* with Kasey?" Sarah winked and chuckled.

Courtney blushed and grinned as she stirred her tea. "Yeah, I guess so!"

"It sounds like you two were so in love!"

"Yes! I had never felt anything like it. Her love was a safe haven—yeah, I guess you could say it was like a cocoon of love—unconditional love. It helped me feel safe enough to admit I needed help."

"That had to be really hard for you. You were denying you needed help because you were always tried to be so strong, right? Or at least, you wanted everyone to think you were strong?"

Courtney nodded. "Right. And then I had to start letting people in, which was terrifying!"

"Yeah, I can imagine," Sarah nodded warmly.

"I'd had the eating disorder for as long as I could remember, and I had no idea how to recover. I just knew I needed to start somewhere."

"So what did you do?"

Courtney took a deep breath. "First, I reenrolled myself in therapy. I called my previous therapist Amy in Michigan, and thankfully, she agreed to do phone sessions with me."

"You really must have liked her, huh?"

"Yes! She was so in tune with my feelings. It felt awesome to have her support. Even though I hadn't spoken with her in years, it only took one session to get her caught up on my relationship with Kasey, my parents' divorce, the eating disorder, everything. Amy was so insightful and never judged me."

"Did that surprise you?" Sarah tilted her head to the side.

"Yeah, I guess it did. I just assumed everyone would judge me just as harshly as I judged myself, but I had been way off base. Thankfully, therapy melted my defenses and taught me self-compassion." When Sarah grinned, Courtney shrugged her shoulders modestly. "Hey, miracles do happen!"

"Anyway, Amy also referred me to a Registered Dietician that specialized in eating disorders. I also saw a naturopath for acupuncture and energy work. I really opened up and shared a lot with them. They were so nurturing and compassionate. They didn't judge me, either. It was awesome!"

"So is that how you stopped judging yourself?"

"Well, it helped, but my pattern of self-doubt ran so deep that no one thing could really fix it."

"So what did you do?"

Courtney smiled at Sarah's sweet tone. "I finished the life coaching program, worked, and focused on therapy. But I realized all my healing was on the conscious level."

Courtney frowned slightly and took a sip of her tea.

Sarah leaned in, looking confused. "But what's wrong with that? The life coaching and therapy helped, right?"

"Oh my god, Sarah, they saved my life—especially Amy. It's just that after a while, I was ready for another layer of healing. I heard all these positive messages from Amy, and I read tons of positive affirmations. I told myself things like 'I'm beautiful. I'm good enough.' Those sounded nice, but at the subconscious level, I didn't believe them."

"At the subconscious level? So you mean that you didn't believe the affirmations deep down."

"Right. The subconscious is basically like an autopilot that's been programmed with instructions we didn't consciously make up. It's where all our buried emotions, old patterns, and memories are stored—and all of those things influence how we behave, even if we're not aware that they do. It's also a pretty big part of our mind— about 90 percent of it. It can really sabotage our progress if we don't work with it. At some point in therapy, for instance, I wanted to exercise less, but I couldn't... well, unless I wanted to be having panic attacks and freaking out all over the place."

"Did you ever cut back on exercise?"

Courtney winked. "You'll see, Sarah. I don't want to ruin the surprise."

"Okay." Sarah chuckled as she reached for her coffee.

"Anyway, I decided to study hypnotherapy."

"You mean like where someone waves a stopwatch in front of people's eyes to hypnotize them?"

"No, silly," Courtney said affectionately. Then her tone became more serious. "But a lot of people do think they're the same thing. Hypnotherapy isn't used on stage. It's more like a guided meditation for therapeutic reasons. You go through it to release old energy and beliefs to make space for new, empowering energy and beliefs about yourself. It was exactly what I needed to unravel my dysfunctional patterns."

"It sounds effective... but weird," Sarah said doubtfully. "I mean, I know it's different, but I still can't stop seeing a stage show when I think about it. Once, when I was in college, I remember seeing a hypnotist get a student to act like a chicken." She put her hands under her armpits, clucked a few times, and grinned.

Courtney laughed. "Well, no, it's not quite like that. It's more like a massage for your soul. People who do it have amazing results."

"So when you went to the hypnotherapist what—" Suddenly Sarah snapped her fingers. "Wait! No, let's come back to that. You left me hanging awhile back! What happened when you came out to the rest of your family and friends? What was it like being in a relationship with a woman?"

"Oh sorry, Sarah, I was getting ahead of myself." Courtney took another sip of her tea and settled in to explain.

Chapter 33

The Gift of Love

"God knows, I tried desperately to be straight, no can do. God knew what he/she was doing when he/she made his/her gay children. I don't need a Bible to know that I am one heck of a fine human being. Meet me through blinded eyes so you may know the beautiful person within." —Shirley A. Walker

Summer 2007

The next step in being true to myself was telling the rest of my family and friends what I suspected would be shocking news for them about my sexual orientation. I felt that they loved me for who I was on the outside, for my sweetness and caring nature. However, I couldn't help but wonder now if they'd love the real me, bisexuality and all. Would they be afraid of me now? Would their religious ideas create a barrier between us? Basically, despite knowing many of them for years, I had no idea how they would react.

As I prepared to call them one at a time, it felt as though every muscle in my body was tensing. I held my breath as I dialed. *I hope they accept me. If not, though, will I know how to breathe on my own?*

I started with my sisters, Kelly then Tracy. After explaining what I'd just gone through with Nathan and Kasey and telling them that I'd discovered my bisexuality at a young age, I finally ran out of air and had to take a breath. As I nervously anticipated each of their reactions, two seconds felt like two years.

Much to my delight, instead of bashing me, my sisters celebrated me. Instead of giving in to fear, they embraced me with love. They said they would miss Nathan, but they fully supported me and wanted me to be happy. *What a relief!*

Thankfully, my experience with several other family members and friends was similar, as I joyfully shared with my journal:

> "I am so thankful for such beautiful, special people in my life. My friends whom I've told about my feelings for Kasey, and about my bisexuality, have been OK. They have understood. They have been so accepting, so supportive, so loving. I am so lucky to have such special people in my life. I hoped they would accept my bisexuality, but I had no idea they'd be so gracious and loving about it."
> —Journal, age 27, Tuesday, 8/2/07, 4:48 p.m.

Mom had also not been kidding when she said she accepted my new relationship. She graciously offered for Kasey to move in with us as Kasey searched for a new home. Having my new partner so close by comforted my soul. In her arms, I felt safer than ever. Whether embraced in a long hug or intertwined as we held each another at night, I felt like I had just come home.

Mom and she became very close. They adored each another and found plenty of topics to laugh about. I was amused by their similarities, such as the ability to "say it like it is."

Fortunately, Mom helped me with some of my coming out process by telling my family in Michigan how wonderful Kasey was. By the time Kasey accompanied me home to Michigan to meet my family in late August, they embraced her with wide, open arms. When they all finally met, they all interacted with such warmth and kindness that they might well have known one another already. I was so relieved and so grateful for my family.

After we returned to sweltering Phoenix, Kasey and I enjoyed many evening walks after work. These gave us a chance to catch up and spend time alone together, while allowing Mom some space too.

One evening as we walked our usual path around Mom's neighborhood, surrounded by bright pink bougainvilleas, scurrying lizards and tall palm trees swaying in the mild evening breeze, I was overcome with relief and a deep sense of peace. I looked out at the horizon, admiring the oranges and yellow tones of the sunset.

Everything we had dreamed of and hoped for was coming true. Kasey and I were an official couple, and now the people we loved the most knew. As a sense of hope returned to me, I had begun eating a little more, and my strength seemed to be rebuilding.

"Courtney, we've been really lucky, you know. Your family was wonderful to me," Kasey said.

"Yeah, Kasey, yours too. When I talk to them on the phone, they make me feel like part of the family. I can't wait to meet them in person."

"If you think about it, Court, we're in the minority. I know some gay people who have been totally rejected by their families."

"Yeah like those LGBTQ youth who are kicked out by their parents." I frowned.

"Makes me sick to my stomach."

Despite the beautiful evening around me, I felt my chest swelling with sad, angry heat. Looking down, I noticed a large stick in the middle of the sidewalk. With a forceful kick, I sent it flying to join a group of nearby stones.

"It also makes me sick how those same youth get bullied at school, and no one steps in to stop it. It's disgusting."

Kasey shook her head. "Are people that afraid of someone who is different from them?"

I stopped walking and looked my partner right in the eye. "Kasey, I want to do something about this. To help our youth. I'm just not sure how."

I had a feeling I wanted to do something significant. I wondered if everything I had recently gone through was not only for my own growth, but so that I could help other people grow too.

"Courtney, I can't even imagine what they go through. It was hard enough for me to accept myself without being bullied."

"You weren't out in high school, right?"

"Nope. Half the girls on my soccer team were probably lesbians, but no one said anything."

I adored hearing Kasey's stories, almost as much as I adored her. "What age did you first know?"

"Well, I was always a tomboy and really into sports. When I was younger, my mom tried to put me in dresses, but I refused. I suspected it in junior high, but I didn't know for sure until high school. All the other girls were into guys, but I was obsessed with my best friend Clara."

"Did she like you too?"

"Yeah. I guess you'd call it a secret love affair. I'd go to her house for sleepovers, but we didn't do much sleeping!" Kasey laughed.

It was hard to imagine Kasey as a teenager, unsure of her sexual orientation. Now, she seemed so strong and sure of herself. "Were you together a long time?"

"Maybe a year. I was totally in love with her, but she broke my heart. She got scared and went back to her boyfriend."

We continued walking, now passing little kids joyfully playing in the park. Kasey continued, her voice fading into sadness. "In college, I was the maid of honor in her wedding. It made me sick to see her marrying a man."

"I'm so sorry." I put my hand on her arm and squeezed. "Was she in your wedding?"

"No, we'd drifted apart by then. Can you believe I wore a wedding dress?"

I giggled and vigorously shook my head. Kasey had a nurturing feminine side, but she expressed it through caring for others, not through clothes.

"Kasey, when you married your ex-husband did you already know you were gay?"

"Yes."

Concerned, I frowned. "Then why did you get married?"

"All my friends were getting married and planning to have kids. I thought it was the right thing to do."

"Wow, it's amazing the lengths we'll go to do what we're 'supposed to' do. What about what feels authentic and right to us?"

"That's why my marriage did not last long. I could not keep up the lie."

"How did your family react?"

"They had a triple whammy… I told them I was getting divorced, which in a Catholic family was already taboo. Then I told them I was a lesbian, and *then* that I was moving to Arizona with my partner."

My eyes widened. "Oh my gosh, did they freak out?"

"Actually, no. They were super supportive. Even my dad, who had paid for the whole wedding. He said he loved me no matter what."

"That's awesome!"

"A few of my friends freaked out, though. One of them told me I was going to hell for being a lesbian. The funny thing was, a few years later, she came out too."

My eyes widened with surprise. "What? Wow!"

"Yeah, I was so mad at her." Kasey's brow furrowed with anger.

"You know, I think that just proves my theory. When people are super judgmental, sometimes it's because they're hiding something about themselves. Like they're projecting their own self-judgment onto someone else so they can avoid looking within. Otherwise, why would they spend so much energy pointing their finger at someone else?"

"That's a good point. Speaking of friends, Courtney, you said that you told a few old high school friends about us recently, right? How did it go?"

I sighed. "Yeah, I e-mailed them weeks ago, but I haven't heard back. It sucks."

"You know what, Court, if someone doesn't accept you for who you are, they're not a good friend."

I could not simply dismiss people the way Kasey said I should. I understood her point, but sadness filled my heart when I thought about it. "Kasey, it just bothers me that so many people hold onto that old belief that being gay is a sin. What happened to critical thinking?"

"You're not supposed to question the Bible, remember?" Kasey's tone screamed sarcasm.

"Well, someone questioned it. If we follow it just as it's written, women would not be allowed to wear pants."

Kasey frowned. "What? That's crazy!"

"Yes, and supposedly people go to hell for breaking promises, lying, gossiping, eating pork or shrimp, and a bunch of other things."[xxviii]

I felt the fire burning in my belly. No one had the authority to tell me I was going to hell for doing what I came to Earth to do—love.

"That's messed up, Court. I think the Bible's been misinterpreted."

"Amen!"

We both laughed.

"Kasey, supposedly there were a bunch of books of the Bible that weren't even included."

"Really? I wonder what those would have said about homosexuality."

"People are just too busy blindly following external 'rules.' I got myself into a lot of trouble doing that, with all those dieting and exercise rules. I had no idea how to check in with body first."

"This world would be so different if people tuned into their own hearts," Kasey said. "Our hearts don't judge right from wrong. They just love others as we love ourselves."

"Yeah, but Kasey, the trouble is that people don't know how to love *themselves*."

I nodded sadly. We turned the corner, our pace slowing down now.

"The Bible is supposed to teach us how to love, not how to judge and hate," I said.

"Exactly. Why would God have made us this way if we weren't supposed to be this way?"

"We both know that. But for someone who doesn't, questioning their religious beliefs might be the scariest thing they ever have to do. It might lead to questioning every aspect of their lives." I couldn't help but smirk. "Believe me, I know how scary *that* is."

"Yes, and worthwhile."

"Even if it's hard, it's the only way to live authentically," I agreed.

We were approaching the house now, and the Arizona evening was coming out in full form. The sky was purpling like the prairie clover that bloomed everywhere in the Sonoran Desert.

"Kasey, the love that we have between us is the most beautiful thing I've experienced!" I said. The night was too beautiful and our conversation too deep for me to say anything else.

Kasey's brown eyes smiled at me. She leaned over and kissed my cheek, then spoke in a soft, feather-like whisper. "Me too, Court. There's nothing more beautiful than love."

She leaned kissed me gently on the lips. My heart began tingling, and the feeling soon radiated through the rest of my body. In her presence, I felt relaxed and at peace, as if I truly was "home."

◎

Autumn 2007

I wondered how Leah would react to the news that I had fallen in love with a woman. I wondered if it would bring up old emotions and hurt for her, since I had cut off our relationship many years prior. Leah had clearly embraced her bisexuality long ago, continuing to date both men and women. Now here I was, finally embracing mine.

Leah and I rarely spoke or saw each another, and then only at occasional family gatherings. Even so, I knew it would only be a matter of time until someone in my family mentioned my news to her. I wasn't surprised when my cell phone rang one autumn afternoon and her name scrolled across the caller ID.

At first, I hesitated to answer, wondering what she would say. Was she still mad at me? Would she be jealous of Kasey? *Oh well, here goes,* I thought as I took a deep breath.

"Hello?"

Much to my relief, Leah was in a super good mood and practically ecstatic to talk to me. Somehow, the sound of her voice felt both familiar and unfamiliar, comforting and disconcerting. It reminded me how much had changed since our teenage years. After we spent a few minutes catching up, the conversation I'd worried about began.

"I heard the good news from my mom. Wow, Court, I'm so happy for you!"

"Thanks! I wasn't expecting to fall in love with a woman, but I'm so happy."

I felt nervous and unsure what to talk about next. Thankfully, Leah had plenty of energy to carry the conversation.

"What is Kasey like? Butch or femme?"

Whoa, is this what LGBTQ folks always ask each other when someone comes out? Way too stereotypical for my taste.

"Um… neither. She's not overly feminine or masculine… just kind of, well, herself. You know, masculine *and* feminine. She's so nice."

"Cool. Well, I can't wait to meet her. Did you tell Gran yet?"

"Yes, I did."

"I admire you. I see her all the time, and I've still never worked up the courage to tell her I have a girlfriend. How did she react?"

"She was okay with it! Both of my grandmas were. It was so amazing, Leah. I was especially nervous when I told Granny Long. She's in her mid-80s and traditional Catholic. She goes to church every week. I had no idea how she'd react."

"Yeah… so what did she say?"

"She said she loves me and that no matter what I tell her, she will always love me. Is that amazing or what? Everybody's been really awesome… my sisters, dad, everyone. They said they can't wait to meet Kasey." Just remembering it made me beam with gratitude.

"Did you tell everyone all at once?"

"No, I've been taking my time… especially with people I don't see all that often. I can't believe how much energy it takes to come out!"

"Yeah, it's really draining. Isn't that weird? Look Court, I gotta go. It's really good to talk to you. I really miss you."

"I miss you too, Leah! I love you. I always will."

"I love you too! I'll let you know how it goes when I tell Gran. Call me again soon, okay?"

"Okay, good luck!"

I had mixed emotions as we hung up. Talking to Leah had felt familiar and unfamiliar, comfortable and awkward, all at the same time. Once, she was my best friend in the world. Today she had felt more like a stranger. Although the conversation had gone well, I had an odd feeling we would not talk again anytime soon.

Chapter 34

You're Going to Eat *That*?

"Fall down seven times, get up eight. That's recovery! People in recovery are tenacious. Be thankful you get up!" —Amy Pershing[xxix]

Summer 2008

Peeling back the layers of an artichoke is best accomplished one petal at a time. It requires patience, perseverance, and trust that the prize, the artichoke heart at the bottom, is worth waiting for. In addition, the petals can be quite tasty too. However, if one is not careful, the sharp ends of the petals can easily pierce one's skin.

I should know. I was regularly peeling them.

Among many other healthy eating lessons, Kasey taught me how to cook and eat a whole artichoke. What a perfect metaphor for my recovery! Peeling one reminded me to enjoy the process while allowing for the challenges and stings. Yet, I could so easily see myself a few years down the road, at a healthy weight, experiencing freedom, rather than obsession, around food. Yet, sometimes I forgot to enjoy the process. Not being at this point just yet was really frustrating and demoralizing.

In the springtime, Kasey bought a house on the west side of town. By now, I had become antsy to move out of Mom's. She needed her own space to grieve, and so did I. Despite the excitement of my new relationship with Kasey, I was still grieving over Nathan. Every so often, Kasey told me that she worried I would want to return to Nathan or be with another man. Therefore, I just needed some space so I could grieve in peace. I moved into my own apartment for a few months and did a great deal of journaling, walking and reflecting.

However, soon enough, living apart from Kasey became far too difficult. By summer, I had moved into her house, which now became our home. We filled it with love and hung our little Chinese girl ornament on our new bathroom door handle. The girls still smiled, as did we. Indeed, we were now living the life we'd dreamed!

Our mornings together seemed especially magical. After months of hiding our love for each another, waking up next to Kasey and kissing and her felt out of this world. We had to stock up on kisses then, because we still needed to hide our relationship at work. I may have wanted to proclaim our love for each other from the top of our work building, but I also wanted to keep my job there.

One of our first mornings living together revealed an interesting, unexpected twist in our relationship.

"Kasey, want me to make your lunch?"

"Sure, that'd be awesome. Really?"

"Yeah, really!" I winked and smiled at her.

She grinned back. "Wow, Court, I'm not used to someone taking care of me."

"Well get used to it!"

Kasey poured a bowl of cereal. As she gathered her things into her workbag, I tried not to pass judgment on her breakfast and failed. *Wow, she is eating three times the amount of cereal I usually eat!*

"What do you want on your sandwich, Kasey?"

"Turkey, cheese, and mayo."

Grabbing two pieces of bread for a sandwich made me feel like I was on another planet. My own sandwich would include only one piece of gluten-free rice bread, with plenty of lettuce and tomato and veggies on the side, of course.

Opening a canister of mayonnaise also felt foreign. Because of the high fat content, I had not eaten it since my early teenage years. I spread the white grossness onto Kasey's bread, nauseated by the sight of the fat-laden creaminess. It actually looked like globules of saturated fat, the kind that sticks to the thighs, bubbling up into every woman's worst nightmare—cellulite. I was not liking Planet Fatso, and I hoped to navigate this foreign land without vomiting all over Kasey's sandwich.

"Is that enough?"

Despite my disgust, I wanted this sandwich to be just right.

Kasey looked at the bread, then at me, and laughed. "No Court, try about three or four times that amount."

"Oh really?" *Is she crazy? Won't she get fat? She eats that much on every sandwich?*

"Yeah, Court. And can you put it on both pieces of bread?"

What?! Tingles of fear and shock rushed through my body. This was totally breaking the diet rules I had followed for so many years.

Apparently, Kasey saw the look of horror on my face. "It's gonna be okay, Court," she said soothingly. "Remember, this sandwich is for me. You don't have to eat it."

As I'd been learning to do in therapy, I breathed and reminded myself that I was safe. "Well, it's good for me to see how a 'normal' person eats," I said at last. But as usual, my cheerfulness covered up what I was really thinking. The mayonnaise represented something bigger. Kasey was strong, I thought. She did not fear taking up space in the world. Nor did she fear being her true self. If she wanted mayonnaise, she was going to eat mayonnaise. *But still, how does she eat these calories without gaining endless pounds?*

"Kasey, do you ever struggle with your weight?"

"No. Sometimes it goes up and down just a little. But I just listen to my appetite and eat what I want."

"You're a healthy eater, though. That must be why your weight stays under control."

"Well, I don't think my weight is something I have to 'control.' I usually eat healthy, but if I want a burger and fries, I eat it."

I frowned, recalling the delicious pecan pie she had recently baked. Kasey loved desserts. For years, I had thought that everyone needed to cut out all desserts and high-fat foods like french fries and mayonnaise to maintain their weight. According to my dieting rules, anyway. *But maybe they were wrong?*

Who knew that such deep life lessons arrived this early in the morning!

"Kasey, by the way, I loved the pecan pie you made. It felt incredible to eat a whole piece!"

She laughed, but not meanly. "Your piece was tiny, Court. But still, I'm proud of you for eating it. I know how hard that must have been for you."

I was so grateful that Kasey had been so supportive of my therapy and recovery from the eating disorder. I just wished that the steps, no matter how tiny they were, weren't so painful sometimes. Indeed, I was recovering. *But can't I fast-forward to recover<u>ed</u>?* I thought constantly.

Still, her kindness lightened my mood. "Thank you, Kasey!" I chuckled myself. "Hey, apparently, you use plenty of mayo *and* salad dressing. Guess that last part is rubbing off on me, at least."

Already, Kasey's influence meant I was now adding salad dressing to my salads. I often teased her by saying her salads looked more like salad dressing soup with a touch of lettuce. Over time, both our salads were finding balance.

"Kasey, so your body just maintains your weight? Have you always worked out a lot?" I continued.

"Not nearly as much as you."

"No, seriously, Kasey."

"Oh, I don't know, a couple times a week."

"How do you trust your body like that?"

"I don't know. I just do."

I nodded as I considered this. I wanted to understand. I ached to trust my own body and feel relaxed and free around food too.

"Look, Court, I gotta go to work. Thanks for the sandwich. I'll see you soon, okay?"

After a soft, romantic kiss, she left for work. I headed to the bathroom to finish getting ready, my mind drifting into deep contemplation. Tears streamed down my cheeks. As I stared into the mirror, I realized with sadness, alarm, and confusion how much work lay ahead of me.

Why have I always felt that my body has betrayed me? Why are the rules different for me? How come Kasey's body can be trusted, but mine can't? Why do I have to work so hard to prevent weight gain? Is it possible that I could let go too? That I could learn to trust my body?

I then looked at even more discrepancies in the rules I held myself to. *Why do I have compassion for everyone else but not for myself? I'm capable of loving. So why can't I learn to love myself? Why don't I care when others make mistakes, but when I do, I beat myself up? If I'm five minutes late to a meeting, I feel terrible. If someone else is ten minutes late, I let it slide. Why am I the only one that has to be perfect?*

In this moment, I felt determined to change these old patterns. I had been learning in life coaching that I had the power to choose new beliefs. It was time, I realized, that I chose beliefs that would uplift my life rather than hold me back.

Suddenly I remembered Navee's comment: "Then you have not yet learned your own power…. be who you came here to be." *Hmm… I think I'm onto something!*

On my way to work, I thought back to the mayo incident. *I used to like mayo. Maybe I will try a little.* I made a mental note to talk to my registered dietician about this, and felt glad and excited that I had made the choice. *This is so empowering, I am learning to be healthy. I am learning to let go, learning to trust… learning to be ME!*

However, my balloons of excitement quickly deflated. The more empowered I was becoming, the harder the eating disorder fought back, and the louder and meaner my self-doubts became. I sighed with worry. *How will I ever get through this? I guess one dollop of mayo at a time.*

Chapter 35

The Ultimate Judge

"Be kind to yourself. Begin to love and approve of yourself."
–Louise L. Hay[xxx]

Autumn 2008

Later that year, I landed some contract work as a wellness coach. After completing the life coaching program, I ached to put my new skills to work. I felt thrilled at the prospect of coaching people to be happy and healthy through self-care. Despite my excitement, however, saying goodbye to my social work clients and coworkers was bittersweet. As for my boss, well, I'd see her every morning and night at home.

This new job seemed to arrive at a perfect time I was learning so many personal lessons on self-care that I thought for sure I could impart some of my newfound wisdom to my clients. During the interview, I had learned that I would be coaching on four aspects of self-care: stress relief techniques and healthy sleep, exercise, and nutrition.

I can do this, I thought. I often shared stress management techniques with my clients and their family caregivers (although I didn't always follow my own advice!). Also, my background as a group fitness instructor would help. And how cool that I could share the new lessons I was learning about exercising for fun and health, not just for weight loss.

My new boss mentioned that some clients would want help managing their weight too. *Argh*, I thought. *Can I handle that?* I'd given weight loss advice to many people before, but then I was in the throes of an eating disorder, not in the midst of recovery. But optimism won out over my hesitation, and I gratefully took the job.

A few months later, Kasey and I relaxed on our back patio couch together one evening after work. We stared out at the beautiful sunset, admiring the purple-and-red paint strokes in the sky.

"How was work today?" I asked her.

"Crazy and stressful as ever. You miss it, don't you?"

Her sarcasm made me laugh. "Actually I do miss working with you, now that you ask."

"How was your new job today?"

"Good, but I thought my title was 'wellness coach,' not 'weight loss coach.'"

"What do you mean?"

"Well, I guess I should have asked more questions before I started this job. I didn't realize how much it would affect me, you know, emotionally. I thought I would get to coach people on all kinds of wellness topics, like stress relief, positive affirmations, deep breathing, all my favorite things. But instead, it seems like ninety-five percent of my clients are obsessed with losing weight. They'll do whatever it takes to lose it."

Kasey nodded, inviting me to continue.

"One of my clients is on this really strict diet, and today he confessed that he totally blew that diet last night. He ate pasta and bread."

"So what?"

"I felt like a priest at the confessional," I said. "He felt terrible about himself, just like I used to. I tried to explain that healthy eating is about balance, not restriction or extremes. He didn't seem to buy it." My shoulders slumped with disappointment. "Sometimes it feels like I'm coaching hundreds and hundreds of me's… the way I used to be. It's like this weight loss fog covers their eyes, and they can't see or think about anything else."

Kasey looked concerned. "Maybe they think their bodies define who they are. But the body is just an earth suit or vessel for our soul. Anyway, how are the weigh-ins going?"

I scoffed, tossing a pillow up into the air and catching it. "Terrible. These weight loss contests are crazy! I have like thirty people at a time lined up to weigh in. A number on a scale does not measure health. I'm spending more energy consoling people about their weight than actually logging in numbers. The shame they feel if they gain one pound is so sad. It's breaking my heart!"

"Ha, maybe instead of numbers, the scale should have two options: 'good enough' or 'not good enough,'" Kasey said wryly.

"Yeah, you got it. Kasey, I explain the natural fluctuations in weight. I tell them they might be more hydrated than they were when they weighed in last time, but they still insist on beating themselves up over it."

Kasey sighed. "Courtney, you can't just wave a magic wand and take away their body shame. I understand, though. It's sad how unhappy most people are with their bodies."

"Yeah, it's like a virus."

"A virus of unhappiness and self-doubt."

We laughed, but the sound was hollow. More like a sigh.

"Want to go in and watch TV, Court?"

I nodded. The evening breeze felt quite cool on my skin, and the inside warmth sounded inviting. After entering the house, we cuddled under a blanket on the couch. Flipping through the channels, we landed on our favorite talent competition show.

"Yikes, Court, look how thin those dancers are." Kasey pointed at the TV with the remote control, her face contorted with concern. The female dancers reminded me of the images in magazines that I had strived to look like for years. Sadness washed over me too.

"Wow, Kasey, they are super thin. They actually look unhealthy."

"No wonder people hate their bodies when this is what we see, you know?"

"That's why I stopped reading most magazines," I said, gesturing at the screen.

"I know they do a lot of airbrushing and photo editing to make people look thinner. Who would even want to be flawless like that? That's too much pressure to live up to."

I used to want to be flawless, I admitted to myself. "It's funny, Kasey. Amy and I just discussed this today in my therapy session. Did you know that the average US woman's dress size is 12 to 14? But guess what 'plus size' is for models."

"I don't know… size 10?"

"Good guess, but not even close. Size 6."

Kasey's eyes opened wide. "What?! Why?"

"I'm not sure, but it sends the wrong message, especially to youth."

"Yeah, that and flat bellies." Kasey looked disgusted. "What were you saying about those the other day again?"

"Oh, just that I see diets and exercises everywhere that suggest they'll give you a flat stomach. Yet, Amy told me that only a tiny percentage of women have the genetics for a flat stomach. I did some research, and it's true. Most of us have an outward curve, because it protects our uterus."

"That's crazy! Then why do people talk about it all the time?"

"I guess they're misinformed. The sad part is how much shame people feel for not having a flat stomach when their bodies aren't even meant to. I know I felt it." In my mind's eye, I saw a full-length mirror and myself standing in front of it, looking down at my own curve and feeling terrible.

"Courtney." Kasey's voice snapped me back to reality. "It was genetically impossible. No wonder it was so frustrating."

"You know what's so interesting, Kasey? Even at my lowest weight, when I was totally unhealthy with hardly any energy, my stomach still poofed out. That tells me something."

"I'm glad you're slowly gaining weight. You look really healthy. Although, you are beautiful no matter what weight."

I blushed. "Thanks, Kasey. I know I still have more to go, but I'm getting there. It's weird… I was so obsessed with losing weight. Now, I have to gain it."

"You don't seem to be too worried about your weight, though."

"That's true, actually. I'm focusing on the emotional stuff instead… you know, what's underneath the eating disorder behaviors, like fear, control, that kind of stuff."

"It's wild how our weight is so connected to our emotions and beliefs. That's why I never judge anyone for their size. Who knows what they've gone through."

"Hmm… I never thought about that."

"Every time we go out in public, I see bodies of all different shapes and sizes. Isn't that the way it's supposed to be? There's so many different people in this world. How boring would things be if we all had the same body."

I nodded. My reality was changing in so many ways. Although it felt scary at some points, it was empowering! "Kasey, today Amy told me about a book called *Health At Every Size.*[xxxi] It talks about the fact that being thin does not necessarily mean someone is healthy. And how a larger body does not necessary mean someone is unhealthy."

"I think a lot of larger women are sexy," Kasey said with a grin.

"Yeah, like Marilyn Monroe? Supposedly, she was a size 14."

"Well, Court, what do you think makes someone beautiful, anyway? It's not necessarily their body."

I smiled, fully reminded of the reasons I fell in love with Kasey.

"Kasey, I love you. I think you're beautiful."

Now it was her turn to blush.

"Seriously, Court. What's beautiful to you?" she asked again.

"Well, I'd have to say a caring, loving heart. When people give or help, this beautiful light shines out of their hearts, and it makes them glow from the inside out."

"I agree. I'd say confidence too. It's hot when someone believes in themselves."

I smiled. I loved the truths I was learning about bodies, beauty, and health, and felt grateful for the opportunity to discuss them with Kasey. My mind then drifted off as I visualized meeting with my clients the next day at work and struggling to make them understand these same truths. *I wonder how much longer I can last in this job,* I thought.

◎

As it turned out, the answer was "not very long." During the next few months, I could no longer ignore the toll this job was taking on my mind, body, and spirit. I craved to help my clients love and accept themselves— not deprive and punish themselves through diets. Night after night, I woke up at 2:00 or 3:00 a.m. with my heart pounding from nightmares of long lines of clients waiting to get on the scale, anxious to receive their "good enough" or "not good enough" rating. And when it came down to it, I thought, were my nightmares really that different from my daily reality?

If I wanted to live authentically and in integrity, I realized I could no longer do that while doing this job. After eight months of doing my best, I told my boss the truth. I explained that I was in recovery from an eating disorder, and this job was too triggering and emotionally challenging for me. He was both disappointed and compassionate. I told him my plans to start my own coaching business, focusing on self-care and self-acceptance.

First, I gave myself a month off. I went to Michigan to visit family for a week. I had intended to spend major time nurturing myself, but I was so excited to start my business that I did little relaxing and lots of business planning both in Michigan and Arizona.

I also decided to return to SWIHA. I needed a new tool for my toolkit—one that could address the deep dissatisfaction and self-loathing that my clients and I had experienced around our weight and ourselves in general. Hypnotherapy had been calling my name for some time. Would it help? I was not sure, but willing to go along for the ride. After all, ever since I started honoring my inner wisdom, it had not led me astray. It led me to Kasey, after all!

Chapter 36

Journey into the Subconscious

"As we let our own light shine, we unconsciously give other people permission to do the same. As we are liberated from our own fear, our presence automatically liberates others." —Marianne Williamson[xxxii]

Summer 2009

"Ahhh…" I exhaled, smiling in satisfaction. After a year's absence, my whole body relaxed as I walked down the light-filled hallways. Today, I had returned to SWIHA, where my heart felt at home—to a place where I had released fears, received profound insights, and discovered deeper layers of my true self. This time, however, I returned stronger, more energized, and ready for a whole new adventure.

After doling out hugs and hellos to familiar faces, I made my way to the introductory hypnotherapy classroom. I found an empty seat next to a friendly faced woman with long curly red hair. We smiled at each another as I sat down.

Just then, flashing a welcoming smile of her own, our new hypnotherapy instructor stepped to the front of the room. She was a relatively short, thin woman with medium-length straight brown hair and a beautiful face. She wore a red satin shirt, a long black skirt, and multi-colored heart-shaped necklaces and bracelets. I had a feeling I would like her.

"Welcome to Hypnotherapy 1," she began warmly. "I'm Linda Bennett. Are you all ready for a journey into your subconscious?" After we all nodded, Linda continued, "First let's dispel the myths about hypnotherapy, shall we?"

For the next few hours, we reviewed the misconceptions, history, and background of hypnotherapy. Linda then prepared us for our first group hypnotherapy experience. Excitedly, I grabbed a yoga blanket from the front of the room. I spread it on the floor near my chair and lay down on top of it, ready, open and willing.

After asking us to close our eyes, Linda invited us to imagine a beautiful light hovering just above our heads.

"Allow the light to enter through an imaginary opening in the top of your head," she instructed. "As this happens, the light melts into a liquid relaxation, which soothes and relaxes your entire body."

As she spoke, I felt the light melting away all the tension and tightness in my body, all the way to the tips of my toes. Then, once my body was calm and relaxed, my conscious mind could get out of the way, allowing my subconscious and inner wisdom to emerge.

"Imagine that you're standing at the top of a staircase," Linda's voice continued. "Way at the bottom you see an image of yourself just the way you want to be… perhaps meeting a goal or being your truest self."

Unable to make out any details, I could vaguely see an image of myself surrounded by a light and glowing from within. It reminded me of Navee's favorite saying: "You are the light!"

Linda continued, "Now, notice the many blocks and limitations covering the staircase. These have been keeping you from meeting your goal. Allow yourself to walk down the staircase, clearing away all the fears, self-doubts, and limitations. With each item you remove, your subconscious simultaneously removes these blocks from within you."

I imagined myself kicking away hundreds of boxes as I descended the steps. Each box represented different forms of negativity just aching to be released from my subconscious—guilt, shame, blame, self-doubt, anger, fears of judgment, and much more. It felt like an instantaneous emotional detox!

Upon reaching the bottom of the staircase, I admired the image of myself, with whom I now stood face-to-face. Tall and confident, she radiated joy. Her weight was healthy, not nearly as thin as I had once been. She seemed at peace inside, connected to her spirituality and strength. I felt elated to discover that this version of myself could possibly exist!

Linda's voice chimed in, "Your subconscious does not know the difference between reality and what you imagine. You've just created a whole new reality for yourself!"

She then instructed us to allow our awareness to come back to the room, to allow us to feel alert and awake again. As I opened my eyes, I felt amazingly refreshed. *Wow*, I thought. *That was incredible!* Every cell of my body now felt whole, complete, and confident.

Linda instructed us to take a break. Still spacey-eyed, my classmates and I followed one another down the hall to the bathroom. Thankfully, following nature's call brought me quickly back to earth.

"I *love* your hair!" an unfamiliar voice said as I walked from the bathroom stall toward the sink.

I turned to look at a smiling face with big, beautiful eyes staring at me. I felt her joy and warmth, just like when I had sat down next to her in class.

"Thanks!" I said as I washed my hands at the sink next to hers. "I love yours too. I noticed it earlier."

"I'm Julie."

"I'm Courtney. Nice to meet you!"

We dried our hands and walked down the hall back to class.

"What do you think so far?" Julie asked along the way. She looked at me with anticipation.

"Oh my god," I said. "I'm hooked! What about you?"

"I moved some major stuff off that staircase!"

We laughed as we re-entered the classroom. As we did, I told Julie that she seemed familiar, as if I knew her from somewhere. Smiling to myself, I wondered, *Is she your answer to my prayers, Universe?* Recently, I had repeatedly said the affirmation, "Thank you, Universe, for a meaningful, balanced friendship where I am seen for who I am!" Was it coming true already?

During the following day's class, Julie invited me to join her and a few other classmates for lunch. I felt a little nervous about meeting new people, but as soon as we sat down at the restaurant, I sensed I was among like-minded souls. I gazed in awe at the sparkling light in their eyes. Our excitement escalated as we shared our ah-ha moments from class. I could hardly believe how easy it was to open up to them! Apparently, my willingness to be real and share from my heart meant I had just attracted in new friends who would match that energy. Although we still had a lot to learn about one another, the comfort and familiarity led me to feel like we were a family reuniting.

◎

"Courtney, how was class today?" Kasey asked as I joined her on the couch after returning home that evening.

"Amazing! I can't believe the whole weekend class is over already. How was your day?"

"Boring and lonesome."

My heart sunk. I was glad Kasey missed me while I was away, but in moments like these, I wished she had some hobbies or friends of her own. I no longer wanted to carry the weight of responsibility for other people's happiness.

"Oh, Kasey," I said sympathetically. "Well, don't worry, I'm home now."

She smiled and nodded. "Tell me more about your day, Court."

"Hypno was incredible. And it feels so good to be at SWIHA again. During the life coaching program, I was still hiding. This time, I feel less scared, like I'm willing to connect with people in a deeper way."

"Awesome! Did you have lunch with your new friends again?"

"Yes, and I made more new friends too. A few of them are even gay. How cool is that?"

"Wow, very cool. Well, I look forward to meeting them. The one you met first, Julie… she's straight, right?"

I sensed Kasey's insecurity. "Yes, totally straight. You have nothing to worry about," I reassured her. I kissed her lovingly and settled into her arms for the rest of the evening, allowing our heartbeats to synchronize and our bodies to melt into relaxation.

◎

Over the next few months, Julie and I grew closer. We talked on the phone regularly and took the next few hypnotherapy classes together. I felt so safe sharing with her. I opened up about things that I didn't share with anyone besides Kasey or my therapist. Somehow, my soul sensed that I was safe with her. She was indeed supportive, caring, sweet, and willing to be real. We were such great mirrors for one another, as our current life lessons were so similar. To have this kind of friendship where I could be seen and safe was something my heart had craved my whole life. I had no idea it was even possible!

After a few more months of hypnotherapy classes, my classmates and I became Certified Hypnotherapists. I found office space at a local yoga studio and excitedly launched my new business, Caring for Your Spirit, LLC.

I focused my hypnotherapy and transformational life coaching services on those whom I called "Caring Warriors." They were giving, caring people, like lightworkers and caregivers, who put everyone else's needs ahead of their own. Through one-on-one sessions and workshops, I taught them self-care and stress relief techniques.

Although it could be very stressful at times, I loved the freedom and creativity of having my own business. Walking the path of my life purpose seemed to melt away any remaining depression. I had always felt called to do something significant in this life, and I had finally discovered what it was! Not only was I on my own journey of healing, but now I could give back by assisting others in theirs.

Chapter 37

Mystery Solved

"Everyone has the right to be respected and the responsibility to respect others." –Bullying.org[xxxiii]

"As humans, we are complex beings with many qualities and characteristics," Linda explained. "Some of these qualities assist us, such as kindness or a drive for success, while others may hinder our growth, such as jealousy."

My classmates and I nodded in understanding. I smiled with gratitude that I had enrolled in some advanced hypnotherapy classes. I was excited for even more healing and emotional freedom.

"Today, you will experience Parts Therapy. You will have the opportunity to confront a part of you that has hindered your growth. The best way to understand is to experience it."

As I looked around the room, I recognized very few students. I would miss seeing my friends, but realized that perhaps today's healing needed to be experienced all on my own.

Linda invited us to take out a piece of paper and a pen, get comfortable, and close our eyes. I had never heard of Parts Therapy and felt quite curious as I closed my eyes and obediently took deep breaths. Linda encouraged us to connect more and more with our inner wisdom with each deep breath.

"What is a goal you have for yourself at this point in your life?" Linda asked. "What is for your highest good?"

A goal came to mind immediately. I was surprised at how quickly answers came when I just quieted my mind and allowed the inner wisdom to rise to the surface. No matter if we were in life coaching or hypnotherapy, any time I calmed down and looked within, I had all the answers I needed. *Why don't I close my eyes and tap into this more often?*

Putting these thoughts aside, I refocused on my goal for today's session: healing from the eating disorder and trusting my body.

"How will you know when you've met this goal? How would that look or show up in your life?" Linda asked.

I did not feel surprised by the answers that came next: allowing my body to gain weight, if that's what it wanted to do; getting in tune with my body's signals so I could tell when I was hungry; no longer being disconnected from all my own thoughts, feelings, and needs; connecting to my body, mind, and spirit.

It would look like knowing when I was hungry and eating, and knowing when I was full and stopping. Listening inside for the foods my body was craving. The same was true for exercise—exercising when my body felt like it, not because "rules" told me how often or how long to exercise. Overall, meeting this goal would mean listening to my body, trusting my body.

"Now," Linda said, "ask your inner wisdom to tell you what keeps you from that goal. What is blocking you? Notice where that block resides in your body."

I felt it in my stomach.

"Notice how it feels," Linda continued.

I felt a tightness and heaviness.

"Imagine you can take that part out of you and sit it down in a chair next to you. Imagine you will have a conversation with it. First, notice how it looks. How does it appear to you?"

I gasped with fear and surprise as I visualized a shriveled-up, dark little creature. She appeared to be half-insect and half-alien with a mean face. She seemed uncomfortable, unhappy, and scared.

I heard Linda's voice. "Ask this part if it has a name. If so, what that name is."

Immediately, the answer popped into my mind: "Chastity."

Chastity? I thought. *That's a weird name for this little creature.*

"Ask the part what its role is in your life. What havoc has it been wreaking in your life?"

I instinctively knew the answer. It had been trying to keep me small and powerless.

"What are some of the ways it shows up in your life?"

This is crazy, I thought. Even so, I decided to remain open and continue. Within my mind, I heard Chastity say, "I'm the one who always tells you that you're not good enough, smart enough, or thin enough."

Something about this imaginary conversation felt oddly familiar. Feeling annoyed and disgusted, I confronted her within my mind. *Why do you have to be so mean and intimidating?*

"I'm not mean. I'm just honest, you stupid, no-good, fatso."

Suddenly, an old memory flashed through my mind. I visualized the wrinkled, mean-looking image from my childhood dreams—C.I.B.! After all these years, I had pushed her as far as possible out of my mind. *But what does Chastity have to do with C.I.B.?* I had the feeling that something was about to click into place.

"Wait a minute, I just realized something!" I said in my mind. "That's why your name is Chastity, isn't it? You have always put me down and chastised me."

I waited eagerly for her response. Apparently she felt no remorse, nor desire to be kind.

"Yes, that's right, you idiot. Whoop-dee-doo. If you were smart you'd know that I'm really good at something else too."

Her demeaning tone was getting on my nerves. I'd listened to it far long enough.

"What's that?"

"Cooourtneeeey. Haven't you realized yet? Think about it!"

Why does she derive some sick pleasure from bullying me? She's so intimidating and mean.

"Wait a minute, that's it! You're my inner bully!"

Chastity nodded. "It took you long enough to figure out, stupid!" She looked away as though she had better things to do.

I breathed in deeply and exhaled loudly. *Oh my gosh, that makes so much sense! She's been bullying me my whole life! I've been bullying myself my whole life.* A deep sadness washed over me at the thought of all I had missed out on. While other kids seemed to be having fun, I was being tortured by my inner bully. While some people seemed to eat whatever they wanted, I had obsessed over every bite of food I put in my mouth.

"Okay," Linda interjected. "Finish up your conversation about the ways this part shows up in your life."

My eyes remained closed as I continued this enlightening conversation with the part of me driving the eating disorder. Anger rushed to my chest as a new insight hit me.

"Chastity? Do you also go by the name of C.I.B.?"

"Congratulations! Finally, you may know what C.I.B. stands for. You did ask me years ago, remember?"

I guessed that meant yes. Her arrogance was getting on my last nerve. If she had been a tangible object, I would have punched her.

"So what's the answer?"

"Do you have to be so impatient? You're pitiful. All right, fine. 'C.I.B' stands for 'Chastity your Inner Bully.'"

I wasn't sure whether I wanted to cry or laugh out loud. *Oh my god, after all this time. She's the one who showed up in my childhood dreams. She's the part of me who's been driving my self-doubts and fears.* I felt surprised, afraid, and excited to bring healing to this situation. My mouth remained open in disbelief.

"You know, Courtney, I want you to have this eating disorder."

"Why would you say something like that?" I found no need to hide my angry defensiveness.

"Duh. Because I want to keep you small."

Just then, Linda's voice came in again, grounding me in reality. She explained that every behavior has a purpose and payoff—a way it serves us.

"Ask the part what positive role it's been playing in your life," she said. "How has it been trying to protect you, help you, support you? What has it been trying to protect you from? Remember that ultimately everyone's doing the best they can… even the parts within ourselves. Instead of getting angry with the part, we need to send it compassion and love. The part has limited knowledge. It doesn't know everything. How has it been trying to help you?"

"Well?" I asked C.I.B.

"The world is scary out there, Courtney. I've been trying to protect you from feeling pain. You know, like anger and sadness and stuff. Those aren't fun to feel."

"Right, but I'm human. Emotions and pain come with the territory."

"Not if you have an eating disorder. You can just hide in your food and exercise and avoid feeling those yucky things."

As her tone softened, I laughed to myself. *She sounds like a frightened child!*

"But, C.I.B., don't you get it? I don't want to have an eating disorder anymore!"

I sat up taller in my chair, ready to put my foot down once and for all.

Linda's voice said, "Now it's time to negotiate. Either the part must go away, or if it stays with you, it has to do something more positive in your life. Claim your power. You decide what will take the best care of you. Reassure the part that it's safe."

I told Chastity that I wanted to be healthy now and I could handle feeling my own emotions. I reassured her that the world is not a scary place but one filled with love, that it's only scary if we give into fear and forget the love. I let her know that even though she looked like a monster, I was going to love her.

"Chastity, thank you for the role you've played in my life. But I don't need you anymore. I release you."

"But is there something else I can help you with?"

I thought about it for a few minutes. "Um... how about if you speak up when I'm hungry? A lot of times when I'm hungry, I forget to eat or don't want to take the time to eat. I'm still learning to listen to what I need and honor it."

"Sure, I can do that."

I felt surprised at how much nicer she was being. *I guess all this time she just needed some love, just like me.*

"But you have to promise not to chastise me when I forget. Just be gentle and compassionate. Can you do that?"

I hoped for the answer I wanted to hear. She hesitated to respond.

"Chastity, again, thanks for trying to help. But I just don't need to be bullied. I deserve compassion. Are you capable of that?"

She must have said yes, because suddenly, her whole image softened and changed. Within my mind, the previously shriveled-up, frightened creature morphed into a beautiful woman wearing a long, flowing skirt. Apparently, she had just needed to know that she was loved and good enough herself. I could see her feeling light and free, dancing in a garden filled with the most vibrant flowers of every color. I had claimed my power back from my inner bully! She was free, and now so was I!

Just then, Linda invited us to open our eyes. As I did, my awareness returned to the room. I had the biggest grin on my face as I processed all that had just happened. I grabbed my pen and wrote vigorously. I had heard the eating disorder's concerns, soothed her fears, and assigned her a new role in my life. I had just peeled away a whole row of artichoke petals in my healing journey.

Wow! I like parts therapy, I thought as I kept smiling. How refreshing it was to realize that as dysfunctional as it seemed, the eating disorder was not out to destroy me. Rather, it tried to help me survive by protecting me from pain. I thought back to the many times I had exercised in the past. Yes, I thought. I often did it when I felt uncomfortable or angry. However, I didn't let myself feel that discomfort or anger. I didn't know how to, so I exercised to escape. Now, here I was… starting to feel safe in the world all on my own. I no longer needed to escape from my feelings. I was awakening to my own power and strength from deep within.

Chapter 38

What Are You Afraid Of?

"Our deepest fear is not that we are inadequate. Our deepest fear is that we are powerful beyond measure. It is our light, not our darkness that most frightens us." –Marianne Williamson[xxxiv]

Winter 2010

As I digested my recent breakthrough in recovery, I continued building my business. I knew I was born to teach, help, and empower other people, which I now did through sessions and workshops. Living my life purpose felt amazing. But still, something felt "off."

One day my life coaching classmate Ashley came over. We often connected for business brainstorming meetings. Ashley had sassy, wavy, shoulder-length blondish-brown hair and bright blue eyes, and her looks matched her bubbly personality. She inspired me with her willingness to take risks, speak her truth, and laugh at herself.

"You know, Ashley, I've been really nervous about something," I told her during one of our meetings. "I've connected with clients on social media. What if they see I'm with a woman?"

As I nervously made my confession, Ashley looked me directly in the eyes, remaining silent. To fill the discomfort of the empty space, I continued. "What if they judge me for it?"

Ashley must have been guided by her intuition, because she seemed to know exactly what to say.

"Courtney, so what?"

"Well, I don't want to lose clients. I can't afford to right now."

"Well, don't you want clients who accept you for who you are?"

Now came my turn for silence. After a few moments, I answered. "Yes, of course."

"Don't you want clients who are in alignment with your values?"

"Yes. I want to work with people who are open-hearted and open-minded." My gaze drifted to the ceiling. *Wow, that's so helpful to realize!* I glanced at Ashley, who was also staring off into space. I could almost see the divine ideas flowing through her mind.

"Courtney, why are you skirting around this? Help the people who need you most. The BLT—um, how do you say it? I have friends and family that are gay and lesbian, but I forget how the letters go!"

We both laughed.

"LGBTQ," I gently corrected her. "I know, it's like a mouthful of alphabet soup!"

"Yes, the BLT-Q community. Gosh, I haven't had a BLT in years."

"That makes me hungry!"

We laughed some more.

"Courtney, you know you'd be accepted there. And they need encouragement and empowerment. Why aren't you the empowerment coach for the LGBTQ community?"

My insides twisted and turned with excitement and fear. *Me? Could I do that? Am I brave enough?* "Ashley, that sounds awesome. But that means I have to be more out... like publically."

A huge smile came over her face. "You got it. And isn't it you who talks about being authentic and free?"

I took a deep breath. Even though even the thought of doing this terrified me, a deeper part of me knew this was my next step.

"You know, Ashley, I do get all fired up about equal rights, especially for LGBTQ people."

"I know, it's ridiculous. There's still a lot of discrimination, right?"

"Yeah, for sure. I can't hold Kasey's hand in public without worrying about offending someone. I get so jealous seeing straight couples with their arms around one another. It's frustrating. People have made stupid comments to me. And the worst part is that my relationship is not recognized legally. We're denied over 1000 rights that married couples have, like automatic hospital visitations, joint tax returns, and joint health insurance." [xxxv]

"I knew there were differences, but I didn't realize *that* many! That's crazy!"

I sat up taller in my chair. "It makes me feel like a second-class citizen. It's so weird, because regardless of who I'm in love with, I am the same person inside. I have the same beliefs, thoughts, and values... I'm the same Courtney!"

"Don't you think the discrimination affects BI—sorry, LGBTQ people on the inside?"

"Oh, for sure. I think it leads to self-hatred and self-sabotage. I want LGBTQ people to know how precious they are." I chuckled. "You can see I get pretty fired up about this, huh?"

Ashley giggled. "Yes, I know. That's why I thought I'd point out the obvious."

"Ashley, thanks for having the guts to call me out on this. I'd love to work with LGBTQ clients... if I can just get past my own fears."

"You're going to have to be really comfortable with being bisexual. But you can do this, Courtney. Just sit with it, and see how it feels."

Later that night, as I lay down to sleep, I thought about what all of this this would really mean. If I were an empowerment coach for LGBTQ clients, I would be subject to ridicule... and possibly hate crimes. I would also have to face one of my deepest fears—people not liking me.

I also wondered how Kasey would feel. She was so private. *How would she feel if I were doing a presentation and pointed at her and said, 'There is my beautiful partner'? Yet if I trust in a divine plan for my life, and I'm truly called to help others, I will get through my fears. I will have some hypnotherapy sessions or do whatever it will take. I will answer that call.*

◎

As I showed up in the world in a more authentic way by not hiding my love for Kasey I slowly regained weight and physical energy. As I spoke my truth, I felt more motivated to live and more motivated to eat. Therapy was also helping me unravel my fears and discover my inner truths. My therapist Amy guided me along the path of discovering how to hear, tap into, and connect with my own authentic voice. The more authentic I became, the hungrier my body allowed me to feel. I wasn't just hungry for food... I was hungry for life!

One cool winter morning as the sun shined in through the living room windows, I settled into the couch, a cup of hot tea in hand. Kasey had already left for work, and it was time for my weekly therapy session with Amy. I took a deep breath, dialed her office, and awaited the comforting sound of her voice.

"Courtney, how are you?" Amy asked as she picked up. Her tone was warm, inviting tone.

What a reassuring way to start our therapy sessions, I thought. Unlike people who ask this question without truly listening to the answer, I knew that Amy actually cared. Her question reminded me that the next hour would be dedicated to me... to the support and nurturing of my own spirit. The tension in my shoulders melted away.

"Well, I'm okay... just tense lately," I said.

When I had first started therapy years ago, I often said I was "good" even when I was depressed or struggling. I did not purposely hide from Amy; I unintentionally hid from myself. I had felt like a locked vault, filled with secrets and a pain I did not even realize were there. By constantly reaffirming that I was in a safe space, Amy helped me feel safe enough to open my vault and explore inside, without shame or guilt about what I found. The further I explored, the more I connected with my deepest truth, and the more I learned about me—including my preferences, needs, feelings, fears and hopes—the stronger I felt. Today in particular, I felt proud that I could answer Amy's 'How are you' truthfully, without shame, guilt, or self-blame.

"Tell me more about the tension," Amy requested gently.

"Well, I've been meeting with Laurie my registered dietician. It's been going really well."

"What have you been working on?"

"I started eating desserts. I still haven't had the *amount* of dessert that a 'normal' person would eat. But this is a huge step for me."

"Courtney, that's wonderful!"

Amy's validation and enthusiasm was such a comfort to my heart. She celebrated my successes, no matter how big or small. Both she and Laurie knew this was far more than simply 'eating dessert.' Having that sweet meant having the courage to confront deep-rooted fears—the very fears that had driven the entire eating disorder.

It also meant facing the emotional pain I had been avoiding my whole life, including a recent emotion—sadness. I felt deep remorse for all the years I had been depriving myself of joy, pleasure, and life.

"The desserts are delicious!" I giggled. Then my voice became more serious. "I'm realizing that I deserve to eat them."

"Yes, you do. You do know there is a food group for desserts, right?"

At first, I wondered if she was serious. Then, I imagined her jovial facial expression with one eyebrow raised, trying to keep a straight face while hiding a facetious smile.

"No, Amy, I didn't know that. Which food group? Don't tell me—it's the veggie group, right?" I played along.

She laughed. "No, it's a different one. It's called F-U-N."

"Fun?" I asked, surprised. "Seriously?"

"Yes! We need to have fun, even in our food landscape. Courtney, what emotions have come up when you're eating dessert?"

"Oh my god, tons of fear. It's been horrifying. I'm afraid of gaining tons of weight and getting in trouble. It's like a hammer hanging over my head, ready to strike any time I get 'out of line.'"

"Courtney, if that hammer could talk, what would it say?"

I paused, closed my eyes, and allowed the answer to arise from my inner wisdom.

"It says that if I listen to myself, I would be totally out of control. I guess this is why I don't trust myself… or my appetite." I hoped for some reassurance.

"Courtney, the most 'in control' thing you can do is listen to your body and honor its needs. This means eating the foods your body intuitively asks you for. If you eat when you're hungry and stop when you're full, your body will go to the weight at which it feels the best."

"So my body knows what to do, and I don't have to control it. Right?"

"Right. Your healthiest weight is not a number on a scale. It's the weight at which your body feels vibrant, energized, and able to move freely. Your body knows what to do."

"I'm starting to see that. I've been adding in foods I haven't eaten in years, like mayonnaise, salad dressing, and coconut ice cream. When I tune in, my body knows how much it wants. I have more energy than I've had in a long time!"

"That's great! I honor your courage, Courtney."

"Thank you. I've gained a little weight, which I guess my body must have needed. I'm surprised at how gradual it's been… not the never-ending amount of weight I always feared."

"How does that feel?"

I smiled. "Like a huge relief!"

We both laughed. If we had been in the same room, I imagined she would be giving me a high-five.

"That's how it works when we tune into our body's cues. Congratulations!"

"Thanks," I said. "I guess maybe my body can be trusted after all." I smiled at this new insight, and my thoughts trailed off. I felt increasingly grateful for Amy. She helped me to see and know me… who I was apart from my parents, apart from the rigid rules I had for myself, and even apart from Kasey. I loved getting to know Courtney. I was realizing that maybe she wasn't so bad after all.

"You know what, though, Amy? I don't have much energy when I over-exercise."

"I'm not surprised. Tell me more."

"Well, I've cut back a little bit. I'm not exercising as intensely as before. I'm doing more walks and yoga. But even with yoga, I do the power yoga, even when my body is tired and would rather do calm, Zen yoga. I have good intentions to listen to my body. Certain days, I even plan to take the whole day off exercise. But then suddenly, I have this urgent need to exercise. And if I don't, it feels like something really bad is going to happen."

"What do you think would happen?

"I'm not sure, but it feels like a matter of life or death. Like if I don't exercise, I'll die. Amy, I'm tired of hurting my body by over-exercising. But I don't know how to stop feeling this way."

My eyes suddenly welled up with tears. "I feel like I've made so much progress in my recovery," I said through them.

"Yes, Courtney you have."

"I know this is the last piece."

Amy didn't respond to that right away. I waited in silence for her next statement.

"Courtney, what if you thought of it as an experiment, like you have with the desserts?"

"What do you mean?"

"Well, decide how much exercise you *think* might feel authentic to your body and try doing that amount... even for a few weeks. Eventually, you'll get really good at knowing which days to move and which to rest. But for now, it sounds like an experiment might help."

"But Amy, that would mean I would have to *feel*." Every cell of my body sunk low with disappointment.

"Yes, and it will be uncomfortable. Courtney?"

"Yes?"

"You can handle it."

My stomach dropped in fear, and with knowing that this was indeed the next step. I wanted to take it, but I was terrified. "When I was a teenager, anytime I didn't exercise, I told myself I was really fat. This is still programmed into me. I don't want to feel fat. It's the worst feeling in the world."

"Courtney, what does 'fat' mean to you?"

Again, I closed my eyes. The answer came immediately. "Imperfect. If I'm fat, it means I'm not perfect."

"And what does it mean to be imperfect?"

"Unlovable. Unacceptable to God."

My eyes filled with more tears as I squirmed in my seat with shame. I hoped to somehow hide my ugliness from God. Then suddenly, a wave of strength came over my body and lifted my spine to a taller posture. *Wait a minute, what am I talking about?*

"If I weren't acceptable to God, then God wouldn't have made me the way I am. I'm exactly who I am supposed to be… even the dark, ugly stuff. That's just part of being human!" I said.

"Yes, and humans do not have to be perfect."

I smiled. "Amy, I know now that I'm lovable, whole, and complete just as I am. We all are. God made us just the way we are supposed to be. I'm ready to confront the exercise. I'm terrified, but I have to do this."

"Well, the beautiful thing is you don't *have* to do anything. It's always your choice."

"Then I choose to. I owe this to myself."

As we wrapped up our session, I committed to doing a lesser amount of exercise. Thankfully, I had already done my exercise earlier that morning, so I could put off my concerns until tomorrow. Or could I?

Later that day, in between seeing clients, I felt like I was sinking into worry-saturated quicksand. *Can I really do this? I'm freaked out. What about when I get stressed*? For so many years, exercise was the only way I could cope.

Give yourself more credit, Courtney, I reassured myself. *You've come so far. You can do this!*

After a record of two days in a row without exercising, my muscles started to feel gross, loose, and fat. Instead of allowing myself to feeling the intense discomfort in my body, I immersed myself into my work. However, I could only work so long. Eventually, I would have to face the withdrawal symptoms.

Upon arriving home from work, the panic and anxiousness set in… especially when I saw that Kasey had changed into her workout clothes.

"Hi Kasey," I said, trying to cover up my nervousness. "Whatcha doing?"

"Going for a walk. Want to come?"

Oh no. Just what I had feared. As Kasey bent over to lace up her sneakers, I salivated at the sight of them.

"Um, I would love to, but I promised myself I would rest today." But how could I possibly not go with her? We always walked together. "Then again, maybe I will go with you. I can just start my exercise detox tomorrow."

Her head tilted, as if she could see right through my lie. "Courtney, you're staying here. You'll be okay."

She gave me a kiss and headed out the door. It felt like my favorite thing in the world had just been ripped away from me. The injustice of it all infuriated me. *How does she know that I'll be okay? I'm not okay at all!*

I broke out in a sweat. I paced back and forth. I felt like hitting or breaking something. Instead, my body shook with angry terror. *I'm the one in control. Damnit, I can go for a walk if I want to.*

Then anxiousness took over. *Maybe if I change my clothes fast enough, I can catch up to her.* I walked into our closet and started changing. Halfway through, I paused. *What am I doing?* I chastised myself.

In my half-unbuttoned collared shirt and workout shorts, I left the closet. I walked into the living room and sat on the couch, seeking relief from the obsessive thoughts reverberating through my mind as if they'd been shouted into my ear.

"I can't take this!" I screamed. Two seconds later, as though my body had completely disconnected from my mind, I observed myself standing up and walking back to the closet. This time I completed my clothing change and felt my feet slide into my well-worn sneakers.

Maybe just this once, I convinced myself.

I was an addict craving her addiction. I approached the front door and reached for the doorknob, preparing to run hard and fast to catch up to Kasey, who was probably halfway through her walk by now, with all this time I'd been wasting. I walked outside and turned to close and lock the door behind me.

Suddenly, the key slipped from my hand. Bending down to pick it up, I felt my hands shaking. "What the fuck am I doing? I'm tired of hurting myself. It ends now." I stomped my foot in an act of power.

However, quickly, the power dissipated into release as my body fell loose and limp to the ground. Hoping the neighbors could not hear me talking to myself in hysterics, I crawled through the doorway back into the house. Helpless, I lay in the foyer crying and pounding my fists against the floor. *What am I supposed to do? I don't want to feel. No God, no.*

Soon, Kasey returned home and saw me hyperventilating on the floor.

She immediately fell to her knees and joined me on the floor, worry all over her face. "Courtney, oh my god, are you okay? What happened?"

"No I'm not okay! I don't know how to do this."

Kasey looked at me with her beautiful brown eyes. So many times, I had felt safe and comforted by her love, as if her love could wash away anything that was happening to me, no matter what it was. Unfortunately, this was not one of the times.

"It's going to be okay, Court."

I frowned at her. "No, it won't. How would you know?" When she attempted to reassure me with a hug, I pushed her away and glared at her. "Get away from me!"

"Courtney, what's happening to you? I've never seen you like this." With a look of utter confusion and fear, she stood up and headed to the kitchen.

Horror filled me. *Oh my god? What did I just say?* I peeled myself off the floor, grabbed my journal, and stumbled to the back yard. Sitting in the grass, I wrote vigorously. *Why can't I handle a day of rest?* I had to get to the bottom of this.

> "After the second day in a row of rest and no exercise...my body is feeling antsy.
> I'm afraid to feel my feelings.
> I'm afraid of my own body.
> I'm afraid of my own power.
> I'm afraid that I <u>am</u> good enough, that my body is good enough already.
> I'm afraid of nothing.
> I <u>feel</u>.
> Perhaps is it that I'm afraid of my life purpose? That I have been all this time... since I was little and heard that voice of wisdom within me. And ironically, it

wasn't just the interactions with my mom. I've kept
myself little."

—Journal, age 29, Friday, 1/29/10, 7:10 p.m.

I stared at what I had written. *That's it? This is what I've been fearing all along for all these years... my power?*

It all made sense. Even though I had felt powerless growing up, I knew that my spirit—my authentic self—was incredibly powerful. But instead of directing my energy toward standing up for myself, I had directed it into exercise. Every time I had lots of energy or felt some emotion, I avoided feeling it by exercising instead. This, of course, would release endorphins, which calmed me down and made me "forget"—that is, push out of my mind—whatever had been bothering me. Exercise also left me happily exhausted. If I used all the energy I had doing aerobics or running, I had no energy to do or say anything differently, like set a boundary or, God forbid, sit down with my feelings and puzzle them out.

I could not wait until next week's therapy session with Amy.

◎

"Amy, I tried the experiment just like we talked about." I practically bounced on the couch with excitement.

"Great. How did it go?"

The words started pouring from my mouth. "I figured it out! I've been afraid of my own power... that is what I was avoiding all these years."

"Wow, Courtney, that's a beautiful insight! So what does this mean for you?"

"It feels like it changes everything! All these years I've been beating myself up and telling myself what a bad person I am. And underneath it all, there's been this incredibly beautiful power. I just didn't see it, because I was afraid of it."

"Why do you sense you feared it?"

"Maybe I was afraid of hurting someone's feelings. I mean, what if I expressed my power and someone doesn't like it? I guess I was afraid of not being liked and afraid of being vulnerable."

"What happens if you're not liked?"

I chuckled. "Well, I guess that would be okay, because now I'm starting to like myself. But what I used to think was that if I wasn't liked, I would end up all alone."

"Oh. But is that really true?"

"No, not at all! The more risk opening up and sharing what I'm really thinking and feeling, the more people seem to listen... at least those who are ready to hear what I have to say."

"Can you think of an instance where it's happened this way?"

I loved her insightful questions.

"Well, I was really proud of myself," I said. "In a hypnotherapy class recently, I stood up and shared that I had had an eating disorder. Before, I was too ashamed to share that with anyone. I was so scared of their judgment. And when I told the class this, I was so nervous that my whole body was trembling inside."

"How did it go?"

"Amazing. Instead of judging me, a few people came up to me after and thanked me for sharing. A few even said they related."

"Courtney, you faced your fear head-on. And it paid off. Congratulations!"

"Huh, I guess I did," I admitted. "Sharing my story in class felt powerful."

Just then, a huge realization came over me. "It's so funny, Amy. For me, exercise has always been about power. It used to be the only way I felt powerful. Oh my gosh, the whole eating disorder was never really about my weight. It was about something deeper."

"You got it, Courtney. For most people, the focus on food and weight is just a symptom. What hides underneath that is usually a ton of emotional pain, low self-worth, shame, all sorts of things. Now you can call on your warrior or queen energy. Beside exercise, what are some other ways you can feel powerful?"

I sat quietly for a moment and allowed the answers to come. "I can speak up when my feelings are hurt," I said at last.

"That's great. What else?"

"I can say 'no' when I want to say 'no.' Which means taking care of myself."

"Mmm… Yes, self-care is extremely powerful!"

"And ask for what I need."

"Yes!"

"I'm tired of numbing my own power," I said firmly. "I want my power to go into my loving myself and standing up for myself. One, because that's what I deserve, and two, because that's what will help me to empower others to find authenticity. You know, Amy, I'm pretty sure I can handle cutting back on exercise now. Exercise doesn't make me a good person. Pleasing others doesn't make me a good person, either. Neither does twisting the truth to say what I think others want to hear. I'm a good person because I am who I am. I finally understand what you meant when you said that my value is constant."

"Courtney, you've done some major work the last few weeks— actually the last few years!"

"You know what else this means? I have just as much power as my mom does." I sat up taller.

"Yes, you do!"

"I have a feeling my interactions with her will be very different now." My smile was filled with sweet satisfaction and hope.

PART IV:

Butterfly Wings

Chapter 39

Will I Ever Feel Good Enough?

"Though no one can go back and make a brand new start, anyone can start from now and make a brand new ending." –Carl Bard

Spring 2010

My latest discovery lifted a veil of darkness from my vision. In my mind's eye, I saw my power as a luminescent, sparkling gemstone, revealing a rainbow of colors, depending on the angle at which the light hit.

Long ago, fear had broken and shattered this gemstone into several pieces, which were then lost and scattered. The fear of my own light led me to give those pieces away to others. I begrudgingly gave one to my mom on a silver platter at age sixteen, on the day she caught James and me sneaking into the house and I surrendered to her authority and rules. Long before that, I gave pieces to my first grade friend Jennifer and teacher Ms. Stout when I made the unspoken vow never to upset anyone ever again. Others I gave to boyfriends, teachers, society, and friends by giving their opinions more importance than my own. Now I was ready to reclaim every angle and particle of my personal power.

Yet once I gathered and reintegrated all these pieces back into one sparking, luminescent gemstone, what would I do with it? I wondered. *How will standing in my power affect my life?* The most powerful thing I could do would be to love and be myself, of course. *But how can I do that?*

During the course of recovery, I felt angry with my mom for her rigid rules and mean comments. I had no idea how to get past the hurt and pain these had caused me, or how to free myself from the shame I still felt. How could I possibly be true to myself when I still felt like a bad person whenever someone else—especially my mom—was upset?

One day before Kasey came home from work, I sat outside in the backyard reflecting on this.

Mom is so different from me. It's like we're from different planets.

Okay, but who cares? Why does that bother me so much? Even if she expects me to be like her, I don't have to. In fact, I can't. I'm unique. Nor do I have to please her anymore. I'm an adult now. I can make my own choices.

In that moment, my entire being became still and calm as awareness came over me. It felt as if the sweet, soft breeze had been listening and had delivered the perfect insights directly to me.

I have to learn how to trust my intuition and my own decisions. I am the only authority in my life. Mom is not holding me back from anything anymore. At this point, the only person holding me back from being me is myself.

I can't blame Mom for my eating disorder. That doesn't serve either of us. Sure, I acknowledge that her behavior and rigid rules played a role in me developing it. In fact, it's been really important to acknowledge my pain around that, especially since I denied it for so long. I feel it, heal it, and let it go.

But on a soul level, I believe I chose her to be my mom before I came to earth In fact, I believe I chose the eating disorder too, for the lessons my soul needed this lifetime, like self-compassion, self-love, and now the reclaiming of my power. It's time for me to accept responsibility, forgive, and move on.

"How can I truly forgive her? How can I fully accept her? God, Universe, Divine Love, Spirit...I need your help, your guidance. Are you telling me that the only way to forgive her is to stand up for myself? To work through my own fear and still speak up? I need to express my feelings, my opinions, my preferences, my passions, my needs. To forgive Mom, I must take responsibility for myself and my own self-care. My inner child must know she is safe. She must feel protected and see that I can take care of myself, that I'm willing to stand up for her. I'm getting there. I'm

288

I recalled an e-mail I had recently received from SWIHA, announcing their annual forgiveness ceremony. I felt drawn to go.

When the evening of the event arrived a few weeks later, I walked into a beautiful candlelit room filled with the sweet scent of aromatherapy sprays. Immediately, I felt a sense of peace and compassion. Prior to the ceremony, I had assumed I would focus on forgiving my mom. I sat down and quickly realized that I was there to forgive someone else too—myself. As I waited for the ceremony to begin, in quiet prayer, I asked the Universe how I could forgive my mother and my inner bully for shaming, restricting, and unintentionally harming me. I especially wanted to forgive my teenage self for cutting myself, drinking rum out of the bottle in my closet, restricting my food, over-exercising, and completely going against my body's natural rhythms, along with all the self-hatred and self-disgust.

The ceremony began. Linda welcomed us and invited us to light a candle in the spirit of forgiveness. She explained that forgiveness does not mean approving of someone's actions, but letting go of the hurt surrounding those actions. That made me feel better, because I would never be okay with someone shaming or guilt-tripping me. I deserved better. At the same time, I wanted to be free, and I wanted my mom and my inner teenager to be free too.

Linda then invited us to close our eyes and imagine the person we were choosing to forgive. As guided, I imagined beautiful angels surrounding my mom and my younger self in light. I still wondered how I could possibly forgive.

Suddenly, the most beautiful and profound answer came, as though those angels I imagined had whispered it to me.

My mother did not know her own light. Her mother, my grandmother, did not know hers. This pattern had existed for many generations within the family. My ancestors did not know their beauty and goodness. I did not know my light either until recently.

I realized that I could heal the entire situation, including my relationships with my mom, grandma, and myself, simply by seeing my own light. It was time to acknowledge my goodness and power— who I truly was! The ultimate healing would be all of us seeing and shining our own light!

Of course, I could not control whether my family members chose to see their own light. However, I thought, being myself just might give them the inspiration they needed to see theirs. In that moment, I committed to love, honor, and nurture myself. That was it— something so simple, yet so profound. I realized then that loving myself was the most significant thing I could do in this life.

©

I had forgiven Mom, but still struggled being around her. In fact, every time she became stressed, upset, or angry, my whole body cringed with fear and shame. Somehow, I still felt that it was my fault and my responsibility to do something to make her happy. Apparently, I had more healing work to do.

As usual, I headed to SWIHA to do it.

"Thanks for saving me a seat, Jules!" I said, taking my place next to my best friend. Class was just about to begin.

"You're welcome, friend. Are you ready for this? I heard it's a really intense."

"Isn't every hypnotherapy class intense?"

She laughed. "Yeah, that's true! This one is about feeling good enough and lovable. Are you ready for that?"

She seemed both serious and sarcastic. Just as I shrugged my shoulders, Linda called our attention and began teaching. I felt captivated and as usual, sensed this would be a life-changing weekend.

"This weekend, you will meet your inner child," Linda explained. "We will help him or her see an old situation through a more accurate lens."

Accurate? I thought. *I wonder what she means.*

"Each of us has faced difficult situations throughout our lifetimes... pain, heartache, abuse. When something challenging happens, we often form negative beliefs about ourselves, especially if that thing happened when we were a child."

A student in a green shirt raised her hand. "Do you mean when someone feels responsible for the way someone else acted, like it was their fault?" she asked when Linda called on her.

"Yes, exactly," Linda responded. "What matters is not what someone has done or said to us, but what we've decided about ourselves because of it."

Several classmates and I nodded. I'd never thought of it that way!

"In fact, we form most of our beliefs about the world and ourselves before age seven. Our logical mind is not fully developed then. This means we have beliefs about ourselves that just aren't true.

"At a deep subconscious level, many people do not feel good enough or lovable. The truth is that everyone's value is constant. We are always good enough and lovable, regardless of anyone else's opinions or actions. But when we are little children, we don't know how to filter negative messages. We think everyone else's opinions are the truth, especially authority figures'. If a mother tells her little daughter that she is selfish, more than likely the daughter takes on that belief about herself. Through the rest of her life, the daughter does everything in her power to prove to everyone how unselfish she is. She becomes the caregiver, the helper, the volunteer, the generous one... to the point of sacrificing her own well-being."

Whoa, I thought. *I relate.*

"As children, we also think others' actions are about us, especially as toddlers when our minds can only comprehend 'me, me, me.' If Dad comes home from work angry, a toddler likely thinks he did something wrong to cause the anger, and it shakes his sense of self-worth."

Another classmate raised her hand. "So there's a lot of repair work to do, huh?"

"Oh, tons!" Linda agreed. "These beliefs stay with us through adulthood, unless we clear them out and form new ones, which most people don't know how to do. Most people operate from a place of unworthiness, and this blocks them from self-care, healthy loving relationships, and going after their dreams. They don't feel deserving of any of these things."

Another classmate raised his hand. "Is this why so many people sabotage themselves? Like every time I start a diet, I end up eating a whole chocolate cake." He laughed.

"Yes, you got it," Linda said. "A classic example is when someone sets the intention to be in a healthy relationship, but they find themselves back with an abusive partner. It's because at a deep subconscious level, they do not feel good enough for anything else.

"Remember the difference between the conscious mind and subconscious mind," she continued. Your mind might *think* you are good enough, but your emotional subconscious may have a totally different awareness."

"Regardless of what has happened to you or your clients—whether it was abuse, trauma, rejection, abandonment, or a relatively smooth life—what specifically happened isn't as important as what you or they decided about yourself or themselves because of it. If your client's friend put them down, did they feel they deserved the negative comment? If a partner broke up with them, did it reinforce their old belief that they are unlovable?"

Linda then taught us the advanced hypnotherapy healing technique and sent us into separate rooms to practice on each other. Julie and I and our friend Christine decided to work together. As a nurse and holistic healthcare practitioner, Christine's caring heart shined brightly. She had short curly brown hair, fair skin, and a sweet, nurturing personality.

Eager to delve into the process, I volunteered to go first. I sat down in a chair, closed my eyes, and let Christine guide me.

"Allow your subconscious to take you to the first moment you did not feel good enough," she instructed warmly.

I took a deep breath and allowed my memory to take me where I needed to go. I had learned to trust that my subconscious would show me whatever was for my highest good and never more or less than I could handle.

A scene began to appear within my mind's eye. Suddenly, I heard my mom's voice abruptly and harshly snap, "Stop!" I literally jumped in my seat with fear, then sobbed like a little kid—unusual behavior for me, especially in front of other people!

Once my tears calmed a little, Christine asked me to describe the scene.

"I'm just playing at the kitchen counter," I explained. "Mom is making dinner."

"How old are you?"

"Three," I said, aware that my voice even sounded like a three-year-old's. "I guess I messed up her papers on the counter. She just yelled at me. I'm so scared!"

"Know that you are safe, Courtney."

"But she hurt my feelings. I didn't do anything wrong. Why did she have to be so mean?"

As I pouted and continued crying, Christine continued reassuring me that I was safe. She then guided me to imagine my current adult self entering the scene and soothing little Courtney however she needed. In my imagination, I lifted the sweet little one into my arms, took her outside into the fresh air, and held her on my lap. In the quiet of my mind, we had a very healing conversation.

"You've been ignoring me!" she pouted.

"I'm so sorry, little Courtney, I didn't mean to," I responded sweetly. "I didn't know you were there!"

"I've been hurt all this time. Why haven't you been taking care of me?" She frowned at me.

"Well, I'll do a better job now. What do you need, sweetheart?"

Her bright blue eyes looked at me through her tears. "I just need love. And to know that I'm safe and good enough. Am I?" she asked.

I smiled and squeezed her tighter in my arms. "Yes, sweet little Courtney. You are so safe and so very good enough! In fact, your light shines so brightly! You are a gift to this world, you know."

An infectious smile came over her face and she dried away the tears. "Will you promise to love me more?"

"Yes, I promise!"

I gave her another big hug, feeling so much love for this precious, younger version of myself.

Just then, Christine's voice instructed me to imagine that my spirit could temporarily leave my body and inhabit my mom's. She encouraged me to think my mom's thoughts, see through her eyes, and even feel what it was like to be in her body. I did so, and immediately, all the muscles in my body tightened and twisted in anguish. I felt like a pressure cooker just waiting to burst.

"What's happening? Are you okay?" Christine asked.

"Yes, I'm okay. But I just remembered that my mom has fibromyalgia. No wonder she was crabby. It's painful in her body!"

Christine made a small noise in sympathy.

I continued: "I get it now. I'm looking through my mom's eyes at my sisters and Dad, who just walked into the kitchen. Intuitively, I can hear my mom's thoughts. She just found out that my dad was having an affair. She didn't feel good enough for him. And, she was terrified that they might get a divorce, because she had no way to support my sisters and me without a job or degree. She was petrified." I took a few deep breaths and continued, "I had no idea. My parents kept that from my sisters and me."

"So your mom was frightened and hurt," Christine clarified. "Is that why she yelled at you?"

"Yes. She was like a pressure cooker—the lid just flew off and she snapped at me. She didn't meant to hurt my feelings. She wasn't mad at me. She was mad at my dad."

"Okay, Courtney. Through your mom's eyes, look at little Courtney on the other side of the counter. What do you see?"

I looked over at the image of my three-year-old self. I felt some of the tension in my mom's body melting away. I sensed the most intense, beautiful, motherly love for the little girl—intense, beautiful love for me! I already knew she loved me, but to actually *feel* the preciousness of that love and see it through her eyes melted my heart. Mom never meant to hurt my feelings. She cherished me! I started to cry again, but this time for a very different reason.

"Does Mom know that little Courtney is good enough?" Christine asked.

"Oh yes. She loves me so much! In fact, she admires me. She's even a little jealous of me."

"Why's that?"

"Because I'm such a happy baby, and people love me. Mom is crabby, and oh my gosh, I just remembered! When I was little, some of my dad's friends nicknamed her 'the bitch.' My mom was really sensitive too. That must have really hurt her feelings." I suddenly felt so much compassion for my mom. Seeing her in her humanness, with insecurities, fears and hurt feelings opened the pathway of forgiveness within me. I could feel the burden of resentment lifting off my shoulders. I could hardly believe the realizations taking place.

"Okay Courtney, once you feel complete, thank your mom for sharing her perspective, and go back into your own body."

I imagined doing so and felt incredibly relieved to go back into the comfort of my own body.

"How do you feel?"

"Good enough!" I proclaimed with a smile. The sensation of "good enough" was spreading warmth and peace through my whole body.

"Courtney, now that you feel good enough, how will this affect your current life?"

"When other people are in bad moods—especially my mom—I can remember that what they're feeling is about them, not me. I don't have to 'save' anyone from a bad mood in order to make myself more comfortable. I'm responsible for me and my moods, not anyone else's."

"That's great! What else?"

"Since I'm good enough, I guess I can stop punishing myself. I can be nicer to myself now."

Christine wrapped up the session and invited me to open my eyes.

"Wow, thank you so much!" I blinked as my eyes adjusted to the light.

Across the room in the observer's chair sat Julie, with tears streaming down her cheeks. I was so engaged in my process, I had forgotten she was there. Tears welled in my eyes again at this realization. My best friend had been right there for me during the most important healing session I had ever experienced. I felt supported, loved, and ready to celebrate.

Note: Courtney would love for you to experience the freedom, healing and empowerment that a 'good enough' session can bring. Check out her services, including hypnotherapy, guided meditation, coaching and more at:
www.authenticandfree.com/services

Chapter 40

Mirror Reflections

"People act out of a need for healing...Forgiveness will provide relief and release. Love will heal anything that is not an expression of love."
–Iyanla Vanzant[xxxvi]

January 23, 2012

"Wow, I wasn't even there and I feel like celebrating!" Sarah said, bouncing in her chair.

"Ha, me too!" Courtney laughed.

"This was a huge turning point for you, wasn't it?"

"Absolutely!"

"You've done some deep healing work, Courtney, even though it was uncomfortable." Sarah looked down at her hands thoughtfully. "But I guess it's okay to feel uncomfortable sometimes, right? If it means we are growing, then that's a good thing." Sarah shifted back in her seat.

"Yeah, recovery wasn't a straight, pretty line like it is in movies; it was filled with ups and downs. It still is, actually. But I think that's life, don't you think?"

Sarah nodded.

"Sometimes I took three steps forward, then two steps back. I got so disheartened sometimes, but Amy would remind me that's the way recovery works. Then I'd get up and take another two steps forward. It was challenging, but more than worth it."

"The 'good enough' session definitely sounded worth it!" Sarah took a sip of her coffee.

"Yes! It was what my soul had been longing for. I finally got it at a deep level—there was nothing wrong with me!"

"So you had your butterfly wings now, right?" Sarah grinned.

"Oh yeah, baby! Finally, I had burst free from the cocoon. I was flying around like a butterfly—or maybe like a fairy." Courtney winked at Sarah.

"I bet your wings were beautiful!"

"Rainbow-colored, of course."

The two women laughed.

"So what did you notice after the 'good enough' session? What changed?"

Courtney paused, then stared down at the table as she recalled. "I felt so different. It was like years of shame had melted away and I was finally comfortable in my own skin."

"Wow, that's awesome!"

"Yeah, it was *huge*! I noticed myself standing up taller and speaking up more. It was as though I broke a vow of silence I never wanted to take and I was finally speaking my truth!" Courtney smiled. "I can hardly believe some of the things that happened after."

"Oooh, like what? Did your inner bully really go away?"

"Well, not completely, but now I set boundaries with her. As my authentic voice got louder, hers got quieter. I mean, I still have self-doubts and body image issues here and there. But I don't let them run my life anymore. I'm the one making the decisions now."

"So cool. Do you think everyone has an inner bully?" Sarah tilted her head to the side.

Courtney looked sideways in contemplation. "Yes, but I bet the loudness varies."

"I bet so too. So what do you do when a self-doubt shows up?"

"Well, I take it less seriously now, because I know deep down that I'm good enough. It's like I can feel my own light now. And I've realized that self-doubts show up louder when I'm afraid. If I notice myself criticizing my stomach, I say 'Wait a minute. What's really going on?' I basically ask myself what I'm afraid of and reassure myself that I'm safe."

"Huh, interesting. Don't you think that's when most bullies lash out? When they feel insecure or afraid?"

"Yeah, exactly! They're kind of like snakes. They only bite when they feel threatened or backed into a corner."

"Kind of like your mom," Sarah pointed out. "She used to yell when she was really stressed or afraid. Not because there was something wrong with you."

"Oh my gosh, Sarah, yes! It felt so comforting to realize that! I think her anger masked all her pain and self-doubt. She just needed relief." Courtney's voice trailed off as she glanced out the window. "Probably from all the trauma she went through as a child."

Sarah raised her eyebrows.

"Well, her dad died of a stroke when she was only nine, and her mom went into a deep depression—slept all the time. Which meant my mom had to grow up really fast and take care of her two little sisters. I don't think she ever had a chance to acknowledge her pain from all of this, or express it in healthy ways. She didn't have emotional support or feel safe looking within, so instead, the pain became anger, which she directed at other people."

"I think a lot of bullies do that, Courtney. They're hurt, angry, or scared, and they think they'll feel better by blaming or hurting others. But they're actually hurting themselves, like a boomerang effect."

"A boomerang. What a good image." Courtney traced her fingers in a loop across the table's surface, mimicking a boomerang's trajectory. "I've realized that when I judge someone else, it's because on a deeper level, I'm judging myself in the same way. It's like the world is a mirror, and everyone is our reflection."

"That's interesting!"

"Isn't it? So there's no need to judge anyone… including ourselves. We're always doing the best we can in any given moment."

"I agree. Just like your mom. When I met her that one time, I could tell that she has a beautiful, caring soul. And that she has an inner light, just like everyone else. I hope she sees it one day!"

Courtney smiled. "I agree, Sarah. She *is* a beautiful person inside and out. I hope she sees that too."

"Okay, so we know that people sometimes act out of fear, insecurity, or envy instead of love, right?"

Courtney nodded.

"But how do we interact with them? I know they might not feel loved, since hurt people tend to hurt others. But is it really my job to help them feel loved? What if it's toxic for me to be around their negativity?"

"Oh Sarah, I couldn't agree more. Sometimes we just have to remove ourselves from negativity, even if it's coming from someone we love. We have to set healthy boundaries, you know? We owe it to ourselves and to the other person. I have no tolerance anymore for abusive or mean comments. Even if that means ending a relationship with a friend or family member."

"Yeah, aren't we supposed to be connecting with our soul family, anyway?" Sarah's dimples appeared as she smiled.

"Good point again!" Courtney nodded.

"Okay, so speaking of people who can be negative, did things get better with your mom after all this?"

"Yes, definitely. We still have ups and downs, and some moments are still tough. But I handle it much better now. Sometimes my inner child gets afraid or goes back to thinking I still need to please her. But in those moments, I remind myself that I have my own power now."

"And how does your power show up?"

"Well, if she says something that hurts my feelings, I tell her. And I don't spend time with her out of obligation. If she asks me to get together, and I don't have time or don't *feel* like it, I say 'no thank you.' To me, that's speaking my truth and being authentic—even if she doesn't like it."

"Wow, that's totally different from the past when you felt responsible for her feelings. You're okay if she's mad at you?"

"Well, it's not pleasant, but yes, I'm okay."

"It's also totally different from when you thought you needed to have the same opinions as her!"

"Exactly! Now I realize that she can have her opinions, and I can have my own. Sometimes I tell her 'Mom, let's just agree to disagree.' She is her, and I am me. Feeling good enough within myself has been amazing. I don't need her approval anymore. I just need mine."

"That is so cool. I know she was supportive of your sexual orientation ever since you came out, but does she *understand* it better now?"

"Ha, yes, definitely. I know bisexuality is a new concept for a lot of people, especially when they're used to boxes like 'gay' or 'straight' and 'black' or 'white.' So, I don't expect everyone to understand it right away. But I do expect them to respect it."

"Oooh, I like that. And it sounds like your mom did respect that part of you all along."

Courtney smiled. "Yes. And she supports equal rights for all LGBTQ people. I'm really grateful that she's open-minded—and that she's become more relaxed over the years. She lets herself eat when she feels like it now too, not at certain times. It just feels good not to be afraid of her anymore. After the hypnotherapy session, it felt like she went from being a scary monster to a scared, furry little puppy!"

Sarah laughed. "You never knew that your mom was scared?"

"No, not at all! She pretended to be so strong. She never let us see her vulnerability, like to ask for help or say 'I'm afraid.'"

Sarah snapped her fingers, as if something had suddenly occurred to her. "You know, people probably kept their distance because they thought she had it all together."

Courtney paused and reflected on that for a moment. "Yes, that's probably true. I want to be more transparent than that. I'm no longer under the delusion that I have to be strong every moment. It's okay to need help. It's okay to cry or even freak out. It's just kinda part of being human."

"Speaking of being transparent… what happened to that idea of working with LGBTQ clients?"

Courtney blushed.

"What, Courtney, were you too scared?" Sarah's tone was both teasing and serious.

"For a while, yes. I was picking and choosing who to tell about my sexual orientation."

"Why?"

"Well, I was afraid of rejection and hate messages."

"It's sad that we have to even think about that. But really, if you accept yourself, why does it matter what anyone says?"

Courtney smiled. "You're amazing, Sarah."

This time, Sarah blushed.

"Well, I just wanted to be me wherever I went. And finally, I realized that being afraid wasn't going to help me or anyone else. I confronted my fears and did what I needed to do… which was show up to help LGBTQ youth and adults."

"How did it go at first?"

"Great! I went to all these LGBTQ networking events, and I felt welcomed with open arms. And so comfortable, because I could be myself. Then I started speaking at LGBTQ events and the local LGBTQ community center. It was amazing."

"I'm so proud of you for showing up." Sarah beamed. "That must've been hard after so many years of hiding."

"Thanks, Sarah. It was so difficult at first, but after I started, I felt different and just… incredible. Now that I had those butterfly wings, I had to put them to good use!" Courtney then flashed a playful smile. "I don't discriminate though."

Sarah raised her eyebrows.

"I work with straight clients too," Courtney laughed. "Seriously, I just want everyone to learn how to accept themselves, regardless of their sexual orientation, gender identity, size or shape. We all deserve self-acceptance, you know?"

Sarah nodded. "So what happened next?"

"Are you sure you want to hear? I want to get to how *you're* doing at some point here."

Sarah rolled her eyes. "Courtney, don't leave me hanging now!" she whined playfully.

Chapter 41

No More Hiding

"You gain strength, courage and confidence by every experience in which you really stop to look fear in the face. You must do the thing you think you cannot do." —Eleanor Roosevelt

Summer 2010

"What are you doing today?" Julie bubbled on the other end of the phone.

"Oh, just showing up and standing in my power, that's all!"

I laughed, and Julie joined me.

"Okay, Court, do tell."

"Well, remember the insight I got at the forgiveness ceremony?"

"About your own light?"

"Yes! It was about *seeing* my own light. Last night during my walk, I realized I also need to *show* my light to others."

"Well, I see your light easily, friend."

"I know you do, Jules. I think you have from the moment we met. Thank you so much for helping me feel safe enough to open up."

"Court, it's an honor to see and know you. You're beautiful inside and out, you know!"

I blushed. Although she was on the other end of town, I felt the intensity of her love as though she was sitting next to me, holding my hand and giving me a big, celebratory hug. "I just want to show up as the real, raw, authentic me no matter who I'm with," I told her.

"Even your mom?"

"Yeah, how'd you guess? I'm on my way to her house right now to confront her."

"*What?* Are you serious?"

"Remember how I told you I gave her my power when I was a teenager? Well, today's the day I claim it back."

"Wow. Okay. What are you going to say?"

"Oh, something like, 'I'll take that back now, thank you very much. I'm ready for it now.'" I giggled, then continued: "I'm not exactly sure, but I need to stand up for myself. I want her to know that she hurt my feelings, and she can't intimidate me anymore."

Julie sighed. "I support you, friend. But remember that she might not have the reaction you're hoping for."

This time, I sighed. *I know Jules is trying to protect me, but does she have to burst my bubble?* "Oh Jules, of course she won't. And I'm okay with that. I need to do this for me!"

"I understand. Just remember one more thing, Court. No matter what we say or do, our mothers are going to drive us crazy."

"Yeah." I rolled my eyes. "Why do they do that, anyway?"

"Silly, it's in their job description!"

She laughed.

I laughed too. "Oh, finally, that explains it!" I said wryly.

◎

As I parked my car in Mom's driveway, I recalled a similar day three years prior, when I came to confess my love for Kasey. Today, I felt stronger than ever. I now knew who I was. I was ready to shine my light and stand in my power. Doing so with Mom was the key to doing so with everyone. If I could assert my power with the one who scared and intimidated me the most, I could assert my power in any situation!

However, despite my newfound strength, this was by far the scariest moment of my life! Far scarier than when I came out or broke up with James and Nathan. My heart beat so quickly it seemed to buoy me up, like a bumblebee's flittering wings support its weight. My hands were shaking too.

Before entering the house, I closed my eyes and imagined a cocoon of beautiful, protective light around me. I attempted to take a deep breath, though the breath sunk no deeper than my lungs. *Who has time to breathe? I have a major boundary to set! Okay, Spirit, I ask for your help. Please surround this interaction with light, love, and peace. Whatever happens, let it be for the highest good!*

Despite my fear and knowing all the ways this interaction could potentially go wrong, I trusted my gut. It had guided me to this moment and directly into this conversation. I entered Mom's house, greeted her with a hug, and sat down on the living room couch. She had just poured herself a glass of iced tea and offered me some, but I politely declined.

"Mom, there's something I want to talk to you about," I said as she sat in the recliner next to me.

"Okay," she said hesitantly. "Is that why you wanted to come over? You hardly ever spend time with me anymore."

I attempted not to roll my eyes. *The guilt trips have really gotten old... no, actually, ancient.*

"Mom, you know I've been in therapy the last few years, and something has been bothering me lately."

"Great," she said sarcastically. "Are you going to tell me what a terrible mother I was? They always blame the mother for eating disorders."

I gave her a look of confusion. *Why is she so defensive? I haven't even said anything yet.* I prepared myself to dodge as many bullets as necessary. "Mom, I've never heard that. My eating disorder wasn't all your fault. I don't blame you for it. But you know, your rules did play a role in it."

"What do you mean, Courtney? You're always complaining about the rules I set for you. They weren't that bad. Ask your sisters... theirs were way worse."

In the past, a statement like this would have sent me into a tizzy, causing me to question myself. Today, I felt angry at her dismissal of my experience. I had feelings, damnit. But even though her defensiveness prevented her from validating my feelings, at least I could now validate myself.

"Mom, I know you loosened up over time, and I appreciated that. I know that you were just trying to protect me. I'm thankful for that."

"You're right, and I wouldn't have changed a thing! I'm proud of the way I raised you girls. You turned out to be successful, caring people!"

"Mom, this is really hard for me, so let me just get it out, okay? I'm glad I had rules. They provided structure. But sometimes they were so rigid. I know you were really stressed, but sometimes you were mean when you enforced them."

"Courtney, I was not mean!" She looked disgusted.

"Mom, please let me finish!"

She rolled her eyes, but let me. I was unsurprised by her reaction so far, but I was determined to be strong even though I was nervous. Being "seen" was the scariest thing in the world for me. I had hidden my true feelings from Mom my entire life. Now here I was, exposing them and putting myself in the line of fire.

"Maybe you don't remember, Mom, but a few times you called me mean names. You threatened to make my life a living hell. Maybe it wasn't a big deal to you, but it was to me. It hurt my feelings. That's all I want you to know… that my feelings were hurt. It wasn't okay with me."

I took a deep breath as I saw her facial expression softening. What she said next nearly caused me to pass out from shock.

"Courtney, I don't remember that, but I'm sorry. I'm sorry for anything I did to ever hurt you."

I paused in silence, breathing in her apology with love. *Did she really just say that?*

I smiled at her warmly. "Mom, thank you! That means a lot to me. I just want to be done with this and move on." I then hesitated. There was one more thing I needed to share with her, one more thing to get off my chest before I could be at peace. "Mom, I used to get so upset that I cut myself."

I braced myself for her reaction. I hoped for sympathy and understanding. I should have known better. Instead, I received a look of disapproval and disgust, as though she thought something was horribly wrong with me.

"I know."

"What do you mean 'you know'?" I asked defensively. "I never told anyone. No one knew. There's no way you could have known."

She stared at me with a blank look on her face, refusing to share how 'she knew.' I felt hurt, disgusted, and devastated. *Doesn't she care? Doesn't that upset her? I cut myself. I hurt myself! Doesn't she get how much that hurt my soul? How much it still hurts?* I wanted to scream in frustration. Instead, I chose to maintain peace. I had certainly made progress today, so I chose to cut my losses and get out while I could.

Not knowing what else to say, we both turned to the TV, which had been playing quietly in the background. Thankfully, *The Ellen DeGeneres Show* helped to lighten the mood. But soon enough, I could no longer tolerate the lingering tension. I could tell Mom was not happy about our conversation, and frankly, neither was I, so I gathered my purse to leave. We hugged, kissed, and out the door I went.

As I pulled out of the driveway, tears of relief and pain poured down my face. *I did it! I spoke my truth! I'm so proud of you, Courtney.*

Despite the ups and downs of the conversation, energetically speaking, I had put my foot down. Indeed, in that moment, I claimed my power back. Although my words were few, they spoke loud and clear: *Mom, I'm empowered now. You are no longer the boss of me. I am!*

I called Julie to share the excitement.

"Hi, Court! How did it go?"

"Oh my gosh, I did it! I feel amazing!"

"Yay you! I'm so proud of you!"

I smiled, and so did my heart. "Thanks, friend. I mean, of course I was a little disappointed by her reaction. But she apologized, which felt incredible. And wow, I was honest! I stood up for myself!" I beamed with pride and self-respect.

"Court, do you think that today you became stronger? Or do you think that you simply *realized* your own inner strength and allowed it to come forth?"

"Oooh, good point!"

"Well, either way, friend, you called on your powerful queen energy, and she stood up for your hurt, angry teenager self."

"Yes, and maybe my teenager self can let go of all her bitterness now. I think she just needed to have her feelings validated."

"Validated by your mom?"

"No, actually. I had thought so, but that doesn't matter. *I'm* the one who needed to validate how my teenage self felt. I'm the one who needed to listen to her concerns."

"Yeah, Court, and maybe she needed to see that you are willing to stand up for her!"

Relief and excitement flooded me. "Jules, it feels like wearing a new pair of glasses. But instead of being able to see the world better, it's like I can now see that I'm good enough, that I deserve to be treated with respect. And you know what?"

"What, friend?"

"I won't tolerate anything less than respect from others... whether it's my mom or anyone else."

"Or yourself. Don't forget you're not excluded from this list."

"Wow, yeah. I have everything I need inside me. I don't need anyone else's acceptance or validation. I mean, that would be nice. But what I need the most is love and respect for myself." I smiled. "You know what? I feel A-M-A-Z-I-N-G! Stronger than ever! I think I can trust myself now... and take better care of myself."

"Yes, please be nice to my friend, okay?"

"It's a deal!"

I headed home, grinning and excited to share the news with Kasey.

Chapter 42

Bisexual Beauty

"Be confident in yourself, you are the only one who knows your own true sexuality. Others will try to tell you differently, but don't listen to them, be proud of what you know you are and don't shy away from it."
—Jarrett, age 18[xxxvii]

Not surprisingly, Kasey celebrated my news about gently confronting my mom. The following morning, she and I went out to run an errand.

"That was a huge conversation with your mom yesterday. Are you feeling all right today, Court?" she asked me as she pulled our car into the shopping plaza.

"Hmm." I scanned my body and noticed a subtle sensation of strength I had never felt before. "Empowered. Strong. Proud of myself."

"That's great!"

I glanced around. "Thanks. Wow, it's crowded here today."

"Well it is Saturday, you know," Kasey said as she pulled into a parking spot far from the entrance. As we got out of the car and headed for the entrance of the bulk foods store, I reached for Kasey's hand, which she accepted warmly. After holding hands for a moment, she let go.

The cumulative effect of this pattern had begun eating away at me. I could not help but feel rejected. A twinge of anger filled my voice as I spoke. "Kasey, I had no idea that being out would be such a pain sometimes."

"What do you mean?"

"Well, why won't you hold my hand in public? Is it because we're gay?"

"Don't be ridiculous. I do hold your hand."

"Yeah, maybe for five seconds. Sorry Kasey, but I'm affectionate. I want to hold your hand." I felt angry tears welling in my eyes, but pride held them in.

"Maybe we can try for ten seconds."

I shot her a dirty look. This was not funny. "No, seriously, Kasey, why?"

"I don't know. I guess I don't want anyone looking at us."

"Like you don't want to make them uncomfortable?"

"Yeah, I guess."

That's ridiculous, I thought. Instead, I said, "Kasey, what if uncomfortable is exactly what they need to feel?"

As we entered the bulk foods store, she frowned. "What do you mean, Courtney?"

"Well, there's a ton of us LGBTQ people in the world, and if we don't start holding hands and showing up, how will people realize how many of us exist? How will they realize that we're just 'normal' people who deserve to be loved just like anyone else?"

"I guess that's a good point."

"If we felt unsafe, that'd be a different story," I explained. "But that's not the case. Kasey, it's not fair. I love you. I want to be able to touch you, just like straight couples can touch each other anytime and anywhere they want."

I was burning with anger, but I had made my point, so I dropped the subject as we focused on shopping. As we tossed walnuts, raspberries, and paper towels into the cart, I wondered if Kasey understood. Apparently not, I decided, because she was still not holding my hand.

After we checked out and unloaded our new purchases into the car, I decided to lighten the mood. "So I'm reading this book called *Sexual Fluidity*.[xxxviii] Ever hear of it?"

"No, what's it about?" Kasey's tone was cautious, as if she was still on edge.

"Well, it's all about sexual orientation. The author, Lisa Diamond, interviewed almost 100 women about their sexual orientation over the course of ten years. Tons of them were surprised at how fluid their attractions were. Some of the lesbians found themselves occasionally attracted to a man, and some of the straight women found themselves hooking up with a girl from time to time. Isn't that interesting?"

"Cool." But Kasey's tone was flat and unenthusiastic as she started the car.

After we drove in silence for a minute, I tried to lighten the atmosphere by sharing more. "Also, most people she interviewed said they are attracted to a person's soul, not their gender. It's really helping me embrace my bisexuality."

"But Courtney, why does it really matter that you're bisexual, since you're in a relationship with me now? You're not planning on leaving me to be with a man, are you?"

Oops, wrong thing to say.

"Oh, Kasey, you don't have to worry about that," I soothed. "But you've known from the very beginning that I'm bisexual. I just don't talk about it much."

"Why, because you want to please me?"

My stomach dropped to the floor with discomfort. "Yeah, I guess so," I responded timidly.

"Well, now that you've done all this healing work, I guess you're done pleasing me, huh?" Kasey snapped.

I rolled my eyes.

"Courtney, I still don't understand why it matters."

"It matters because I want to be honest about who I am, Kasey. I am attracted to all genders, not just to women like you are," I said as evenly as I could.

Kasey sighed audibly as she pulled the car into the driveway, she changed the subject. "Anyway, thanks for agreeing to have dinner with my friends Barb and Marilyn tonight. I haven't seen them in forever, and I've wanted them to meet you." She was trying to sound chipper, but the attempt didn't feel sincere to me.

"Sure, no problem, Kasey. I'm looking forward to it." I opened the door and gratefully breathed in the fresh, open air. Hopping out of the car, I shook the negativity off my body. After such an awkward start to our day, I wondered what the evening would bring.

"We're so happy to meet you, Courtney!" Barb enthused that evening.

We had arrived at Barb and Marilyn's house and warmly exchanged hugs. After a few minutes of chitchatting, they offered Kasey and me wine. Kasey accepted, but I shook my head. I had learned to have fun without alcohol. Plus, I no longer liked the way it made me feel, especially the next day. The ladies poured three glasses of wine and led the way to the back patio, where we sat down to chat.

"Courtney, tell us more about what you do," Marilyn asked.

"I have my own business," I explained. "I empower people to be their authentic selves… especially self-acceptance and self-love for LGBTQ people. I do life coaching, hypnotherapy and a few other modalities."

"She's teaching now too," Kasey chimed in.

"Teaching where?" Barb asked.

"At SWIHA," I responded.

"Oh, how lovely," Marilyn said.

I suddenly felt uncomfortable, as though our friends were evaluating me. I decided to change the focus to them. "What do you both do?"

"I own a gardening business," Barb answered.

"And I teach third graders," Marilyn said.

I smiled. "Oh, that's great!"

"Ever hear from your ex-husband?" Kasey asked Marilyn.

"Ugh, no, and thank goodness. I don't know how I was married to him. I'd never be with a man again."

"Yeah, me either," Kasey said. "Actually, though, we can't bash men completely… Courtney's bisexual."

"Oh?" Barb said.

"Yeah," I said with a half smile. Inside though, I was annoyed. *Why did Kasey have to bring it up? It was already a sore subject.*

"Well, why are you bisexual if you're with Kasey now?" Barb asked.

Oh my god. Seriously? Attempting to remain patient and understanding, and well-aware of Kasey's discomfort around this subject, I quickly conjured up my response. "Just because I'm with Kasey doesn't mean my sexual orientation changed. But I do plan to be with Kasey for the rest of my life."

"I was bisexual for about ten years," Marilyn said before taking another sip of wine. "Then I realized I just wanted to be with Barb for the rest of my life."

My blood was boiling now. *Is she trying to put me down? Did she not hear me? How much wine has she had? Being bisexual is not a phase. Maybe it was for her, but it certainly isn't for me.*

"How do you feel about her being bisexual?" Marilyn asked Kasey.

"Well, I don't really like it," she answered, avoiding my glance.

"It's part of who I am, Kasey," I snapped.

"Maybe we should talk about something else." Barb offered, and quickly changed subject to their latest vacation plans.

I wasn't listening, though. I was angry, and I felt deceived. *Why didn't Kasey tell me this earlier in our relationship?* I then thought back over the last several years. *I guess she really did seem paranoid whenever a guy looked at me. She made stupid, insecure comments. Why was I more concerned with pleasing her than being me? I shouldn't have to hide my bisexuality.*

My newfound strength meant seeing life through a new lens. Instead of just sitting down and not rocking the boat as I'd learned to do as a child, I was now thinking critically about what resonated with me and what did not. Tonight's interactions certainly did *not* resonate with me. I pretended to have a good time for the rest of the night, though Marilyn's comment kept spinning in my mind like a hamster wheel. I was still furious a few hours later when we said our goodbyes and left.

"I can't believe Marilyn said it like that," I said when we were on the road.

"Said what?" Kasey said.

"She *used* to be bisexual? It's not something that just goes away."

"Well, maybe for some people it does."

313

I raised my eyebrows doubtfully. "It felt like she was totally denying my experience. Like she was saying, 'Oh, that's just a phase. You'll get over it.'"

"Don't you think you're being a little too sensitive?"

I rolled my eyes and decided to be quiet for the rest of the ride home. Kasey had had plenty to drink, and it probably wasn't worth talking about right now anyway, I decided. *I'm glad I met them for Kasey's sake. But I don't want to hang out with them again,* I vowed.

After a few moments, Kasey attempted to strike up conversation again. "What did you think of my friends?"

My whole body remained frustrated and tense. I kept my answer brief. "They were nice."

"That's all you have to say?"

"Look, I'm tired, Kasey, okay? Let's just talk more tomorrow."

I had known that feeling "good enough" would bring changes to my life. But what kind of changes were on the horizon? Would our relationship still be "good enough" for me?

◎

The next morning, Kasey and I rolled out of bed and opened the blinds to let the bright Arizona sunshine into the house. Like every Sunday morning, I made the coffee and tea while she went outside to get the paper. I decided not to discuss what had happened last night. The pot had been stirred enough for one weekend.

After a brief phone conversation with Julie, I told Kasey my friend and I were going out for a hike that afternoon.

"What? You always spend Sundays with me." Her tone sounded sad and hurt.

"I know, but I need some friend time too."

"But it's the middle of the summer. Won't it be too hot?"

"We're going late enough in the day. I'll take plenty of water."

"Okay," she sighed reluctantly, tossing the paper down on the table.

Despite Kasey's unhappiness about the hike, I met Julie at a trailhead at the base of South Mountain, my favorite mountain range, later that day. After a hug, we began a leisurely hike in the oven of a Phoenix afternoon. As we ascended the first hill, sweat began pouring from my face.

"How was your evening with Kasey's friends?"

"Oh my god. It was rough, Jules. How about your evening?"

"Mine was good. But tell me more about yours."

As usual, her tone was upbeat and inquisitive. I explained last night's interactions. "Jules, I've called myself a lesbian many times over the past few years," I said at last. "I guess it just seemed easier. But that's not being true to who I am. I'm not a lesbian. I'm bisexual… or I guess I could call myself 'sexually fluid.'"

"Well, isn't that just a label, anyway?"

"Yeah, that's true. Labels can be so limiting. I just know that reading this *Sexual Fluidity* book is helping me feel more 'normal.'"

"I didn't know you wanted to be 'normal,'" Julie teased. "Wouldn't that be kinda boring?"

We laughed and then hiked along in silence for a few minutes, feeling the sweltering sun beating down on our skin.

"I can't help it of others don't understand me, but at least I'm starting to understand myself."

"I can't say I relate, since my sexual orientation is pretty self-explanatory."

"I love you, straight friend."

We both laughed.

"It bothers me that so many people don't understand bisexuality. Why, Jules? Why don't they get it?"

"Maybe because it doesn't fit into a nice pretty box. It's not black or white."

"Sexual orientation is not black or white at all, though. Sure, for some people, it is gay or straight… simple, clear-cut. But most people are somewhere along the spectrum."

"Spectrum… you mean like a range?"

"Yeah, exactly. It's called the Kinsey Scale,[xxxix] and it's like a line. On one end is attraction to opposite sex only. On the other end is attraction to same-sex only. I fall right in the middle, attracted to both sexes equally."

"And you said a lot of people fall somewhere along the middle of the line?"

"Yeah, a lot more than we realize. A lot of people won't let themselves go there, because of fear or society's judgments. Or they don't want to face discrimination."

"Well, if you ask me, love is love. Doesn't attraction have many layers, anyway? From my experience, it's not just physical. It's also mental, emotional, and spiritual."

"Yes! When I first met Kasey, we connected on the emotional and spiritual levels. The physical came after."

"Then you look at the fact that everyone has masculine and feminine energy within them. Oh, it's so interesting, Court."

"Isn't it beautiful, actually? I just wish Kasey didn't feel threatened by me being bisexual." I sighed.

"Exactly. Isn't bisexuality the *potential* to be attracted to any gender? It doesn't mean you're attracted to everyone and sleeping with them all."

We laughed.

"Right. And it doesn't mean I need an open relationship with more than one partner either. I know that some bisexual people go that route. I think that's great, as long as everyone's honest, upfront and on the same page about it."

"Hey, it's not just the bisexuals. Tons of gay *and* straight people have healthy open relationships too."

I took a deep breath. "I also know a lot of bisexual people like me who are content in monogamous relationships. I mean, if something were to happen with Kasey and me, who knows what I'd want in the future. Right now, though, I just want to be with her."

"Court, I know you like to see the positive side of things, but remember that things haven't been exactly hunky dory between the two of you lately."

"That's true." I sighed again. "The more empowered I am, it's like she doesn't know what to do."

"Yeah, the rules are changing as you get to know you!"

"The biggest problem is that she wants me home all the time. She hates it when I teach at night or on weekends. But I know that part of my life purpose is to teach, which means being gone some nights and weekends. I love being out and about teaching and interacting with people."

"Well no wonder! You've just gotten your wings! Butterflies like to fly all around, you know, exploring, visiting different-colored flowers."

She smiled at me, and I felt a sense of hope as I visualized delightful butterflies flying all around, being their authentic selves. "Yeah! A few years ago, I was content hanging out with Kasey in our little love nest. I was in such a period of healing, and I liked that it was just the two of us. But now my needs are changing."

Julie nodded and patted me on the shoulder. "Just remember to honor those needs. And keep being Courtney, no matter what!"

Chapter 43

Out and Proud

"Authenticity is a collection of choices that we have to make every day. It's about the choice to show up and be real. The choice to be honest. The choice to let our true selves be seen."
— Brené Brown[xl]

October 2010

Life was telling me that I needed to be more authentic and more transparent about who I was, and this included my bisexuality. And while I'd done a lot of healing, the thought still scared me. I often wondered if I'd be able to answer the call.

A few months after the dinner with Barb and Marilyn, I felt thrilled to receive a phone call from Brandi, the president of Phoenix Pride. I was hoping my business could host a vendor table at OUTdayPHX, a large celebration of National Coming Out Day in the city. Brandi not only said yes to my request, she asked me to be the presenting sponsor! This meant I would be the opening speaker, setting the stage for numerous community members to tell their coming out stories, including two celebrities—comedian Ant and actor Heather Matarazzo. Before our phone call, I was feeling ready to show up and assume my leadership role in the LGBTQ community… and now, here was my opportunity!

Prior to the event, I felt both excited and nervous. I gently reminded my ego that this was not about me; it was about being of service and empowering others. If my story could help someone, then I had an obligation to share it.

I had been distraught by stories of several suicides among LGBTQ youth that had hit the news that autumn. I was sick to my stomach with grief, especially once I realized these suicides were not isolated events—they happen every day whether or not someone reports on them. I realized I had even more of an obligation to share my story, and I felt honored, though nervous, to do so.

On the morning of the event, I was floating with excitement... even though I had hardly slept the night before. It felt like my feet were not even touching the ground! I was grateful to Brandi and Phoenix Pride for this opportunity, and so grateful to Kasey for helping me prepare the supplies for my vendor table. We arrived safely at the event, set up the table, and watched as hundreds and hundreds of people took their seats.

I can hardly believe this, I thought. Suddenly, I flashed back to my high school graduation speech. *That was the first time I ever spoke in front of hundreds of people. But then I was hiding. I was in total denial of my sexual orientation—total denial of my emotions, pain, struggle, and my power. I can't wait to feel the difference. Today as I take the podium, I will be honest about who I am and what I've been through. Today I show up as me... the real, authentic Courtney Long.*

As the event began, Micheal, a much-loved leader in the local LGBTQ community, took the stage. He was the Deputy Director of 'one n ten', the local organization that serves and empowers LGBTQ youth. In his lighthearted, jovial style, Micheal welcomed everyone to the event, then began reading my biography in preparation for me to take the stage.

Suddenly, a wave of calm washed away the nervousness in my body. I noticed myself standing up taller. *Okay, Universe, here goes*, I thought. *Thank you for this beautiful opportunity! Please help me to touch their hearts and souls.*

On cue with the applause, I walked to the podium and took my place. Looking out at the crowd, I saw hundreds of smiling, eager faces. Some were people I already knew and loved. Some were new to me. However, I felt a sense of comfort, as though I was among family. In fact, I was among family—my soul family.

"Did you know that you're *courageous*?" I said assertively. "Did you know that you're beautiful, lovable, whole and complete... just as you are?"

I paused, allowing the audience to breathe in the truth of these words.

"We are here today to honor and celebrate everyone who has had the courage and strength to come out. I congratulate you. I also want to thank each person who has surrounded them with love, support, and acceptance."

I waited as the audience warmly applauded in gratitude for their courage and their supporters.

"I realized at age fifteen that I was bisexual and very attracted to women. But it wasn't until about four years ago, at age twenty-six, that I had the courage—and a reason—to come out when I feel deeply in love with my beautiful partner Kasey."

I pointed to Kasey standing in the back of the room, and the audience looked her way as they applauded. I beamed with love as I continued. "I've found that in order to feel accepted by others, I first must accept myself. I must feel confident about who I am, not question myself or my sexual orientation… and not to hide it, just because others may feel uncomfortable with it. If they do, it is their issue, not mine. As a nurturing person who cares about others, that's not always easy. But it's the truth.

"I want to know, how do you feel deep within yourself about being lesbian, gay, bisexual, transgender, or queer? Do you see being LGBTQ as a blessing? A strength? A gift?

"It is! It's is a beautiful opportunity to love and embrace ourselves. In a society that does not always understand us, it is essential that we understand, love and embrace ourselves."

I heard the applause and saw audience members nodding as if they related.

"Being LGBTQ is sometimes a beautiful opportunity to open people's hearts and minds. To teach others about *love*. Our love sees beyond gender, beyond boxes and boundaries. Of course, we cannot control whether others allow their hearts to be opened. We cannot force other people to accept us. All we can control is how we feel about ourselves."

As I spoke my truth, my strength grew. I imagined a beautiful light all around me, uplifting and supporting me as I delivered this message of love. "We are all deeply saddened by the astonishing number of LGBTQ youth in pain, turmoil, even committing suicide. What is even sadder is that the self-doubt, fear, and suicides are not a rare occurrence. They are happening every day.

"As for the bullies, those who live in fear, ignorance, and intolerance... I want to ask them, 'What are you hiding from yourselves? What are you afraid of seeing within yourselves?' The world is a mirror. If we hate others, it's really because we hate something about ourselves. The bullies need to accept themselves. And stop projecting their own self-hatred onto LGBTQ youth."

The audience again applauded. My passion escalated as my voice now became louder, more powerful and even more inspired. "It is time we stop bullying others, and it is time we stop bullying ourselves. That is what we are doing every time we criticize ourselves or tell ourselves we are not good enough, not smart enough, not pretty or handsome enough. Every time we ask ourselves to be anyone other than who we truly are. All this criticism and self-doubt needs to stop. Just because others may judge us does not mean we have to judge and bully ourselves.

"For the youth, if for no one else, it is our *obligation* to feel good about ourselves. To be a message of hope. Let's show the youth and everyone else that being LGBTQ can be a blessing! That we are happy, healthy, and grateful for who we are. Each of us has beauty and strength within us. Are you willing to find yours and allow yourself to shine?

"We have this beautiful opportunity to shine our light and to be a beacon of love. Others might be inspired by us being who we are. It might give them permission to be who they are, whether that relates to their sexual orientation, their talents, gifts, spirituality, or any aspect of their life.

"Together, let's shine our lights and stand in our power. When one of us hurts, all of us hurt. And... when one of us shines, it gives other people permission to shine. When we all shine together, we are a sight to see!

"I challenge you... what is one way you can allow yourself to shine? Not just to "be out," yet to truly shine and feel confident? I dare you to accept, embrace, and express your authentic self. I dare you to be the shining light of inspiration that you truly are!"

As I finished, tears filled my eyes. Shockingly, a few escaped, trickling down my cheek. No more hiding! After years of concealing my feelings, in this moment, as I looked out at the crowd, I felt safe enough to show my vulnerability. Hundreds of people could see my tears. Much to my delight, I felt safer than I had ever felt. Standing in the energy of the words I had just spoken, I felt honored to be among such courageous, beautiful souls. In a momentous way, I had just shined my light and stood in my power.

After the applause ended, Micheal and I exchanged hugs. I effortlessly exited the stage and floated to the back of the room, landing directly into Kasey's loving, warm embrace.

The rest of the afternoon brought more tears as person after person shared the pains, triumphs, and surprising twists and turns of coming out. Some of the speakers had been disowned by family, some even by their own parents or children. Some had been homeless. I felt saddened, inspired, and in awe of the courage and beauty of the human spirit. Almost all spoke of the shame and self-hatred they had experienced until they learned to accept themselves. As the event came to a conclusion, I silently thanked Ashley. *I guess she was right, after all.* I smiled to myself. *I am right where I belong.*

Note: If you or your organization or group would benefit from an uplifting, empowering workshop or webinar with Courtney, check out the variety of topics available at: www.authenticandfree.com/events

Chapter 44

Self-Love

"To love yourself as you are is a miracle, and to seek yourself is to have found yourself, for now. And now is all we have, and love is who we are."
—Anne Lamott[xli]

January 23, 2012

Enthusiastically engaged in conversation, Sarah and Courtney had not even noticed the multitude of customers flowing in and out of the coffee shop. The late afternoon rush was just arriving, umbrellas in hand.

"How exciting, Courtney. Things were going so well for you!"

Courtney smiled as she caressed her teacup, which the barista had graciously refilled. "Can you believe it? All the pieces of my life's puzzle were falling into place–life purpose, spirituality, romance. At some point, I stopped needing the antidepressant!"

"No more depression?"

"Nope. I healed the root causes. I mean, I still have dark moments… but they're mostly just normal human emotions, like sadness or anger."

Sarah smiled. "So you're not afraid of feeling your emotions anymore?"

Courtney paused to reflect. "Sometimes, yes. Sometimes I'd still rather distract myself. But, then at other moments, I cry, scream, or feel whatever I need to feel."

"Sounds freeing… but not always fun."

"Good point! Recovery itself has not been easy or fun. But it's been worth it. Now that I know who I am, no matter how dark life seems at times, I know my light is always shining… even when I don't see it."

Sarah cocked her head. "Then how do you know it's shining?"

Courtney grinned, crossing her legs. "Because of my soul family. If I ever forget who I am or go into fear, they shine a light back on me and help me remember."

"That's beautiful! It's amazing you found people you connect with on such a deep level."

Courtney nodded enthusiastically. "I'm so grateful. They accept me, and the coolest part is that I accept myself. That has changed everything!"

"Do you think accepting yourself helped you recover from the eating disorder?"

"Oh my gosh, more than anything. Thank God Amy taught me how to. And Kasey's love helped. My soul family's love helped. But what I needed the most was to love myself."

Sarah tilted her head again. "But wait, isn't it kind of arrogant to love yourself?"

Courtney laughed as though she had been anticipating Sarah's question. "I hear that all the time. Nope. Arrogance is thinking you're better than others. I don't think I'm better than anyone. I think I'm beautiful inside and out, and so is everyone else! We're all one."

"Oh, I see! I like that." Sarah's smile grew even wider.

"Sarah, I think loving yourself is knowing yourself. Seeing your strengths and shadows… your light and darkness."

Sarah nodded. "Okay, I think I get it. It sounds like self-love is just giving yourself permission to be human. And that means permission not to be perfect too."

"Yes! And it also means knowing our spiritual essence—our light. I mean, when most people criticize themselves, they criticize their looks, body, or their personality, but those things don't define who we are. They are surface-level—like the rind of a watermelon."

"Yeah, and, I mean, even watermelons are all different shapes and sizes. Right? Each one has different dents or scars."

"Ooh, good point! And on the inside, watermelons are pretty much the same—juicy deliciousness. Just like our true essence—the energy of love that flows through everything—that's what we're made of!"

"That's funny… I never thought of myself as a watermelon!"

The two women giggled.

"Now I'm hungry! We should get some food! Maybe even watermelon." Courtney laughed even harder.

"It sounds like realizing that we're all energy has helped you to realize who you are on the inside, right? That you're not your body."

"Exactly. I also realized that loving myself is not just about me. It helps me love everyone else better. Now, I don't come from a place of emptiness or need, like 'I love you so that you'll love me and help me feel less incomplete.' Nope. Now, 'I love me and feel whole and complete within myself so that I *can* love you.' I see my beauty so I can see everyone else's too."

"You know, I think I'm starting to love myself. But I wonder if I could *really* love myself."

"Of course you can! You're worth loving, you know, Sarah. You're precious. We all are. That's the way we were made!"

Sarah crossed her arms as she absorbed the conversation.

"So Courtney, you love yourself all the time?"

"Deep down, yes. When I look at myself in the mirror, I feel love now, instead of hatred. But I still get mad at myself. Sometimes I still beat myself up for making a mistake. Then I quickly reassure myself that it's okay to make mistakes."

"I hope so. I make plenty of them!"

Sarah and Courtney laughed again.

"Sometimes I even laugh at myself and feel thankful, because making a mistake reminds me of how far I've come," Courtney continued. "I don't have to be perfect to be loved. I am lovable just as I am." She paused to take a long sip of tea. "Hey, want to hear a funny story?"

"Sure, I could use a good laugh."

"The other day, I treated myself to lunch at this outdoor restaurant. They happened to have live music that day. The musician was awesome. As I was leaving, I thanked him, and we chatted for a few minutes. Then I got in my car and noticed I had dark chocolate all over my tan pants."

"Oh no! Where did it come from?"

"I forgot about the piece of dark chocolate in my purse… it must have melted in the sun. There was chocolate everywhere!"

"So you were talking to the musician with chocolate all over you?" Sarah giggled.

"Yes! *And* when I glanced in the rear view mirror, I realized I had a huge glob of chocolate on my neck! I was a chocolaty mess. There's no way he didn't notice it."

"That's hilarious. So how did you react?"

"I laughed! I was a little embarrassed, but mostly it was entertaining."

"Hmm. You know, maybe you could market this self-acceptance by starting a new fashion trend."

"Chocolate makeup?" Courtney giggled as she glanced at the clock on the coffee shop wall. "I'd love to tell you more about self-love, but it's getting pretty late, so we may have to save that talk for later."

"It's a deal!" Sarah said. "I'm sure you have a lot more to share about it. Oh, and could we talk more about the blessings of being LGBTQ sometime? Also, I'd love to hear more about bisexuality… you know, from a spiritual perspective."

"Oh Sarah, like that isn't one my favorite topics! I feel a lot of us LGBTQ people are here as spiritual messengers. But I guess we'll have to save that for later."

"Okay, but before we go, what about Leah? Did she ever learn to love herself? Did she come out to your grandmother?"

Courtney looked outside as regret clouded her face. "Well, Leah actually passed away a few years ago."

Sarah's hand flew to her mouth. "Oh you're kidding. I'm so sorry."

"Yeah, it was really sad and unexpected. After that conversation about me coming out, I only saw her one more time. I definitely miss her."

Sarah patted Courtney's hand. "I'm so sorry. But I'm sure she watches over you and supports your work."

After a few moments of silence, Sarah conjured up a question. "I hate to ask about another sad thing now, but what happened with you and Kasey? You broke up last year, right? You seemed so in love."

Courtney gave a sad, audible sigh. "Yeah, we were. But as I recovered and connected with my power, certain dynamics in our relationship didn't work anymore."

"Like what?"

"Well, Kasey wanted a partner to nest with at home. I realized I'm kind of like a fairy, flying from place to place. I don't like to be cooped up in one place. I wanted to be out teaching and traveling."

"Oh, gotcha. That's rough."

"Yeah, it was devastating. I would have never expected it. We had been together for four and a half years. I was so scared, sad, and lost at first."

"I can imagine."

Sarah's empathy shined through her green eyes.

"Being authentic is not always the easy road. But I would rather take the risk to listen to be vulnerable and express my feelings than be stuck in a bunch of dysfunction, you know?"

Sarah nodded.

"It definitely means facing fears of rejection and abandonment. But, now I trust that I will never again reject or abandon myself. I'm here for myself now." Courtney leaned back, smiling with satisfaction. "With that said, it still hasn't been easy to say 'no' or end a relationship to be true to what I feel. I trust my inner wisdom to guide me down the path for my highest good. But still, the easier road *seems* to be to stay, do what's expected, and not rock the boat."

"So you got out of the Long family boat of silence, huh?" Sarah teased.

"Yes! I had fun dancing and skipping around the shore. Then I got in my own boat and decorated it and rocked it whenever I wanted to."

Sarah and Courtney both laughed.

"So, you're single now, right?"

"Yep. I dated this incredible guy briefly. We learned a lot from each other, but we went our separate ways."

"Why?"

"Well, he wanted to focus on self-love, and so did I."

Courtney shrugged as Sarah's eyes widened with awe. "Wow, talk about being authentic!"

"Amazing, huh? I'm so grateful to be single right now. It gives me space to hear my own opinions without anybody else's influence. It's weird that I don't always know my own opinions, you know? But after a lifetime of practically being invisible to myself, I'm still learning how to be authentic."

"Courtney, don't you think it's more of a journey than a destination?"

The corners of Courtney's lips turned upward into a grateful smile.

Chapter 45

Celebration of Wings

"Became aware of what your body can do each day. Remember it is the instrument of your life, not just an ornament."
—Margo Maine and National Eating Disorders Association[xlii]

June 2011

A month after Kasey and I broke up, I felt a strong desire to soak in some sunshine. I felt emotionally raw and sensed that nature would provide just the healing energy I needed. Therefore, one Sunday morning I headed to my favorite park to journal in the grass.

During my drive there, I reflected back to the days of my youth when being alone outside had felt like my only opportunity to fully be me. The trees, dandelions, and grass had been my escape and hideaway. Now, I still longed to be outside—only now, the outdoors gave me time to breathe, rejuvenate, and connect with my inner wisdom to make sure my actions are in alignment with my authentic self.

Upon arriving at the park, I found a tall, old pecan tree and sat down beneath its branches. With my back pressed against the sturdy trunk, I buried my feet in the lush, green grass. Pulling my journal onto my lap, I took a few deep breaths, and closed my eyes. My mind drifted back to the start of college. Just like my recent breakup with Kasey, the breakup with James had felt devastating. Yet, something positive arose from that devastation. Despite my current emotional pain, I trusted this time would be no different.

My friend's e-mail thirteen years prior echoed through my mind. *Courtney, you have just opened your wings, spread them, and are flying… Now that you are on your own, you need to get into your groove, figure out what you like, what you want, and exactly who Courtney Lynn Long is. What do you want? What will make YOU happy?*

How funny, I thought. *Here I am, in a similar situation. Only this time, I'm free from my inner bully and free to be me.* I smiled, overwhelmed with gratitude and love. For the first time in my life, I felt strong and solid, like the tree against which I rested. No longer could others' whims, opinions, or actions sweep me away. Before I realized it, I was relaxing deeper and deeper, drifting into a peaceful nap beneath the tree. I had set the intention for a day of healing, but I had no idea that would come through a lucid dream!

A gust of wind carried me away, gently delivering me to the top of a mountain. *That's a nice feeling*, I thought, noticing a light tingling in my shoulder blades. I looked from side to side, smiling as I admired the purples, blues, and oranges of my butterfly wings.

"C'mon, Courtney, let's go!"

I turned with curiosity in the direction of the voice. Nearby stood a young teenage girl with long wavy hair, bright blue eyes, and wearing baggy clothes. She smiled at me, then looked down at the set of colorful butterfly wings in her hands.

"Need help?" I offered.

"Yes, please!"

With gentleness, I took the wings from her hands and fastened them to her back.

"There you go, Teenage Courtney."

She smiled.

"Do you mind if I call you TC?"

"No problem! But Courtney, what if I don't know how to fly?"

Her sweetness melted my heart. "TC, all you have to do is close your eyes and imagine the beautiful light shining in your heart. Trust in it. It will lift you up to where you need to go!"

Together we closed our eyes. I saw the light in my heart burning like a candle flame. Soon enough, the breeze lifted us. As our wings flapped, our bodies soared through the clear, pale blue sky. TC and I breathed in the sweetness of the air as we floated around freely, lightly, without fear or restriction.

"This is better than the rules at home!" she exclaimed.

I smiled at her, in full understanding. *What a free, loving spirit she is. And now she gets to fly!* "TC, this is what I always dreamed of. Freedom, peace, and hope... just like the butterfly."

Suddenly, as we soared past a mountain peak, three sunshine-yellow butterflies fluttered around flirtatiously. I smiled at them, admiring their playfulness and light, free spirits.

"Courtney, what if the butterfly weren't a butterfly?"

"What do you mean, TC?"

"Well, the butterfly shares so much joy with the world, just by being itself. I feel uplifted just looking at them."

"Me too!"

"So what if the butterfly said, 'Oh, I'd better look like an alligator so I can fit in?'"

I smiled at her creativity. "No way! The butterfly would do a crappy job of trying to be an alligator. It'd be impossible, don't you think, TC?"

"Yeah. And what if the butterfly tried to hide its colors and flaws to be like all its butterfly friends?"

"Oooh, good point. I see where you're going! Each butterfly has its own unique colors and design. When each one shines, our world is colorful and beautiful. What does this all mean to you, sweetheart?"

"I guess it means it's okay to be me, even if I'm different from my friends." Her innocence shined through her blue eyes.

"Exactly! You are enough!" I proclaimed with glee, feeling the exhilarating rush of wind across my face and hair.

We continued soaring, now far beyond the mountains and directly into a garden, where we could rest. We looked around, breathing in the lush green grass, shimmering tulips, roses and daffodils, and admiring the large, iridescent water fountain at the center.

"Hey, Courtney, look! There's a caterpillar!" TC pointed to a green plant. On one leaf, the fuzzy, aqua-and-black caterpillar was eating away, gobbling down to its heart's content. "Why does the caterpillar eat so much?"

"I imagine so it can grow and keep up its strength before going into the cocoon. That huge transformation requires some serious energy!"

TC laughed, sensing my playfulness. "Hey, Courtney? I don't see caterpillars going around saying, 'I'm eating too much, I'm too fat' or 'I gotta cut back and go on a diet.'"

My delight at her comment rumbled deep in my belly and trickled out through my voice, turning into hysterical laughter. "Oh my gosh, you're right, TC!" I said when I found my voice again. "The caterpillar trusts its appetite. It does not worry about its weight, because it knows what it's here to do: grow, transform, and soar."

We rested on the lip of the water fountain now, allowing the cool water to splash on our faces.

"But Courtney, why can't I grow, transform and soar? I'm too ugly and fat." She looked down with shame.

"TC, come here. I want to show you something."

I motioned for her to stand on the ledge of the water fountain. Side by side we stood and looked down. Our bodies' reflections materializing before us. Although our wings remained retracted behind our backs, the sun still shown through them, revealing their brilliant colors. For the first time in my life, I deemed the image staring back at me acceptable. In fact, TC's body was acceptable too. It always had been!

"TC, when I was your age, I freaked out about my weight. I just wanted something I could control."

She looked at me with curiosity. "Yeah, you did a lot of exercise like me, huh? Did it help?"

I frowned and shook my head. "It made me feel powerful, but no, it never helped me feel good deep inside. In fact, it caused more harm than good. I disconnected from my body's cues. I had no idea when I was tired, hungry, or full. I swallowed my anger, which didn't help, either. But I powered through, harming my body, because I was obsessively focused on outside rules. And sadly, that meant shutting down my authenticity."

"What's 'authenticity'?"

"It means being yourself."

"But didn't you want to fit in? How can you fit in if you're different?"

I smiled at her thirteen-year-old wisdom. "Well, if you're different, maybe you can find some other friends who are 'different' too, and you can all be 'different' together!"

"But what if I upset someone... like Mom?" She grasped a strand of her long hair, her eyebrows angling downward into worry.

My heart broke for her. "Your mom loves you so much, TC. She gets stressed and yeah, she can be rude and bossy. Just know that it's not your fault. You're not responsible for how she acts. And, you are powerful and beautiful as you are!"

"Do you really think so?"

"I *know* so," I reassured her. "It's also okay to say what you're really thinking and feeling, even if it's scary at first. Just say something like 'Mom, I know you love me, and I love you too. Can we come to a compromise?' She may still say 'no,' but at least you will have tried and can stand in your power.

"Also, remember that you don't earn love by being who you think others want you to be. In fact, you never have to earn love at all! Just like everybody else, you were born lovable. You were born just the way you were meant to be!"

She grinned at me. "That sounds awesome!" As she took a deep breath, I witnessed her shedding pounds of emotional weight.

However, those pounds returned soon. "But, Courtney, how could I ever accept my body? I hate it!"

I patted her shoulder. "Okay, TC, look in the water again. Will you do this exercise with me?"

"But I already did my kickboxing workout today."

"Oops, sorry. I don't mean physical exercise. I meant mental and spiritual exercise."

"Okay." She nodded. I appreciated her openness to experimenting.

"TC, what body part do you hate the most?"

"My stomach."

"Why?"

"It's fat and ugly!"

Duh, I should have known. I directed my next question to her stomach. "Okay, fat and ugly stomach, why are you in TC's life? What do you help her with?"

TC looked utterly confused. "What does my stomach help me with? Huh?"

"Yeah, why do you have a stomach?"

She looked sideways pensively. "To digest food, I guess... so I have energy."

"Anything else?"

"I don't know! What about your stomach?"

I smiled. "I had to go on a long journey before I could come to terms with mine. Trust me, I get it. Especially since my stomach naturally curves outward, no matter how much or little I weigh. So now, I embrace it. The curve reminds me that I am a woman and that I've been through a lot to be emotionally healthy and strong."

"Wow, really?"

"Yeah. Also, my stomach tells me when something is not okay with me. You know what 'gut feeling' means, right?"

She nodded.

"So my gut helps me know when I need to say 'no' or set a boundary."

"You mean like be honest with someone about how you feel? Your stomach helps you do that?"

"Yes! It helps me be more authentic."

"Wow, that's so cool!"

"Yeah, so since my stomach does so many cool things, who really cares what it looks like?"

"But what about when other people don't like my body... like someone I have a crush on?"

I nodded. "What do you think matters most: what other people think or what *you* think?"

She glanced down briefly, then looked up at me, smiling. "What I think."

"You're amazing, TC! Will you say some affirmations with me?"

"Sure!"

We refocused our attention on our bodies' reflections in the water. I felt tickled that I now saw my body accurately, rather than exaggerating the size of my thighs or stomach. In fact, I could hardly believe my newfound willingness to accept what I had always seen as flaws. Sure, I still had my moments of self-criticism, but overall I knew that my body does not define me. I prayed that even a little of this attitude would trickle over to my teenage self.

"Okay," I said. "Now repeat after me. Here goes… Body, I forgive you."

She looked me in the eyes with surprise, then back at her reflection. "Body, I forgive you," she repeated softly.

"Body, I love you. Body, I accept you," I continued.

She slowly repeated the affirmations. With each word we spoke, I felt more and more love tingling throughout my body. *What a difference to send love, instead of hatred, to our bodies!* I thought.

Soon enough, tears streamed down both our faces.

"Courtney, I forgive you. Courtney, I love you. Courtney, I accept you."

After her turn, we turned to face each other and embraced.

"TC, I'm so proud of you for being who you are."

"But Courtney, what else do I need to know? I'm only thirteen. There's a lot ahead of me, right?"

"Yes, so much."

"Can you give me a sneak peak?"

I paused in contemplation. I was convinced that everything in my life had happened by divine order so that I would become who I am today. Did it really need to be any different for her? On the other hand, though, there were a few things I wished I would have known back then. Perhaps I could share, just this once.

I beckoned her to sit beside me on the fountain's lip again. When she joined me, we gazed into the smooth, bluish-gray water. Images materialized magically, one by one, showing different moments of my life. The first image was Brent.

"Hey, that's the boy I have a crush on!"

"Yes, TC, I know. I want you to know something about him. Although he seems confident, inside he's insecure. That's why he needs lots of attention from girls. Don't take it personally, okay? There's nothing you need to change about yourself."

"Okay," TC responded, wide-eyed.

"Also, sweetheart, don't buy into anyone else's version of 'happily ever after.' You'll discover your own truth. You don't need a knight in shining armor or a princess girlfriend to complete you. Just be who you are and love yourself. The right people will come into your life."

Her eyes widened, but she nodded.

The next image that materialized was my high school graduation speech. TC grinned and bounced a little. "Oh, cool! I'm going to give a speech... to that many people?"

"Yes, sweetheart. You will give others advice about being happy."

"Oh, wow!"

"The only drawback is that you won't be happy inside. You'll be in total denial of your true feelings. It's okay, just something to be mindful of. You don't have to put on a smiling face if that's not what you're feeling."

"Okay. What else?"

"Well, it will be really similar in college."

Now, an image emerged of me teaching kickboxing. "Sweetheart, you're going to feel isolated, and you'll get depressed. Don't be afraid of it. Just know that better times await you. At some point, you'll learn to go into your heart and gut to detect what you really feel. Feeling your emotions is the key to your healing—that and self-acceptance and self-love."

But TC looked distracted. "Oooh, who's that handsome man?" She pointed to the next image in the water, a scene of me having coffee with Nathan.

"Oh, that's the most amazing boyfriend you'll ever have. You'll be happy with him until you get on your healing and spiritual path. Sadly, he cannot go with you."

"Oh really?" She frowned. "That *is* sad."

I hesitated to give her the full story; she would need to experience the magic of self-discovery herself. Instead I said, "Sweetheart, at times you will feel so insecure and unsure of who you are that you'll look to others to validate you... even at the expense of breaking someone else's heart. It won't be pretty, but you'll learn a lot from it. Eventually you'll get through the guilt and learn to forgive yourself."

"Have you forgiven yourself?"

I smiled at her intuitive nature, even as I felt a twinge of sadness. "Just like self-acceptance, forgiveness is a process. I've gone through many layers, but I still have more to go."

We glanced into the fountain again. Images of loved ones appeared and faded, including Leah, my parents and sisters, James, Chelsea, Nathan, Kasey, Julie, and everyone else near and dear to my heart.

"Wow, that's a lot of people!"

"Yes, you'll love many. And they will love you too! Sweetheart, no matter what happens, the most important thing to remember is that you're beautiful and good enough just as you are. Can you remember that?"

"I can try! What other advice do you have for me?"

"Hmm… You can do and be anything you want in this world. Get to know your strengths. Don't give your power away to anyone. Your opinion of yourself is far more important than theirs! Don't believe everything everyone says. Take ideas within and see how they resonate with *you*. Find your own spiritual truth. Trust your intuition."

She sat staring off into the sunshine, and I knew she was absorbing my words. With a deep breath, I continued. "You don't have to be perfect. What's perfect is being yourself… in your humanness and imperfections. The more authentic you are, the more opposition you may face. Some people will feel threatened or jealous because they're not living as their authentic selves. It's okay if you upset someone; who you are or what you tell them might be exactly what they need to see or hear. Not everyone will like you, and that's okay! There will always be people to love you. You'll connect with other authentic people, and the connections you'll make will be so meaningful! Other than that, TC, it's all in divine order. You'll have no regrets, and someday you'll even thank your painful experiences for all they taught you."

"So everything will turn out okay?"

I hugged her. "Yep. You're already great at loving and accepting others. Just remember to be yourself, accept yourself, and love yourself too!"

She smiled.

"And TC, even in the darkest moments, remember that the light in your heart is always shining."

She gave me a big, loving hug in return. I glanced into her bright blue eyes and felt a sense of hope. During this brief but magical journey, she had transformed before my eyes. She stood taller, her inner light glowing brightly through her radiant smile. A dose of love from her future self, me, had transformed her shame into the seeds of self-acceptance!

Suddenly, I heard the sound of a crow cawing overhead. The familiar sound transported me back into reality. I looked around at the grass, flowers, and pecan trees. Turning my head, I glanced behind my shoulders. There was the tree I had been napping beneath. I no longer saw my wings, but energetically, I sensed they were still there.

Grabbing my journal, I allowed the inspiration to flow through my pen:

"My Dear Courtney...

I give you permission to be yourself.

I give you permission to say what's on your mind.

I give you permission to be vulnerable.

I give you permission to be sexy.

I give you permission to acknowledge, honor and cherish yourself.

I give you permission to love without fear.

I give you permission to laugh, to smile.

I give you permission to scream, to cry.

I give you permission to rest, to relax.

I give you permission to take long hot baths in the middle of the day.

I give you permission to honor yourself—even if it means someone may be disappointed. You never know, the outcome may surprise you. By honoring you, you honor others.

I give you permission to be open to miracles and happy surprises.

I give you permission to play.

I give you permission to be silly.

I give you permission to be serious and even stern at times.

I give you permission to celebrate and dance.

I give you permission to jump up and down with joy in public if you so choose.

I give you permission to be genuine... to let yourself be seen and heard... by you and by others.

I give you permission to sparkle and shine.

I give you permission to take up space in this world.

I give you permission to just be your beautiful self.

I give you permission to live.

I give you permission to breathe.

I give you permission to BE.''

Tears poured from my eyes, streaming quickly down my face. *I am free*, I realized. *I am* free*!* After several moments of basking in the salty sweetness of my tears, I continued journaling:

''I have nothing to hide from anyone. I have learned much, yet there is much more to learn. I have discovered much, yet there's far more to discover. I have loved many, and there are many more to love. My heart has expanded far and wide. And yet there's much more room to open wider.

I've discovered much magic in this world, like the magic of the sun shining overhead and glistening on the rocks. Yet, there's more magic to discover. I've grown more connected to life, yet my roots can go deeper. I've seen many rainbows, and there are far more rainbows to see. Each one brighter and more vivid than before. There's much beauty to be awake to. I can't believe I wasn't aware of it before! There's much fun to be had. Much freedom and self-expression to be experienced. Much peace and stillness to feel.

Find my way I must. Cross pathways and fallen tree trunks, I must. Experience the coolness of rivers, I will. Laugh, cry, scream, feel my emotions, I commit to. Opportunities to inspire, shine, show up... I cherish. Genuine smiles that come from the inside out, I will share. I'm here now, fully alive, fully engaged, fully awake.

I'm grateful to my incredible family and soul family. I'm grateful for every experience I've had— the tough ones especially. I know I still have more artichoke layers to shed. More authenticity to reveal. I'm excited to see what lies ahead!

Though I admit, not every day or moment is easy. Some just plain suck. And that's okay. At least every day is real. Now that I'm willing to see and feel the darker stuff, the lighter parts are even brighter. This is life, after all. Light, dark, and everything in between.

There's much to do here in this world. Much to see and much love. It's not about being better than one another. It's not about who has the prettiest hair. Nor is it about who's the most authentic. It's about being comfortable in self. It's about saying 'yes' when I mean 'yes.' And 'no' when I mean 'no.' Loving from the depths of my soul. Not expressing love out of fear of rejection.

I guess earlier in my life, I just misunderstood what life was about. I didn't used to like life. I thought life was about winning approval and favor of others. Impressing people, looking good, dressing nice. I thought that career was about earning a bunch of money to buy all the things I wanted.

So what is life about? Loving. Not just loving others. A lot of people are good at that part. Loving ourselves. Learning to love life. Learning to feel safe. Connected. Life is about connecting. Seeing beyond separation. Our soul knows that we are all one. And we all deserve love and self-acceptance."

—Journal, age 31, Sunday, 6/12/11, 10:43 a.m.

Chapter 46

I Am Beautiful

"The most radical and revolutionary act that any human being can commit within their lifetime is to love themselves as they are."
—Panache Desai[xliii]

January 23, 2012

"Courtney, I've been mesmerized by your story. Are you sure you're not hypnotizing me?"

Courtney winked at her. "Yes, Sarah, I've been subliminally implanting messages in your subconscious this whole time. 'You are lovable… You are good enough,'" Courtney chanted in a deep, scary voice.

The two women glanced at each other hesitantly, then cracked up into belly-deep laughter.

"So back to my original question, Sarah. How are you?"

"Oh yeah, that question."

Courtney smiled warmly.

"Well, Courtney, I'm better now."

"How so?"

"After hearing your story, I realized that I've been taking my inner bully way too seriously. Just because she says nasty things doesn't mean they are true."

Courtney nodded.

"You know, I've been attracted to women my whole life… as long as I can remember. When I was younger, I didn't know what it meant. I just thought I needed to fix it or make it go away."

Sarah rolled her eyes as Courtney listened calmly.

"I loved my ex-husband Ryan" she continued, "but it felt like there was something missing. I married him for all the wrong reasons—mostly because I thought I was supposed to." Sarah bit her lip nervously.

"Living the dream, right?" Courtney's tone was sarcastic, but gentle.

"Yeah, someone else's dream, but not mine! My dream was to be an actor and live in Southern France with the love of my life—who of course I pictured to be a woman." Sarah leaned forward, repositioning her auburn hair behind her ear. "Like I told you at the time, when Ryan and I divorced and I came out to my kids, there was quite an uproar. My mom disowned me, which hurt so bad. I was no longer welcome at my church. I started to question myself. I wondered who I was and if life was worth living." Sarah glanced down at her hands, her expression forlorn. "My kids had a hard time accepting my first female partner. It was not a fun time for anyone, that's for sure."

"That must have been heart-wrenching, Sarah. How did you get through it?" Courtney asked gently.

"At the time, it sucked. But I knew I couldn't give up. Trust me, I wanted to sometimes. But I kept telling myself it would get better. It had to."

Courtney smiled. "I'm so glad you realized that."

"You know, after talking with you, I realize that my family and church members were projecting their own fears onto me, and they chose to listen to that fear instead of to love. And just like you said with the mirror concept, they were actually judging themselves... not me."

Looking her deep in the eyes, Courtney said, "There's nothing wrong with you, Sarah."

Her friend smiled shyly. "I'm starting to see that!" She paused for a few moments then asked, "Courtney, how do you know who the authentic you is?"

"Hmm... good question. Who would you be if you weren't worried about hurting anyone's feelings? Who would you be if you could set aside all your fears? Who would you be if no one were watching? And, who would you be if everyone were watching?"

Sarah wrinkled her nose, head tilting sideways. "I have no idea. Hmm, I'll have to think about that."

"To say it more simply, the authentic you is the person inside, the one who's always been there, hiding beneath the fears, masks, and costumes. She just needs to know it's safe to step out and show up."

An ear-to-ear grin came over Sarah's face. "Hey, Courtney, when we're authentic, we don't have to follow other people's rules or fit into their boxes. We get to blaze our own path. Right?"

"Yes, Sarah! I love that! We don't belong in boxes, anyway. I'd rather dance around the outside of them."

Sarah laughed. "Okay, so now I've got to ask, who is the authentic Courtney?"

Courtney nodded and considered for a moment. "On a spiritual level, I think the authentic me is my essence. You know, my soul. Energy. The same light and love that flows through all things."

"It's hard to define it with words, don't you think?"

"Yeah, it's something that needs to be felt. On a human level, the authentic me is many things. She's sweet and loving, but she can also be firm and fiery. I used to judge that fiery part of me, because I didn't want to be a mean and angry person. But of course that wasn't good, because I was taking the fiery anger out on myself."

"Now what do you do with it?"

"Well, I realized it wasn't good to throw fireballs at other people either." Courtney laughed. "So I looked at what fire and anger are designed to do. They are designed to ignite, like a call to action encourages people to, well, take action!"

"What's your call to action?"

"My life purpose. You know, helping people connect with their light and power, so they can feel good enough and lovable *now*, not once they lose 20 pounds or have the perfect partner. There's so much love in this world, and I think another part of being authentic is letting that love in. We deserve it!"

"Wow, that gives me chills!" Sarah held up her arms, and pointed to the rows of goose bumps. Courtney grinned.

"Also, Sarah, I've very proud to report that the authentic me exercises when she *feels* like it, not because she *has* to. No more strict rules around exercise."

"Yeah, so you really did cut back?"

Courtney smiled. "Yes, can you believe it?"

The two women high fived across the table.

"I still like to hike and things, but I listen to my body and rest when I need to. I started some dance classes too."

"Oooh, how fun!"

"It's been awesome! I'm not running from anything anymore, so now exercise can be fun and playful."

"Wow, no more abuse of your body."

"Nope! It's all about self-care from here."

Sarah smiled. "So tell me more. What else do you like about being authentic?"

"Hmm… well, my favorite part is giving myself permission to be whomever I feel like being moment by moment. No one else can give me that permission; I have to give it to myself. Sometimes I feel like being my fire fairy self. Sometimes I'm a powerful warrior. Other times I'm my inner child, wailing and crying like a baby. Sometimes I'm jealous or insecure. And it's all okay. I embrace all of me, every part of Courtney that shows up. Just like colors of the rainbow, all together they make up me."

"I bet there are a lot of rainbows and sunshine in your life nowadays." Sarah winked as Courtney breathed a sigh of relief.

"Yes, ma'am. But, there's clouds and rain storms too."

Sarah raised her eyebrows.

"Hey, clouds are okay! We need rain. It's cleansing. Just like tears are cleansing."

"Oh, please do explain," Sarah said playfully.

"Not a big fan of crying, huh?" Courtney teased.

Sarah shook her head vehemently.

"Well, for me, another part of authenticity is being willing to feel my emotions. I don't have to be happy and cheerful all the time. And I don't have to pretend to be happy when I'm not. There's a whole range of emotions that I get to feel now… sad, angry, indifferent, grieving, frustrated, hopeful, everything. Life is definitely more interesting now that my palate of emotions is full."

"And it sounds like you *like* being alive now, even though life is filled with ups and downs. How come?"

Courtney smiled. "Life may be challenging, but at least it's real. And at least I know who I am now. So, what about you, Sarah? Who's the authentic Sarah?"

Sarah paused to think. "Well, I'm outgoing sometimes, but other times I'm shy and reserved. Instead of judging myself for that, why don't I just accept it, and acknowledge that's part of me?"

"I love that! I think being authentic is not about fixing or changing ourselves. It's about learning to embrace all of ourselves, strengths, weaknesses, darkness and light."

"Hmm... I definitely have a dark side," Sarah said.

Courtney raised an eyebrow and smiled.

"But I don't have to be scared of it anymore, huh? It's just part of who I am. Also, I'm definitely insecure sometimes. But now that we're talking, I realize that sometimes I'm confident too. Like when I'm speaking up for my kids." Sarah pursed her lips in thought. "Hey. Maybe I'm more confident that I give myself credit for!"

Sarah closed her eyes for a few minutes, deep in contemplation. Courtney finished the last of her tea, which by now had become cold. She glanced at Sarah, waiting for her next response.

Suddenly, Sarah's eyes opened. "That's it, Courtney! I am beautiful just as I am! I'm beautiful in my moments of confidence. And I'm even beautiful in my moments of insecurity. I am who I am!"

Courtney smiled with her whole body.

"Sarah, I already thought... err, *knew*... that you are beautiful." Courtney put her tea mug aside and leaned in closer. "In this moment, Sarah, you are even more beautiful, in fact! I don't know if it's your confidence, or your connection to you... but wow, you are shining big time!"

After blushing, Sarah pointed outside. "Oh Courtney, look!"

As Courtney looked through the coffee shop window, a huge smile came over her face. "Sarah, I hadn't even realized it had stopped raining."

"Me either! And you see what I see, right?"

"Yes, I do," Courtney said in a tone of sweet satisfaction.

The two women quickly stood up and walked outside. Many passers-by had stopped in their tracks and were also staring into the distance with looks of complete awe. There in the sky danced every color of existence… all in a beautiful spectrum.

"Not only is it a rainbow," Sarah said excitedly. "It's a double rainbow!"

Courtney breathed in the beautiful sight, feeling complete gratitude for life itself. "What do you think it means?"

"Hmm… perhaps one represents releasing the past with light and love. It all happened just like it needed to. We acknowledge our feelings, release and move on. That's the dimmer rainbow. The slightly clearer, brighter one represents the future, filled with sunshine, clouds, tons of love—oh, and butterflies."

"Oh yeah. I like that, Sarah."

"But then where's the present?"

"The present is the beauty of this moment—the beauty that resides within us."

The two women took in a calming, empowering breath of fresh air.

"Wow, Courtney. Too bad we can't fly to the rainbow." Sarah glanced at Courtney, who mirrored the gesture with a sideways glance.

"Who says we can't, Sarah? The only one who limits us is ourselves."

"That's true," Sarah answered with a wink.

Courtney then smiled a mischievous smile. "So, ready to spread your wings and soar?"

If *you* are ready to spread *your* wings
and soar as the authentic you….

Join the Authentic and Free Community!

Sign up for Courtney's inspirational e-newsletter and receive
"10 Tips for Authentic Body Image: Ways to Love Your Body
and Love Yourself"

www.authenticandfree.com

Looking for resources?

For a list of helpful resources related to body image,
eating disorders, LGBTQ empowerment,
and being authentic and free, visit:

www.authenticandfree.com/resources

References

[I] Dr. Wayne Dyer, PhD, author of *Your Sacred Self: Making the Decision to Be Free, The Power of Intention, Inspiration: Your Ultimate Calling,* and numerous other books and products, www.drwaynedyer.com and www.hayhouse.com

[ii] Anthony J. D'Angelo, Founder and Chief Visionary Officer of Collegiate EmPowerment, www.collegiate-empowerment.org, author of *Inspiration for LGBT Students & Their Allies* by Anthony J. D'Angelo, Mike Esposito, Stephen D. Collingsworth, Gabriel Hermelin, Ronni Sanlo, Lydia A Sausa, Dr. Ronni Sanlo, Shane L. Windmeyer, The Collegiate EmPowerment Company, November 5, 2002

[iii] *The Dance: Moving To the Rhythms of Your True Self,* by Oriah Mountain Dreamer, HarperOne, first edition, August 21, 2001

[iv] *Women Food and God: An Unexpected Path to Almost Everything* by Geneen Roth, Scribner, February 8, 2011

[v] *The Four Agreements: A Practical Guide to Personal Freedom* by Don Miguel Ruiz, Amber-Allen Publishing, November 7, 1997

[vi] *Accessing the Vibration of Mindfulness* by Panache Desai, audio recording from presentation at Celebrate Your Life conference, Mishka Productions, Phoenix, AZ, November 6, 2011, www.panachedesai.com and www.celebrateyourlife.org

[vii] *One Day My Soul Just Opened Up: 40 Days and 40 Nights Toward Spiritual Strength and Personal Growth* by Iyanla Vanzant, original edition, Touchstone, January 5, 1998

[viii] *The Four Agreements: A Practical Guide to Personal Freedom* by Don Miguel Ruiz, Amber-Allen Publishing, November 7, 1997

[ix] Dharma Talk given by Thich Nhat Hanh on July 20, 1998 in Plum Village, France. See also *Answers from the Heart: Practical Responses To Life's Burning Questions* by Thich Nhat Hanh, Berkeley: Parallax Press, 2009

[x] *The Gifts of Imperfection: Let Go of Who You Think You're Supposed to Be and Embrace Who You Are* by Brené Brown, Hazelden; first edition, September 1, 2010

[xi] *Women Food and God: An Unexpected Path to Almost Everything* by Geneen Roth, Scribner, February 8, 2011

[xii] Doreen Virtue, PhD, best-selling author of *Healing with the Angels* book and oracle cards and the *Messages from Your Angels* books and oracle cards and numerous other products, www.angeltherapy.com and www.hayhouse.com

[xiii] *The Present Moment: 365 Daily Affirmations* by Louise L. Hay, Hay House, Inc, August 1, 2007

[xiv] *The Art of Extreme Self-Care: Transform Your Life One Month at a Time* by Cheryl Richardson, Hay House, Inc, reprint edition, May 1, 2012

[xv] *The Scarlett Letter* by Nathaniel Hawthorne, 1850, available by Dover Publications, May 2, 1994

[xvi] *The Power of Now: A Guide to Spiritual Enlightenment* by Eckhart Tolle, New World Library, 1st edition, August 19, 2004

[xvii] *Anorexia Nervosa,* National Eating Disorders Association, http://www.nationaleatingdisorders.org/nedaDir/files/documents/handouts/Anorexia.pdf and *Eating Disturbances,* Eating Disorders, www.eatingdisordershelpguide.com/disturbances.html

[xviii] *Statistics: Eating Disorders and Their Precursors,* National Eating Disorders Association (NEDA), http://www.nationaleatingdisorders.org/uploads/file/Statistics%20%20Updated %20Feb%2010,%202008%20B.pdf and *Eating Disorder Statistics,* National Association of Anorexia Nervosa and Associated Disorders, Inc® (ANAD), http://www.anad.org/get-information/about-eating-disorders/eating-disorders-statistics/

[xix] Alan Cohen, author of *Why Your Life Sucks, Enough Already: The Power of Radical Contentment,* and numerous other books, www.alancohen.com and www.hayhouse.com

xx *A Matter of Significance: Recognizing Your Value*, Daily OM, April 5, 2011, http://www.dailyom.com/cgi-bin/display/printerfriendly.cgi?articleid=27896

xxi *Daily Guidance from Your Angels: 365 Angelic Messages to Soothe, Heal, and Open Your Heart* by Doreen Virtue, Hay House, Inc, gift edition, October 15, 2008

xxii Marianne Williamson, spiritual author and lecturer, www.marianne.com

xxiii *The Tao of Pooh* by Benjamin Hoff, Penguin Books, 1983

xxiv *Simple Abundance: A Daybook of Comfort and Joy* by Sarah Ban Breathnach, Grand Central Publishing, 10 Anv edition, November 15, 1995

xxv Dr. Darren R. Weissman, author of *The Power of Infinite Love & Gratitude: An Evolutionary Journey to Awakening Your Spirit*, Hay House, Inc, February 1, 2007, and numerous other products, www.drdarrenweissman.com and www.hayhouse.com

xxvi *A Garden of Thoughts: My Affirmation Journal* by Louise L. Hay, Hay House, Inc, hardcover, January 1, 1999

xxvii Anne Parker, Wellness Counselor, Miraval Resort, Tucson, Arizona, 2011 Guide, http://www.docstoc.com/docs/82060623/You-wont-find-you-anywhere-else

xxviii *Hello, I'm a Detestable Abomination. Looking at Leviticus and Deuteronomy* by Kathy Buldock, Jun 29, 2010, Canyonwalker Connections Repairing the Breach Between the Church and the GLBT Christian Community http://canyonwalkerconnections.com/2010/06/im-a-detestable-abomination-looking-at-leviticus-and-deuteronomy/

xxix Amy Pershing, LMSW, ACSW, Executive Director and Co-Founder of Pershing Turner Centers, http://pershingturnercenters.com; Clinical Director, The Center for Eating Disorders, http://www.center4ed.org

xxx *You Can Heal Your Life* by Louise L. Hay, Hay House, Inc, gift edition, September 1999

xxxi *Health at Every Size: The Surprising Truth about Your Weight*, Linda Bacon, BenBella Books; second edition, May 4, 2010, pp. 12-14

xxxii *A Return to Love: Reflections on the Principles of a 'Course in Miracles'* by Marianne Williamson, Harper Paperbacks, March 15, 1996, www.marianne.com

xxxiii www.bullying.org, dedicated to increasing the awareness of bullying and to preventing, resolving and eliminating bullying in society

xxxiv *A Return to Love: Reflections on the Principles of a 'Course in Miracles'* by Marianne Williamson, Harper Paperbacks, March 15, 1996, www.marianne.com

xxxv *The Ten Lies about the GLBT Community Told by Conservative Hate Groups: a Straight Christian Perspective* by Kathy Buldock, Nov 29, 2010, Canyonwalker Connections Repairing the Breach Between the Church and the GLBT Christian Community, http://canyonwalkerconnections.com/2010/11/ten-myths-about-the-glbt-community-a-christian-perspective/

xxxvi *One Day My Soul Just Opened Up: 40 Days and 40 Nights Toward Spiritual Strength and Personal Growth* by Iyanla Vanzant, original edition, Touchstone, January 5, 1998

xxxvii Quotes from Bi Youth, Bisexual Resource Center, http://biresource.net/biquotes.html

xxxviii *Sexual Fluidity: Understanding Women's Love and Desire* by Lisa M. Diamond, PhD, Harvard University Press, April 15, 2009

xxxix Kinsey's Heterosexual-Homosexual Rating Scale, developed by Alfred Kinsey and his colleagues Wardell Pomeroy and Clyde Martin in 1948, The Kinsey Institute for Research in Sex, Gender and Reproduction, Indiana University Bloomington, http://www.iub.edu/~kinsey/research/ak-hhscale.html

xl *The Gifts of Imperfection: Let Go of Who You Think You're Supposed to Be and Embrace Who You Are* by Brené Brown, Hazelden; first edition, September 1, 2010, p. 49

xli *Becoming the Person You Were Meant to Be: Where to Start* by Anne Lamott, Oprah.com, October 13, 2009 http://www.oprah.com/spirit/How-To-Find-Out-Who-You-Really-Are-by-Anne-Lamott

[xli] *20 Ways to Love Your Body!!* compiled by Margo Maine, PhD, National Eating Disorders Association,
http://www.nationaleatingdisorders.org/nedaDir/files/documents/handouts/20WaysTo.pdf
[xli] *The Ultimate Vibrational Relationship Rx* by Panache Desai, audio recording of presentation at Celebrate Your Life conference, Mishka Productions, Phoenix, AZ, November 5, 2011, www.panachedesai.com and www.celebrateyourlife.org

About the Author

Courtney Long, MSW, LC, CHt, ATP®

In addition to writing, Courtney is a Guide to the Authentic and powerful speaker. She inspires youth and adults to experience the sweet freedom of an authentic life through individual empowerment sessions, workshops, webinars and more.

Courtney holds a Masters Degree in Social Work (MSW) and Bachelors Degree in Psychology (B.A.) from the University of Michigan, with emphasis on diversity and social justice. She is a Transformational Life Coach, Spiritual Coach and Certified Hypnotherapist, trained at the award winning Southwest Institute of Healing Arts in Tempe, AZ, where she is now a faculty member/instructor.

Courtney is based in Phoenix, AZ though her sessions and workshops are available worldwide. In addition to *Authentic and Free,* she has self-published a guided journal for self-care: *Rejuvenating Refuge: Uplifting Journal for Caring Warriors.*

www.AuthenticandFree.com

www.facebook.com/CourtneyLongAuthor

Made in the USA
Charleston, SC
01 August 2012